PSYCHO
TH]

M000314671

PRINCIPLES AND APPLICATION

By

FRANZ ALEXANDER, M.D.

AND

THOMAS MORTON FRENCH, M.D.

with

CATHERINE LILLIE BACON, M.D.
THERESE BENEDEK, M.D.
RUDOLF A. FUERST, M.D.
MARGARET WILSON GERARD, M.D.
ROY RICHARD GRINKER, M.D.
MARTIN GROTJAHN, M.D.
ADELAIDE McFADYEN JOHNSON, M.D.
HELEN VINCENT McLEAN, M.D.
EDOARDO WEISS, M.D.

UNIVERSITY OF NEBRASKA PRESS
Lincoln and London

Bison Books in Clinical Psychology
George Stricker, General Editor

UNP

Copyright, 1946, by The Ronald Press Company
Renewed © 1974 by John Wiley & Sons, Inc.

First Bison Book printing: 1980
Most recent printing indicated by first digit below:
1   2   3   4   5   6   7   8   9   10

Library of Congress Cataloging in Publication Data

Alexander, Franz Gabriel, 1891–1964.
  Psychoanalytic therapy.

  (Bison books in clinical psychology)
  "Contains the results of an investigative work . . . of the staff of the Chicago Institute for Psychoanalysis."
  Reprint of the ed. published by Ronald Press Co., New York.
  Bibliography: p. 343.
  Includes index.
  1. Psychoanalysis. I. French, Thomas Morton, 1892–   joint author. II. Chicago. Institute for Psychoanalysis. III. Title. IV. Series.
RC 504.A42   1980   616.8'917   79–24893
ISBN 0–8032–1007–8
ISBN 0–8032–59034 pbk.

Published by arrangement with John Wiley & Sons, Inc.

Manufactured in the United States of America

PREFACE

This publication contains the results of an investigative work to which every member of the Staff of the Chicago *Institute for Psychoanalysis* has in some way contributed—a concerted effort both to define those basic principles which make possible a shorter and more efficient means of psychotherapy and, whenever possible, to develop specific techniques of treatment. It is not, however, the purpose of the book to indicate that there is a short-cut to the practice of psychotherapy. The material herein presented makes it evident that greater, not less, knowledge of the manifold intricacies of human behavior is necessary before one can acquire skill in finding for each individual the most suitable and economical form of treatment.

This book is truly the work of the Institute as a whole and presents as closely as possible the views of all the members of the Staff concerning fundamental issues. During seven years of collective research and during the actual writing of this work, the Staff has come to an agreement on the principles and practices as here set forth, making due allowance for individual differences in the detailed evaluation of therapeutic factors and in the manner of conducting treatments. Some of these differences will be apparent to the acute reader. It is admitted that psychotherapy is still more an art, requiring a constant intuitive response to the patient, than it is an exact science. The effort here has been to express this art in generally valid scientific terms, keeping in mind the fact that scientific formulations must of necessity lag behind the art of treatment.

The present volume is addressed to psychiatrists, psychoanalysts, psychologists, general physicians, social workers, and to all whose work is closely concerned with human relationships. The findings of the research are based on 292 Institute cases treated since the project was begun in 1938, and on an almost equally large number of patients seen in private practice.

We wish to acknowledge the help of the following persons, who have contributed richly to it, not only with their own case material but in general discussions: Edwin R. Eisler, M.D., Louise S. Fred, Maxwell Gitelson, M.D., Maurice Levine, M.D., Milton Leonard Miller, M.D., Fritz Moellenhoff, M.D., George Joseph Mohr, M.D., Gerhart Piers, M.D., Leon Saul, M.D., Lucia Tower, M.D., Carel Van der Heide, M.D., and George Wilson, M.D. Appreciation is due also to Miss Roberta Collard, the Institute librarian, for her assistance in the preparation of the index and bibliography.

The difficulty of publishing a book containing the collective contributions of a number of coworkers is well known. It is the editorial achievement of Helen Ross and her assistant, Helen West Cole, that has made it possible for us to offer an integrated text instead of a symposium. The editorial work in such a venture is far greater than is usual in symposia; in fact, it represents as much creative effort as that of the authors. It is impossible to express adequately the indebtedness of the collaborators to the editors for their selfless and devoted endeavors to make this a readable publication.

The study and the book itself have been made possible through the generous support of a great humanitarian, Mrs. Albert D. Lasker. Mrs. Lasker was quick to see in the Institute's first observations implications for improving the mental health of the country, and graciously subsidized its program of research in order that more people might, through psychiatric treatment, come to lead happier and more efficient lives. For the inspiration of her confidence in this work, and for her financial aid, the Institute acknowledges a deep debt of gratitude.

F. A.
T. M. F.

INTRODUCTION

Like most psychoanalysts, we have been puzzled by the unpredictability of therapeutic results, by the baffling discrepancy between the length and intensity of a treatment and the degree of therapeutic success. It is not unusual for a patient to get well as the result of a few consultations; for even a severe neurotic condition with psychotic elements to yield to brief therapeutic work. Yet another case which seems comparatively mild may not respond to a systematic treatment of many years. That there is no simple correlation between therapeutic results and the length and intensity of treatment has been recognized, tacitly or explicitly, by most experienced psychoanalysts and is an old source of dissatisfaction among them.

Among psychoanalysts there were two types of reaction to this dissatisfaction. One was constructive—like Ferenczi's relentless experimenting with technique in an effort to isolate the factors responsible for therapeutic results. The other was a self-deceptive defense in the form of an almost superstitious belief that quick therapeutic results cannot be genuine, that they are either those transitory results due to suggestion or an escape into "pseudo-health" by patients who prefer to give up their symptoms rather than obtain real insight into their difficulties.

It is argued by some psychoanalysts that quick therapeutic results cannot indicate deep, thoroughgoing changes in the dynamic structure of the personality, that years are required to bring about such fundamental changes. Others excuse the lack of therapeutic result in prolonged analyses by the patient's "resistance." They have comforted themselves by saying that the patient is not yet "fully analyzed" and they are convinced that further treatment will eventually bring the desired results. Then, when results still do not come, they often take refuge in deciding that the patient is a "latent schizophrenic."

We shall not attempt to refute all the unwritten superstitions in our field. Every science has prejudices concerning its unexplored territories. But it is in just this borderland between the known and the unknown that new scientific progress takes place, usually beginning with a critical examination of those unproven assumptions by which the mind protects itself against the discomfort of admitting ignorance and against the uncertainties of the unknown.

Our study started by questioning the validity of certain traditional beliefs, certain psychoanalytic dogmas: (1) that the depth of therapy is *necessarily* proportionate to the length of treatment and the frequency of the interviews; (2) that therapeutic results achieved by a relatively small number of interviews are *necessarily* superficial and temporary, while therapeutic results achieved by prolonged treatment are *necessarily* more stable and more profound; and (3) that the prolongation of an analysis is justified on the grounds that the patient's resistance will *eventually* be overcome and the desired therapeutic results achieved.

WHAT IS PSYCHOANALYSIS?—At the outset it should be made clear that the expression "psychoanalysis" applies to three different things. It is (1) a psychodynamic theory of the development of the personality, (2) a method of investigation, and (3) a therapeutic procedure. The method of investigation and the therapeutic procedure have remained practically identical for a long period. In the past this coincidence of the method of therapy with that of research had valid reasons. The essence of psychoanalytic therapy is to bring into the patient's consciousness emotions and motivations of which he is not aware, or in other words to extend the patient's conscious control over his behavior. This requires a thorough knowledge of the patient's personality structure.

Although Freud's original aim was therapeutic, the method he developed, psychoanalysis, served the double purpose of therapy and research. While he was trying to find a means of curing emotionally upset people, he was at the same time securing data by which he built up a new discipline, a dynamic theory of personality. Freud's technique of therapy was of necessity influenced by his investigative interest, and although he corrected it from time to time to accord with new discoveries, it was inherited by his followers in a highly standardized form and used with little modification for almost forty years.

So long as little was known about the pathogenesis and pathology of neurotic disturbances, it was unavoidable and so justifiable to study every case *in extenso*. Each patient was at the same time both an object of therapy and a subject of research. With the advance of knowledge in this field, however, we can now use generalizations and principles tested by our extended experience to develop a more flexible and economical procedure adjusted to the individual nature of the great variety of neurotic patients.

At the beginning of our collaborative investigation, there was a tendency among us to differentiate sharply between "standard" psychoanalysis and more flexible methods of psychotherapy. Gradually, however, it was recognized that in every case the same psychodynamic principles are applied for the purposes of therapy: inducing emotional discharge in order to facilitate insight, and exposing the ego to those unresolved emotional constellations which it has to learn to master. French was the first among us to state explicitly that there is no essential difference between the various procedures, that the differences lie merely in the extent to which the various therapeutic principles and techniques are utilized. In other words, we are working with the same theories and techniques, the same kit of tools, even though we are trying to refine them so that we can make them accomplish specific purposes more efficiently and in less time. We therefore regard all of the work set forth in this book as "psychoanalytic."

PSYCHOTHERAPY AND PSYCHONEUROSIS.—Every scientific therapy is based on knowledge of the disease which it attempts to remedy and on an understanding of the curative process. Such a therapy is etiological, in contrast to a merely empirical procedure which effects improvement or cure without being based on a thorough understanding of just why and how results are achieved. Although, even in its most primitive form, psychotherapy was never a completely empirical procedure, it has only recently advanced into this rank of etiological therapies.

Many of the therapeutic factors employed in psychiatric practice—emotional support, abreaction, insight, persuasion and, above all, the phenomenon of transference—are constantly used in everyday life. Everyone who tries to console a despondent friend, calm down a panicky child, or help someone to live through an harassing experience, in a sense practices psychotherapy in that he tries *by psychological means* to restore the disturbed emotional equilibrium of another person. We all know intuitively that abreaction has a curative effect, that a disturbed or confused individual needs emotional support, and that we can help him by lending him our own reasoning faculties. In this fashion, we all practice a combination of supportive and insight therapy.

Methodical psychotherapy is, to a large degree, nothing more than the systematic, conscious application of those methods by which we influence our fellow men. Psychotherapy becomes a *scientific* practice when it replaces intuitive knowledge with well-established principles of psychodynamics.

This etiological basis of psychotherapy receives renewed importance when we consider the area of its usefulness.

Every neurosis and every psychosis represents *a failure of the ego in performing its function of securing adequate gratification for subjective needs under the existing external conditions.* This statement is valid for all forms of mental disturbance—whether they are caused by demonstrable organic damage to the brain tissue due to organic, chemical, bacterial causes or are psychogenic disturbances which develop as a result of traumatic life experiences. Psychotherapy in the latter type of cases aims to restore this ability to the ego by psychological means.

When we speak of the ego we refer to the organ system whose anatomical and physiological substratum is made up of the highest integrative centers of the central nervous system. The functioning of this organ system can be studied either by the methods of anatomy and physiology or by those of psychology. When we use the term "ego" functions, we are referring to the psychological approach. If we study these functions by the method of anatomy or physiology, we speak of "cortical" or "subcortical" functions of the brain.

In the ego function, both perceptive and executive activities can be distinguished. The *perceptive faculty* consists of internal perception (of the subjective needs and impulses of the organism) and external perception (of the environment by the sense organs). These functions find expression in the anatomical-physiological structure of the central nervous system and correspond to its afferent nervous pathways. The *executive faculty* of the ego consists in finding ways and means for the gratification of the subjective needs of the organism by adequate activities effected through the efferent nervous pathways.

The perceptive and executive functions of the ego are inter-related, inasmuch as the executive function is dependent upon the perceptive faculties: the ego must register the subjective needs before it can attempt to gratify them, and it must inform itself about the existing external conditions because the gratification depends upon the external conditions. The *integrative function* of the ego, then, consists in the complex harmonious coordination of simultaneously existing, partially conflicting, subjective needs and impulses with each other and with the external conditions upon which their gratification depends. This activity was first described by Freud as the "reality principle" and later analyzed in its finer details by French in his studies of goal structures.

This complex synthesizing function of the ego can be disturbed in various ways. Among these disturbances we distinguish the various types of mental disease. Briefly, mental disturbances can be classified in two large groups: (1) psychiatric conditions due to organic changes in the brain tissue. In these conditions the ego functions are disturbed because the brain tissue is altered by mechanical, infectious, or toxic influences or by the progressive degeneration of aging. In such conditions psychotherapy has only an occasional and accessory application. And (2) psychiatric conditions due to injurious experiences in interpersonal relationships. These conditions may be either acute or chronic. Our study has been concerned primarily with this second group.

It will be noted that in this volume we have not included a case treated according to the strictly classical psychoanalytic procedure. This omission is intentional, first because the psychoanalytic literature abounds in such presentations, and second because we have found in our studies that few cases, if any, require strict adherence to the standard technique throughout the course of treatment.

FRANZ ALEXANDER, M.D.

CONTENTS

PART I

PRINCIPLES OF PSYCHOANALYTIC THERAPY

PART II

APPLICATION OF PSYCHOANALYTIC THERAPY

PSYCHOANALYTIC
THERAPY

"A man must either resolve to put out nothing new, or to become a slave to defend it."

—NEWTON

Chapter 1

THE SCOPE OF PSYCHOTHERAPY

Life is becoming increasingly complex, the interdependence of the members of society more and more intricate. Individual self-sufficiency has almost completely disappeared and we are, to an extreme degree, dependent upon each other in assuring ourselves of the basic necessities of life. And yet, in spite of our great interdependence, we live in a free and competitive society wherein each person strives to be "an individual" with his own specific self-assertive aspirations. We are at the same time friends and rivals. Not only in the individual is this conflict found; nations have been brought by technical developments of recent years into such a close interrelationship that now even here self-sufficiency is impossible and nations must also work in "antagonistic cooperation" with each other.

These diametrically opposed principles of competition and cooperation are reflected in each individual as a personal conflict—one which he must settle for himself; and a successful solution in our present age is the exception rather than the rule. The result is an overwhelming number of emotionally unbalanced persons.

The Function of Psychiatry

To help man find his place in this complex social structure without falling victim to a psychoneurosis, and to help him recover from those insidious emotional maladjustments which are well-nigh universal, is the great function of psychiatry.

This clash between social and antisocial trends (which is found to some degree in every healthy person, accounting for the widespread recognition that "everyone is a little crazy") is characteristic of the neurotic but in an exaggerated form. Conflicting standards contribute more than anything else to

3

that emotional insecurity which is the most common basis of neurotic disturbance. Although the patterns or symptoms may vary greatly, we find this basic struggle in an astounding number of persons. It is one of the fundamental conflicts of our present cultural era.

This conflict between help-seeking dependence and self-assertive rivalry has been found to be the nuclear conflict in such widely different conditions as neurotic criminality and some types of psychosomatic disease. Neurotic delinquents, for instance, often commit aggressive antisocial acts under the impulse to prove to themselves that they are courageous and independent, and thus compensate for that desperate dependent need to seek love and help which they must internally repudiate.

Many persons who suffer from peptic ulcer display a similar conflict but in a socially acceptable form. They defend themselves against their immoderate need to be loved by an exaggerated display of efficiency and accomplishment. They take on more responsibilities than they can stand until the original repressed longing for rest and help becomes excessive. This constant, never sufficiently relieved desire to be loved mobilizes their digestive functions to such a degree that eventually organic changes in the stomach and duodenum take place. In other common psychosomatic disturbances also, we have found this basic conflict in varying manifestations. Individuals suffering from essential hypertension, for example, are caught between their hostile competitive tendencies and their passive dependent wishes.

All these problems of emotional maladjustment have been aggravated by the war and will be accentuated in the period of reconstruction. Already psychiatry is being called upon to contribute on a large scale to the rehabilitation of acute cases of war neurosis. It must be prepared to give help also to the huge number of breakdowns which result from the unavoidable dislocations of life caused by military service, interruption of civilian concerns, hasty marriages, and the loss of near relatives.

THE PLACE OF PSYCHOANALYSIS.—Psychoanalysis, in common usage, is both a practice and a theory; it is concerned with techniques and with principles. From the microscopic study of many individuals under psychoanalytic treatment, a theory of personality development has been devised—a theory which, as in every science, is constantly changing with new discoveries. These principles of the dynamics of personality have wide application. They are not limited to the practice of psychoanalysis, nor yet to the wider field of psychotherapy in general. They extend to many fields, to every sphere of activity in which the human being is an object of study.

In this volume we are concerned with a limited aspect of this broad subject—the application of psychoanalytic principles and techniques to the treatment of persons suffering from all kinds and degrees of emotional disturbance.

Since the dynamic principles of psychoanalysis can be employed in many types of psychotherapy, the choice of the particular method to be used should be determined by the nature of the therapeutic problem. The traditional psychoanalytic method of daily interviews, continued over months or years, is only one of the possible technical procedures and is not necessarily the most economical, the most penetrating, or the most effective technique in every case. It has proved itself best suited to severe chronic cases of psychoneurosis and character disturbance, but even in such cases the therapy will become more efficacious if the procedure is modified to conform to the varying needs of the individual patient and of the different phases of treatment.

In the Chicago Institute, we lay stress on the value of designing a *plan of treatment,* based on a dynamic-diagnostic appraisal of the patient's personality and the actual problems he has to solve in his given life conditions. In devising such a plan of therapy, the analyst must decide in each case whether a primarily supportive or uncovering type of treatment is indicated, or whether the therapeutic task is mainly a question of changing the external conditions of the patient's life.

The traditional attitude in psychoanalytic therapy has been to let the treatment take its own course, the more-or-less passively watching therapist following the lead of the patient's material as it unfolds before him. This therapeutic orientation can be followed only so long as the same procedure is used in every case. As soon as the therapist takes the more active role we advocate, systematic planning becomes imperative.

In addition to the original decision as to the particular sort of strategy to be employed in the treatment of any case, we recommend the *conscious use of various techniques in a flexible manner,* shifting tactics to fit the particular needs of the moment. Among these modifications of the standard technique are: using not only the method of free association but interviews of a more direct character, manipulating the frequency of the interviews, giving directives to the patient concerning his daily life, employing interruptions of long or short duration in preparation for ending the treatment, regulating the transference relationship to meet the specific needs of the case, and making use of real-life experiences as an integral part of the therapy. These various aids to a more flexible and more efficient psychotherapy will be discussed in detail in later chapters.

None of these modifications is, in itself, novel; all have been used on occasion by a large number of psychoanalysts as more or less accidental or "practical" measures. Our contribution consists in the psychodynamic clarification of their therapeutic usefulness and in demonstrating the advisability of their systematic incorporation as integral parts of the therapeutic procedure.

We seek also to develop a more economical procedure, both of time and of effort. This means we must find the technique most applicable to the individual case. Our collective research in certain psychosomatic disturbances has started us on this path; it is no longer necessary to study each of these cases *in extenso.* To our present contribution in this sphere we hope to add findings in other disease syndromes, with the aim of developing new techniques and shortening the process of therapy.

One of the most significant results of our studies is the extension of dynamic psychotherapy to the mild chronic and the acute neuroses, and to the incipient cases of emotional disturbance. Not only do such cases offer the greatest possibility of therapeutic success, but helping them is of much greater social value than helping the severe chronic cases.

These less serious types are extremely prevalent in the present phase of our cultural development, much more so than the severe chronic cases. Moreover, their influence upon the life of the nation is far greater than that of the severely incapacitated psychoneurotics. Of the latter, many have ceased to take any active part in life and have, in their withdrawal, become almost as isolated as if they were psychotic. On the other hand, the great numbers of emotionally disturbed persons who do not fall under any definite psychiatric classification and who formerly have not been recognized by others or by themselves as disturbed, are active in life and exert a tremendous influence on society—as fathers and mothers, as employers and executives, foremen and laborers, as statesmen, politicians and teachers, as physicians, lawyers and ministers.

Psychoanalytic therapy has in the past been confined to the treatment of severe chronic neurotics. It is obvious that the traditional procedure of applying the same technique to every patient can be followed only if the analyst selects for treatment those cases which require this type of treatment, excluding all either too severe or not severe enough for psychoanalysis. Such a selection of patients has had both practical and theoretical consequences. By excluding from psychoanalytic therapy both the psychotic and those suffering from the simpler neuroses, it has hampered the natural development of psychiatry and has even allowed psychiatrists to ignore the necessity for making a sound definition of psychoneurosis itself.

Since, until recently, most of the cases regarded as suitable for the psychoanalytic procedure were chronic neurotics whose illness had begun in childhood, the infantile neurosis was postulated as the etiologically important factor in every neurosis. All of the later traumatic experiences and the actual life situations were dismissed as "precipitating factors." This emphasis on the traumatic infantile experiences in the etiology of neurosis is justifiable only for the severe chronic psychoneuroses and the psychoses; it is not valid for the acute neurotic breakdown (easily recognizable) and has little value in the treatment of mild chronic cases who (often dismissed as being a little odd or "just not easy to get along with") have suffered experiences in early life which, although warping, were not incapacitating.

Neurotic tendencies lie latent in every person. When anyone is exposed to difficulties beyond his powers of adaptation, these latent tendencies may be called into action and an acute neurotic state develop. Acute neurotic states may occur in persons whose ego has always functioned well in the past. That Freud expressed this same view in his original etiological formulation was forgotten under the pressure of evidence of many years, gained solely from the treatment of the severe chronic neurotic. Now, however, recent discoveries in war psychiatry and in experimental psychoneurosis with animals force us to a less dogmatic, more comprehensive concept, which might be called a relativistic concept of neurosis.

PSYCHONEUROSIS DEFINED.—Psychoneurosis is a failure of the individual to deal successfully with a given situation, a failure to find socially acceptable gratification for subjective needs under given circumstances. This failure depends upon the balance between the ego's adaptability and the difficulty of the confronting problem. When the situation demands greater powers of integration than the ego possesses, a neurosis develops. Whether the ego became incapacitated in childhood, adolescence, or adult life, and how it is limited by constitutional endowment, are secondary questions. According to this concept of the causation of neurosis, both unfavorable constitutional endowment and infantile experiences on the one hand, and traumatic experiences of later life on the other, must be taken into consideration.

Freud expressed this view in his original etiological formulation: "For the consideration of the causes of neuroses, we may arrange neurotic diseases in a series in which two factors —sexual constitution and experience, or, if you wish, libido-fixation and self-denial—are represented in such a way that one increases as the other decreases. At one end of the series are the extreme cases of which you can say with full conviction: These persons would have become ill because of the peculiar development of their libido, no matter what they might have experienced, no matter how gently life might have treated them. At the other end are cases which would call for the reversed judgment, that the patients would undoubtedly have escaped illness if life had not thrust certain conditions upon them. But in the intermediate cases of the series, predisposing sexual constitution and subversive demands of life combine . . . Within this series I may grant a certain preponderance to the weight carried by the predisposing factors, but this admission too depends upon the boundaries within which you wish to delimit nervousness." [1]

Since psychoanalysis has dealt chiefly with chronic cases, the significance of this formulation has gradually been forgotten and infantile neurosis as the etiologically important factor in every neurosis has been postulated. Freud's original formulation, however, has had impressive verification in cases of acute war neuroses.

In those cases of psychosis and psychoneurosis severe enough to come to our attention, the relationship of unfavorable constitutional factors and traumatic experiences in infancy to traumatic experiences in later life is demonstrated in the following diagram.

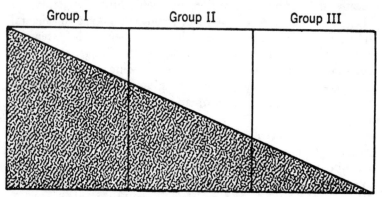

Group I   Group II   Group III

(Shaded area represents unfavorable constitutional factors plus traumatic experiences in infancy and childhood. Blank area represents traumatic experiences in later life.)

[1] Sigmund Freud, *A General Introduction to Psychoanalysis*, Boni & Liveright, Inc., New York, 1920.

Group I includes chronic cases with psychotic symptomatology who develop psychopathological symptoms under practically every life circumstance. (In general, this group is not treated by psychoanalysis.) *Group II* includes cases of psychoneurosis: depressions, compulsion neuroses, character neuroses, anxiety neuroses, a large number of conversion hysterias, some chronic vegetative neuroses. (This group constitutes the scope of standard psychoanalytic practice.) *Group III* represents neurotic breakdowns in formerly well-adjusted individuals subjected to extremely traumatic conditions. This group may show the symptomatology of Group II although they do not have the typical neurotic history (infantile neurosis). Many acute war neuroses are examples. (To this group belong a large number of the cases reported in this study.)

The Goal of Psychiatry

Psychiatry started with the care, observation and description of extreme cases of mental disturbance (psychosis) who required hospitalization. Then Freud and his school made the psychoneurotic a legitimate object of psychiatric study and therapy, thus giving doctors an added incentive for gaining a fuller knowledge of the psychodynamics involved in mental illness. The next logical step in this development is the extension of psychoanalytically oriented therapy to the simpler cases (the acute and the mild chronic) and the incipient cases of psychoneurosis—with the purpose of arresting the progress of, and the expectation of being ultimately able to prevent, psychoneuroses.

This is the supreme aim in every field of medicine. The limitation of therapy to the severe chronic cases has hampered the natural development of psychiatry toward this goal. The extension of dynamic therapy to include the acute, the mild chronic, and the incipient cases of neurosis removes this block.

Both therapy and prevention are served in the successful treatment of many cases. Thus the successful handling of an acute neurotic breakdown is prevention in that it might gradually develop into a chronic condition if the course of the disease were not halted. The intimidated ego, experiencing new failures in its early spontaneous efforts toward rehabilitation, would find its chances for coping with the life situation further diminished. In another way, the relief of any psychoneurosis is preventive in that the intimate associates of the neurotic, his family group, experience relief also. Often another breakdown within the family may be warded off by a beneficial change in the personality of one member or, when this is not possible, simply by the emotional support the therapist provides.

A more widespread help for emotionally disturbed people becomes possible with the more rational attitude toward psychiatry which is emerging in the general public. A visit to a psychiatrist is no longer fraught with opprobrium and anxiety but is becoming as acceptable as consultation with any other specialist in the field of medicine. People are becoming increasingly aware that emotional disturbance is accessible to rational treatment. This new attitude, made evident in the newspapers, periodicals, and current literature, and on the stage and screen, introduces a new chapter in the history of psychiatry—the prevention of emotional illness.

Still another result may be expected from this extension of psychodynamic therapy to the simpler neuroses. Our present theoretical views of the dynamic structure of the human personality have been greatly influenced by the study of chronic neurotics whose behavior has for many years carried the scars of traumatic childhood experiences. The study of disturbances in previously healthy persons will gradually correct these views. From dynamic psychopathology, the broadening scope of psychoanalytic therapy should lead to greater knowledge about the dynamic structure of the total personality, to dynamic psychology.

The development of a flexible use of the sound principles of psychodynamics is imperative. Neither the hit-and-miss variety of merely empirical psychotherapy based on intuition and common sense, nor the prolonged standard psychoanalytic procedure, can fill this need.

If we had to meet this social obligation with only that procedure which was developed to treat chronic psychoneurotics in time of peace, we should find ourselves woefully unprepared for the variety of disturbances left in the wake of war. If we were bound to a procedure which is so costly of time and effort, we could not begin to reach the vast numbers of people in need of help.

Only by a more flexible use of the therapeutic principles of psychoanalysis, adapted to the individual nature of each individual case, can our therapeutic heritage from Sigmund Freud be made truly useful—not merely for a small group but for society at large.

Franz Alexander, M.D.

Chapter 2

THE DEVELOPMENT OF PSYCHOANALYTIC
THERAPY

Before going into a detailed discussion of this new therapeutic orientation, we shall return to some psychoanalytic experimentations of the past which led up to the present more flexible techniques.

Sigmund Freud, the founder of psychoanalysis, was one of the great experimenters of all time. He subjected every formulation to the test of new experience with the result that his original theories underwent important changes. A review of the development of the so-called standard psychoanalytic technique will show the ever-changing character of his work, in which distinct phases can be differentiated.

First Period—Cathartic Hypnosis

When he took up the psychotherapeutic approach to emotionally disturbed patients, Freud was a physician and a neurologist. Accepted medical treatment at that time consisted either in administering drugs or performing a surgical operation. Therapy was then (and often still is) regarded as a procedure in which the physician "does something to" the patient—the classic example being a surgical operation by which a foreign body or a diseased organ is removed. A similar procedure is the giving of an emetic or a cathartic which brings about a dramatic process in the body leading to cure; or the giving of an injection, as in chemotherapy, by which the invading micro-organism is exterminated. Each of these medical procedures is a circumscribed performance, a therapeutic act which may or may not have to be repeated to bring about the desired effect.

The method of psychotherapy first developed by Freud, in collaboration with Breuer, was *cathartic hypnosis*. As even its name shows, cathartic hypnosis was also considered a dramatic one-act performance, in which the patient got rid of a spiritual foreign body—his repressed traumatic memories and pent-up affects.

In hypnosis the ego not only gave up its control over the emotions, but it also abandoned its function of testing reality. The hypnotized patient was asked questions with the purpose of uncovering the origin of his symptoms and of allowing him to discharge his repressed feelings. This discharge of emotion was considered of great therapeutic value and the method was therefore called "cathartic." Breuer and Freud soon saw, however, that simply discharging emotions did not cure the patient and that the hypnotic procedure had to be repeated again and again to obtain results.

In using this method, Freud made three significant discoveries: (1) that hysterical symptoms have their source in emotional disturbances of the past; (2) that these disturbing events are capable of undergoing complete repression from consciousness; and (3) that although discharge of repressed emotions (abreaction) in hypnosis gives temporary relief, it has no lasting therapeutic value in itself.

This insight into the cause and course of hysterical symptoms induced him to search for therapeutic techniques which would yield permanent results. He argued that since in hypnosis the patient is able to express his emotions only because his conscious personality—or more precisely, his critical faculty—is temporarily eliminated, the real therapeutic task must consist in making the conscious personality capable of facing the emotions which were so intolerable that they had to be suppressed. Even a repetition of the hypnotic experience does not improve the ego's capacity for dealing with the repressed emotions, since in hypnosis the ego is (in a sense) not there. His problem, therefore, was to find a method by which the patient retained the full functions of his conscious mind and yet could be induced to face that which it repudiated.

Second Period—Waking Suggestion

The next step was an experiment with *waking suggestion.* This can be considered the second period in Freud's scientific development. Freud would lay his hand on the patient's forehead and assure him that he could recall the past if he tried.

In the history of psychoanalysis this period was of the shortest duration. It is difficult to establish precisely how long it lasted. It started after 1895 and was given up before 1899 when Dora's analysis [1] was completed. It is certain, however, that after a relatively short period Freud learned that he could not, by suggestion alone, force his patients to remember those traumatic events which led to the neurotic condition, to face in themselves what they had not dared acknowledge before. As a result, this phase left the least impression on the therapeutic procedure.

Third Period—Free Association

Having convinced himself of the futility of a frontal attack, Freud now developed a new strategy—the method of *free association.* In free association, Freud found a means of unlocking the unconscious mind of the patient while the patient's consciousness was retained. The patient was required to tell whatever entered his mind without exerting any conscious selectives or applying any logic to the train of thought. What the patient expressed was drawn, therefore, from the whole span of his life experiences—from his thoughts and feelings, fantasies and dreams, of past and present. Dreams became an important source of unconscious material, not only because of their content but also because of the train of associations they aroused. Repressed feelings were thus allowed to come to the surface in an indirect manner.

Freud's main interest at that time remained focused upon the reconstruction of the pathogenic past. He hoped and expected that, while the patient in his daily interviews was giving expression to his uncontrolled train of thought, he would

---

[1] S. Freud, "Fragment of an Analysis of a Case of Hysteria," *Collected Papers,* Vol. III, p. 13. Hogarth Press, London, 1924.

gradually—almost in spite of himself—recall the events of the past which had disturbed him. The patient's conscious defense against his repressed emotions Freud tried to eliminate by what he called his "basic rule"—namely, that the patient reveal everything that occurred to him during the interview whether it be painful or embarrassing or seemingly unimportant.

The free associations were thus used as a substitute for the direct memory of hypnosis. In hypnosis, however, recollection of repressed events was not used alone to reconstruct etiology but also to discharge those emotions which were linked with the traumatic experiences of the past. When he replaced hypnosis with free association, Freud was still concerned with the therapeutic importance of the discharge of emotion. He expected the patient to recall the past gradually and, at the same time, to rid himself of the repressed feelings associated with the painful past. Free association differed from cathartic hypnosis in that the patient's recollections and discharge of emotion took place in small quantities over a long period, rather than in the more dramatic hypnotic session.

At that time, Freud did not see as clearly as he did later that the real therapeutic problem was not merely to make the patient recall a trauma and discharge those emotions connected with it, but rather to produce certain permanent changes in the ego which would make him capable of remembering painful events and dealing with emotional constellations which had previously been unbearable. This he must have sensed without stating it explicitly. One of his reasons for discarding hypnosis was, to be sure, that not everyone can be hypnotized; we find indications, however, that he saw even then that ego resistance had to be dealt with by bringing about a permanent change in the ego, not merely by rendering it defenseless through hypnosis.

Fourth Period—Transference Neurosis

It is in his report on Dora's analysis, published in 1905 but completed in 1899, that Freud gives his first account of *transference*—his most important discovery—which provides the most powerful instrument yet found for overcoming the patient's resistance to facing disturbing emotional experiences. In this treatment, he was still far from recognizing the full therapeutic significance of the transference phenomenon with all its technical implications. From that time on, however, a consistent development can be observed. After this discovery, the search for memories—that is to say, the intellectual reconstruction of the patient's life history—gave place more and more to the utilization, for therapeutic purposes, of the emotional attitudes developed by the patient toward the physician during analysis. The handling of transference manifestations and the patient's resistance gradually became the center of the therapy.

The emotional reaction of the patient toward the analyst Freud called "transference" because he saw that the patient transferred onto the analyst his neurotic behavior patterns that were based on past experiences, that the patient now entertained toward the therapist the same feelings and conflicts he had had in his childhood toward some person of authority. This re-living of his neurotic past in his relationship to the therapist in the form of an experimental neurosis of the present, Freud called *transference neurosis*.[2] The transference neurosis is a milder edition of the patient's real-life neurosis, of which he is cured step by step in the analysis.

In the transference phenomenon, Freud recognized the same principle so well known in immunology. The organism, receiving small quantities of injected toxins or bacteria, develops defenses against them. These antibodies enable the organism to protect itself against the invasion of the original toxins and bacteria when reexposed to infection. In the transference neurosis, the patient learns to deal with small quantities of the same emotional tensions which he could not master in the past and against which he could defend himself only by repression, by excluding the intolerable emotions from consciousness.

---

[2] The expression "transference neurosis" was also used by Freud in a different sense, referring to certain types of neurosis like hysteria in contrast to a narcissistic neurosis like the manic-depressive conditions. It is not in this sense that the expression is used in this book.

After Freud recognized that all the deeply ingrained emotional patterns of the patient, the whole infantile nucleus of his personality, gradually came into free expression during the treatment as the defenses against them were overcome, the transference neurosis as a dynamic reenactment of the pathogenic past became the basis of modern psychoanalytic therapy.

Later, as we shall see, transference analysis transformed therapy into a methodical training of the ego, gradually enabling the patient to deal with conflictful psychological situations which he had avoided before on account of earlier traumatic experiences. Although both principles—the old etiological reconstruction of the past, and the newer analysis of transference manifestations—continued side by side in theory and practice, their mutual relationship was not fully clarified for a long time.

Fifth Period—Emotional Reeducation

After Freud's discovery of the significance of the transference, it took about fifteen years for psychoanalytic therapy to emancipate itself from the formulations based on the one-act drama, cathartic hypnosis, and become transformed into a procedure aimed at achieving permanent changes in the ego's functional capacity by a slowly progressing emotional training —more an educational process than a therapy in the original sense.

This transformation is not yet complete. The present-day standard technique, and particularly our therapeutic attitudes and thinking, still display many features which belong to the earlier phases. The main purpose of this book is to hasten this transformation and to encourage the development of more pertinent forms of psychotherapy.

ARENA OF PSYCHOTHERAPY.—Some analysts still work on the assumption that the curative process takes place mainly on the couch, the doctor by his interpretations performing a "therapeutic act" upon the patient. They have not yet fully appreciated the significance of the fact that psychoanalytic treatment is a part of the patient's ego development. For the most part, this assumption that the therapeutic process is confined to the couch is an uncritical carry-over from the past. Any psychodynamically well-trained therapist (should he seriously try to figure out the therapeutic significance of the events in the patient's daily life) would agree that under the influence of the emotional and intellectual experiences on the couch, the patient becomes capable of having beneficial experiences in his life—at his office with his colleagues, superiors and inferiors; with his wife or his lover; with his children—and that the therapeutic achievements result in part from these life experiences.

Although we are still influenced by the dramatic curative happenings of the hypnotic sessions, common sense requires every sound therapist to reckon with the effect of the patient's daily life and, if absolutely necessary, to interfere. Many practitioners, however, consider it a "practical compromise" and not a desirable part of the treatment to offer any direction to the patient in regard to his daily life. Consequently, a divided attitude has developed: as a scientifically trained therapist, the physician feels he should center his whole attention on the interviews; as a man of common sense, he knows he must guide the patient's daily activities to some degree. The common failure lies in not making this guidance an integral part of the whole treatment.

The analytic sessions may be considered catalytic agents, speeding up and making possible new relationships and experiences. The influence upon the ego of these experiences of daily life is as great as and often much greater than that of the interviews. Having the courage of one's convictions and speaking up in the office for the first time may be the beginning of a profound change in a patient's capacity for self-assertion which had been inhibited by a suppressive home atmosphere in his early childhood. Although this becomes possible only through the experience of the analytic interviews and follows the first successful self-assertion of the patient toward the therapist, the therapeutic influence of such an actual experience is much greater than that of the interviews themselves which are but a "shadow play" of real life.

The practical consequences of the assumption that the therapeutic process is confined to the interviews, are enormous. It is responsible for many unjustifiably prolonged treatments, for the unnecessary insistence upon daily interviews when weekly interviews may suffice or may be preferable. It is responsible for our fear of interrupting the treatment, even at the right moment. It is responsible for our not clarifying one of the most general experiences of psychoanalytic therapy—the mysterious post-analytic improvement. This orientation is also responsible for not recognizing those phases in psychoanalysis when daily interviews become detrimental to the cure, giving the patient an excuse for avoiding experiences in life and substituting for them the safe experiences of the analytic sessions.

SIGNIFICANCE OF RECOVERED MEMORIES.—The belief that the recovery of memories is, in itself, one of the most important therapeutic factors, is still held by many psychoanalysts and in a sense can be considered to be a residue of the period of cathartic hypnosis. The persistent emphasis upon intellectual reconstructions of memory gaps can possibly be traced back to the relatively short period of waking suggestion; but it was the still greater emphasis during the free association phase on the intellectual understanding of the past that made psychoanalytic treatment almost synonymous with genetic research. As a result, the filling in of memory gaps became crystallized as the therapeutic goal of psychoanalysis.

This exaggerated emphasis has long hampered both the understanding of why patients remember repressed events and the correct evaluation of their therapeutic significance. It was not until 1930 [3] that the recovery of memories was demonstrated to be not the *cause* of therapeutic progress but its *result,* and that recollection of repressed childhood memories occurs, as a rule, only after the same type of emotional constellation has been experienced and mastered in the transference situation.

---

[3] F. Alexander, "Zur Genese des Kastrationskomplexes," *Internationale Zeitschrift für Psychoanalyse,* XVI Band, 1930.—"Concerning the Genesis of the Castration Complex," *Psychoanalytic Review,* Vol. XXII, No. 1, January 1935 (translated by C. F. Menninger, M.D.).

All repressions follow the pattern set up by the child when he first repressed painful emotions his weak and inexperienced ego could not cope with. Recently repressed emotions are more easily recaptured than the corresponding infantile material. When the patient has learned to accept recently repressed material that has been brought to consciousness within the transference relationship, his ego becomes more permeable and he is enabled to recover earlier memories of the same emotional coloring, with which his mature ego can now contend successfully. The real therapeutic accomplishment consists in the patient's successful mastery in the transference relationship of a previously unbearable emotional conflict. Remembering the original traumatic experience may be considered an indicator of progress. The fact that the patient can now remember something he could not before, simply shows that his ego's capacity to face a certain type of unbearable emotional constellation has been increased through the treatment.

This, as was noticed later, is really but an elaboration of a brief remark made by Freud in one of his papers: "From the repetition-reactions which are exhibited in the transference, the familiar paths lead back to the awakening of the memories, which yield themselves without difficulty after the resistances have been overcome." [4] It is unfortunate that this isolated remark of Freud's was not developed earlier and in greater detail, with all its significant consequences for therapy.

The recovery of memories is not only a barometer of progress indicating the ego's increased ability to face repressed emotional situations; it has the additional therapeutic value of helping the patient learn how to discriminate between the past and the present situation. For example, a patient's early manifestations of aggressiveness have been intimidated by a father who required complete submissiveness from his son. As a result (following the principle of "spreading" or generalization of emotional reactions) the patient has become inhibited in all situations in which he faces a person of authority. By reviving the past emotional reactions toward the father, we

_____
[4] S. Freud, *Collected Papers*, Vol. II, p. 375, Hogarth Press, London. 1924.

enable the patient to develop the power to differentiate between the original childhood situation and his present status. He will then realize that he is no longer helpless and can afford to resist the oppressive attitude of others.

The principal curative powers of this treatment, however, lie in the fact that he can express his aggressiveness toward the therapist without being punished, and can assert himself without being censured. This actual experience is needed before the patient gains the emotional perception that he is no longer a child facing an omnipotent father. This type of emotional experience as it occurs during treatment, we call "corrective emotional experience" and we consider it the most important factor in all uncovering types of therapy.

It is not necessary—nor is it possible—during the course of treatment to recall *every* feeling that has been repressed. Therapeutic results can be achieved without the patient's recalling all important details of his past history; indeed, good therapeutic results have come in cases in which not a single forgotten memory has been brought to the surface. Ferenczi and Rank were among the first to recognize this principle and apply it to therapy. However, the early belief that the patient "suffers from memories" has so deeply penetrated the minds of the analysts that even today it is difficult for many to recognize that the patient is suffering not so much from his memories as from his incapacity to deal with his actual problems of the moment. The past events have of course prepared the way for his present difficulties, but then every person's reactions are dependent upon behavior patterns formed in the past.

Merely remembering an intimidating or demoralizing event does not change the effect of such an experience. Only a corrective experience can undo the effect of the old. This new corrective experience may be supplied by the transference relationship, by new experiences in life, or by both. A genetic reconstruction of the past is less important for the patient than for the physician; to him it is essential because only in the light of the past will he be able to understand and interpret the meaning of the patient's transference behavior. It is on this understanding that he bases his treatment and helps the patient to find a better and happier way to live.

Conclusion

We have given this brief outline of the history of basic psychoanalytic principles in order to show the logical development of our flexible approach to psychiatric problems. It is by no means a comprehensive statement of the history of psychoanalysis from Freud to the present. If it were, many more names would have to be included to show their influence on the growth of this discipline.

In historical perspective, our work is a continuation and realization of ideas first proposed by Ferenczi and Rank.[5] They advocated an emphasis upon emotional experience instead of intellectual genetic understanding of the sources of the patient's symptoms. They held that emotional experience should replace the search for memories and intellectual reconstruction. At the same time, they proposed another radical departure from the usual procedure by setting a date of termination for treatment. In this respect also, they were groping in the right direction; unfortunately, they did not draw the correct technical conclusion (as to termination) from their correct evaluation of psychoanalysis as a kind of emotional training. Enforced termination was not a method which could be used successfully in the majority of cases and, because of this one faulty technical generalization, the many valid parts of Ferenczi and Rank's contribution did not find adequate recognition.

The briefest of historical outlines would be incomplete without some mention of the work of Jung and Adler, both of whom were associated with Freud in the early days of psychoanalysis. Each developed a school of his own and each has made well-known contributions both to psychodynamic theory and to psychotherapeutic techniques based on psycho-

---

[5] S. Ferenczi and O. Rank, (Developmental Goals of Psychoanalysis) *The Development of Psychoanalysis*, Nervous & Mental Diseases Pub. Co., New York, 1925 (translated by Caroline Newton).—*Entwicklungsziele der Psychoanalyse*, Internationaler Psychoanalytischer Verlag, Wien, 1924.

dynamic principles which it would be of interest to discuss if only space permitted.

A review of the literature in the field of psychoanalytic therapy of the last decade would reveal a large body of ideas and observations similar in direction to the views expressed in this book. Of the more recent contributions, the work of Oberndorf [6] comes nearest to the orientation of this study. To give anything like an adequate account of recent work in this field would go far beyond the limits set for this volume.

The purpose of this brief review has been merely to recall the main trends in the development of psychoanalytic therapy from the earliest technique of cathartic hypnosis to the present, and to show that our main contribution to the growth of psychotherapy is a return from stereotyped thinking to experimentalism.

Franz Alexander, M.D.

---

[6] C. P. Oberndorf, "Factors in Psychoanalytic Therapy," *American Journal of Psychiatry,* 98 :750, 1942.

Chapter 3

THE PRINCIPLE OF FLEXIBILITY

As long as the psychoanalytic method of treatment was considered a single procedure, the analyst—whether he was aware of it or not—selected his patient to fit his technique; only a few tried to adapt the procedure to the diversity of cases they encountered. Such a state of affairs is far from satisfactory. In all medicine there are very few instances in which the therapeutic tool is rigidly fixed and the patients made to conform. The logical solution to the problems of therapy is rather the converse. Not only do their ailments differ greatly, but the patients themselves present many physical and psychological differences. In psychotherapy, as in all therapy, the physician must adapt his technique to the needs of the patient.

Today the tendency among psychoanalysts is to be less rigid in matters of technique. In the research cases described in this volume, the psychoanalytic method has been used in a flexible manner. We have experimented with frequency of interview, the use of chair or couch as the situation required, interruptions of long or short duration in preparation for terminating the treatment, and the combination of psychotherapy with drug or other treatment. Above all, we have sought to learn how to control and manipulate the transference relationship so as to achieve the specific goal and fit the particular psychodynamics of each case.

When a patient consults us, we do not accept him for any specific method of psychotherapy; the procedure is based upon diagnostic opinion. Yet, not even after the initial diagnostic appraisal can we foretell what technique will be necessary for a later phase of the treatment. As we now practice psychoanalytic therapy, we seldom use one and the same method of approach from the first to the last day of treatment.

The number and variety of psychotherapeutic techniques will probably continue to multiply. Our aim, however, is always the same: to increase the patient's ability to find gratifications for his subjective needs in ways acceptable both to himself and to the world he lives in, and thus to free him to develop his capacities.

This therapeutic aim can be achieved by the use of various therapeutic techniques. Only the nature of the individual case can determine which technique is best suited to bring about the curative processes of emotional discharge, insight, and a thorough assimilation of the significance of the recovered unconscious material, and, above all, the corrective emotional experiences necessary to break up the old reaction pattern. Whether the abreaction and the corrective experience take place on the couch during free association or in direct conversation between patient and therapist sitting vis-à-vis, whether it is effected through narcosis, or whether it occurs outside the analytic interview in actual life situations while the patient is still under the influence of the psychoanalytic interview—all these are technical details determined by the nature of the individual case. In some cases the development of a full-fledged transference neurosis may be desirable; in others it should perhaps be avoided altogether. In some it is imperative that emotional discharge and insight take place very gradually; in others with patients whose ego strength is greater, interviews with great emotional tension may be not only harmless but highly desirable. All this depends upon the needs of the patient in a particular phase of the therapeutic procedure.

Is Such a Psychotherapy Psychoanalytic?—Some psychoanalysts who have used the standard method exclusively may feel we are not justified in calling all these different techniques "psychoanalytic." They may argue that the expression should be reserved for the procedure developed by Freud and practiced by his followers for the last forty years.

Whether the designation "psychoanalytic therapy" is justified depends upon one's definition of psychoanalysis. That

concept of psychoanalysis which is based on superficial conformity to the requirements of daily interviews, uninterrupted
free association and the use of a couch, and which regards the
transference neurosis as inevitable, obviously does not include
the flexibility we advocate. However, if one defines psychoanalysis by more essential criteria as any therapy *based on
psychodynamic principles* which attempts to bring the patient
into *a more satisfactory adjustment to his environment* and
to assist *the harmonious development of his capacities,* then
all forms of therapy, however flexible, having this basis and
this goal, may be considered psychoanalytic.

Yet even the so-called standard psychoanalytic therapy does
not consist merely in the patient's dreams, fantasies, free associations, and the analyst's interpretations thereof. Even this
technique often entails direct questioning by the analyst, steer-
ing the material in the direction which seems most significant
to the course of the analysis. It may require advice to the
patient concerning the conduct of his affairs outside the treatment; it may even, in some instances, demand active interference by the analyst.

Then too, assimilation of newly acquired insight cannot be
credited to the analyst's skillful interpretations alone, any more
than the healing of an incision can be said to result solely from
the surgeon's skillful suture. Just as the healing of a wound
is a natural function of the human body, so the integration of
new insight is a normal function of the ego. The surgeon
endeavors to create the best possible conditions for the healing
of the wound; the psychoanalyst tries to create the most
favorable conditions for the integration, by the ego, of its
recently liberated psychic energy. Integration is the ego's main
function; the psychoanalyst merely supports it by proper management of the transference relationship.

And finally, the analytic process is not confined to the
analytic interview. Abreaction and the development of new
emotional reaction patterns take place not only in the presence
of the therapist but throughout the rest of the day or week—
at home, at the club, in the office. The importance of this fact
has been gradually impressed upon us and we have become

progressively aware that what transpires during this interval between the therapeutic sessions is of tremendous significance to the patient's progress toward health. Moreover, actual events within the family life or in business or other pursuits may help or hinder therapeutic progress. The careful analyst, therefore, is actively concerned not only with the analytic situation but also with the patient's other relationships, how they are affected by the analysis and how they in turn affect the analytic work.

Frequency of Interview

PROCRASTINATION: REGRESSION.—The standard procedure of daily interviews tends, in general, to gratify the patient's dependent needs more than is desirable. In a large number of cases the same results—emotional insight and relief of anxieties—could have been achieved with fewer interviews and less time if a technique of changing the frequency of interview according to need had been used from the very beginning of the treatment. Just as a person who is fed every half-hour never becomes conscious of the feeling of hunger, so the analytic patient whose needs for dependence are continually gratified never becomes emotionally aware of them. In such a situation, reducing the frequency of interview will suddenly bring into consciousness the dependent needs, together with all the reactive resentments for their frustration.

One should not forget that daily interviews exercise a seductive influence on a patient's regressive and procrastinating tendencies. The neurotic's proneness to evasion (after all, the most fundamental factor in his withdrawal from the actual life situation) is favored by the expectation of an almost infinite number of interviews. "If not today, tomorrow we will solve the problem—or next month, in the next half-year, the next two or three years."

This expectation of a protracted treatment has its therapeutic value, of course, in a patient who comes to the analyst in despair, sensing his utter incapacity to endure his given life situation. The initial improvement in severe neurotics is, to a large degree, due to the soothing effect of the procrastination sanctioned by the psychoanalytic technique. One relieves the patient by allowing him to evade the pressing issues of his life and to regress to a more comfortable infantile position, not only in fantasy but in reality, in the real relationship between patient and analyst.

By allowing such an actual regression, however, we later find ourselves involved in new difficulties. The initial soothing effect of the prolonged outlook gradually becomes corruptive and the therapist, faced with the task of driving the patient from his comfortable infantile position, realizes anew how difficult it is to force anyone to give up acquired rights.

When pregenital material (that which applies to sensations experienced in early infancy) appears in psychotherapy, it is frequently considered significant traumatic material when it may actually be merely an escape back to the early pretraumatic, highly dependent emotional state in which the patient felt safe and contented. Although it is true the deeper a patient sinks into a dependent transference neurosis the more regressive pregenital material he will produce, it is a fallacy to consider an analysis in which the patient brings up much regressive material as more thorough than one primarily centered around the actual life conflict. Regressive material is a sign not of the depth of the analysis but of the extent of the strategic withdrawal of the ego—a neurotic withdrawal from a difficult life situation back to childhood longings for dependence gratifiable only in fantasy.

In every neurosis we look for that time in the patient's life when he refused to yield to the ever-changing requirements of the process of maturation, to "grow up." This refusal may take place in almost any phase of life from early infancy through adulthood, and the severity of the neurosis is determined in part by how early in life the individual set himself against growing up. This point marks the beginning of the neurosis. When regressive material is brought which antedates this point, it should be evaluated, therefore, as a sign of resistance and not as deep penetration into the sources of the neurosis.

The more skillfully a treatment is conducted, the less time will be spent with such regressive material. It is the therapist's duty to lead the patient from his retreat back into the present, and to induce him to make new attempts to solve the problem from which he fled into the past. With the correct interpretation and handling of the transference relationship, the need for such deep regressions can be almost entirely avoided.

It should, therefore, be a general principle in all psychotherapy to attempt to check this regressive tendency from the very beginning of the treatment, allowing no more procrastination and regression than is absolutely necessary to calm panic, anxiety, and despair.

INTENSITY: EMOTIONAL LEVEL.—An extreme generosity with interviews is not only uneconomical but, in many cases, makes the analysis emotionally less penetrating. Daily interviews often tend to reduce the patient's emotional participation in the therapy; they become routine, and prevent the development of strong emotions by allowing the patient to verbalize his transference feelings as they emerge. This is particularly the case with aggressive impulses felt toward the analyst, for if the patient can give vent to them daily in small amounts he never becomes aware of them in a convincing manner. When the intensity of such hostile impulses is too low, it may be well to let it increase by lessening the frequency of interviews; when it is very great, more frequent interviews become imperative.

It is a common experience that an analysis in which the emotional level is low progresses extremely slowly. The whole procedure becomes intellectualized, without the real emotional participation of the patient. In general, stronger emotional participation brings the issues more clearly to the foreground and makes insight more vivid, thereby speeding up the progress of the treatment. Consequently, every analysis should be conducted on as high an emotional level as the patient's ego can stand without diminishing its capacity for insight.

This level, of course, varies from case to case. Roughly speaking, in patients with a so-called "weak ego" (poor integrative power), the emotional discharge and accompanying insight must take place very gradually. Such severely neurotic individuals cannot tolerate intense emotional participation and require small abreactions in almost daily interviews over a long period. Patients with good integrative faculty ("strong ego"), who can endure more intense sessions without developing too strong defenses, often need relatively infrequent interviews. With many such patients, as soon as a fairly good rapport has developed—which in some cases may require only a few interviews—the entire treatment may be carried out in infrequent interviews. These are apt to become more dramatic and of greater emotional intensity than the psychoanalytic interviews in the standard technique.

MANIPULATION OF FREQUENCY.—Every psychoanalyst must at some time have unwittingly frustrated a patient—when circumstances forced him to cancel an appointment or when, for some reason, the patient had to leave without seeing the physician—and found that association material which had seemed meaningless or obscure because of the small amount of emotion involved, had suddenly become crystal clear. Vacations which were not intended to be technically indicated interruptions of treatment but were solely to refresh the analyst, have often had a similar vitalizing effect upon a treatment become stale in the routine of daily interviews. Many psychoanalytic treatments owe their progress to such an accident which precipitates more relevant material than can the most astute interpretations on material devoid of emotion.

The point to be considered, then, is how to use such incidents intentionally as an integral part of the therapeutic procedure, how to manipulate the frequency of interview so as to secure the patient's emotional participation and to maintain it at the desired level.

Frequency of interview must be regarded as a relative affair. Weekly interviews in some instances may be regarded as the normal frequency, in others constitute a drastic reduction, in still others take on the character of an interruption of treatment. For instance, a patient who has been seeing the physician five times a week might find three times a week a radical reduction, whereas an interval of an entire week might be tantamount to an interruption of treatment.

When the therapeutic relationship has become well established and the patient's ego defenses have been sufficiently analyzed, the patient reaches a fairly stable equilibrium. In this equilibrium—which, in standard psychoanalysis, may develop in some patients after three or four months—the patient feels much as if he were to say, "Yes, I am acting like a child —but what of it? This is not real life anyway." This partial insight into his dependence retains a kind of theoretical quality since it has been gained on the basis of relatively unimportant matters. It therefore becomes almost imperative to increase the emotional intensity in order to make the patient's insight more realistic and convincing. In this phase of the treatment, a radical curtailing of the frequency of interview (from five a week to two or even one) tends to make the emotional insight much deeper and speeds up the analytic process.

It must be borne in mind, however, that reducing the frequency of the interviews can cause stronger emotional participation only if the patient has already developed a fairly intense transference relationship. A patient who is not yet interested in the analysis will not react to the reduction of interviews by developing more intense transference feelings. In most cases, therefore, it is advisable to ensure interest by a series of interviews before reduction of frequency can serve as a method of intensifying the emotional participation.

The opposite procedure of shifting from infrequent interviews to more frequent ones may become necessary in other emotional situations. It is a common observation that in some patients accustomed to daily interviews, a few days' intermission may increase the resistance to such an extent that the patient becomes unable to continue the treatment, may never return to it. This is true of the resistance which develops from repressed hostile impulses, from intense feelings of dependent coloring incompatible with the patient's self-esteem and pride, or from erotic feelings toward the analyst which produce anxiety. In such situations, an intellectual check of the too-strong emotions is needed. More frequent interviews at this point allow a gradual discharge of the emotional tension which has accumulated during the intermission. (Occasionally the opposite technique can be used with success.)

The "acting-out" character also benefits from careful manipulation of the frequency of interview. Since these individuals (feeling no restraint within themselves) tend to act on their impulses without regard for social standards, they frequently clash not only with convention but with the law. The psychiatrist must represent prohibition in his own person and must anticipate his patient's impulses in order to help him by restraint. It is obvious that such patients will at times require almost constant contact with the therapist.

Another important reason for manipulating the frequency of interview lies in the tendency of psychoneurotic patients (with the exception of the "acting-out" character) to substitute experiences of the analysis for life experiences. The transference neurosis comes to serve the purpose of the original neurosis: withdrawal from real participation in life. The original neurosis was a withdrawal into fantasy; the transference neurosis is a withdrawal into the relatively harmless realm of the therapeutic relationship. When the frequency of interview is reduced, the patient is given less opportunity to substitute these safe analytic experiences for life experiences. The sooner a patient can translate what he learns during the treatment into actual life experiences, the faster the analysis will progress.

ECONOMICAL PSYCHOTHERAPY.—From the beginning, the therapist must persist in trying to counteract the patient's tendency to sink himself into a safe, comfortable transference neurosis.[1] Without this continuous, alert pressure from the analyst, even relatively mild neurotic disturbances may lead to a disproportionately prolonged treatment. A correct evaluation of how fast an analysis can progress, how intense an emotional strain the patient can stand, will decide whether the procedure

[1] Cf. S. Rado, "The Relationship of Patient to Therapist," *American Journal of Orthopsychiatry*, Vol. XII, No. 3, July 1942.

will assume the character of the standard psychoanalysis or that of so-called brief psychotherapy.

The nearer the analyst can keep the patient to his actual life problems, the more intensive and effective the therapeutic process is. From the point of view of genetic research, it might be advisable to encourage the patient to wander way back into the Garden of Eden of his early youth; therapeutically, however, such a retreat is valuable only insofar as it sheds light upon the present. Memory material must always be correlated with the present life situation, and the patient must never be allowed to forget that he came to the physician not for an academic understanding of the etiology of his condition, but for help in solving his actual life problems.

The therapeutic maxim of an economical psychotherapy, therefore, must be to allow as little regression as the patient can stand, only that procrastination which is unavoidable, and as little substitution as possible of transference gratifications for life experiences.

PREPARATION FOR INTERRUPTIONS.—In most cases of standard psychoanalysis, the neurotic gratifications of the transference relationship sooner or later outweigh the patient's therapeutic desire for recovery. Freud expressed this as follows: "This transference soon replaces in the patient's mind the desire to be cured." The reason for this is that after the resistance against the emotions in relation to the therapist has been analyzed, the transference neurosis loses much of its painful aspect and the patient's shame for his dependence upon the analyst, his guilt for his hostile impulses, diminishes. The original neurosis was a combination of gratification, conflicts, and suffering; the transference neurosis repeats all these features but, with progressive analysis of the ego's defenses, the conflictful elements diminish and its gratifications increase.

No wonder the patient is not inclined to give it up if he can afford to continue treatment. It is naïve to think that most patients stick to their prolonged treatments so consistently, often year after year, only because of their desperate desire to be cured. This may be true in the first phase of the treatment, but later they cling to it because it gives them neurotic gratification without much suffering. It is, nevertheless, true that the patient can frequently be observed behaving more normally in his daily life during this phase because, in a sense, the transference situation serves as a crutch and at the same time lessens his neurotic needs.

As the patient has no emotional need for a change, it may be extremely difficult to break up this inertia—particularly if there are no external inconveniences connected with the analysis, such as an excessive financial burden or awkward time arrangements. Freud was aware of this impasse in standard psychoanalysis when he stated that in the early years of his practice he had difficulty in persuading his patients to continue their treatment; later he had difficulty in inducing them to give it up. Today an efficiently handled psychotherapy does not allow such a dilemma to occur but combats the growing inertia while still in an incipient stage.

The status quo can now be disturbed only by diminishing the gratifications of the transference neurosis through as radical a reduction of interviews as is at all tolerable for the patient, leading up to an interruption of the treatment which will serve as a test of his capacity to use in his daily life the new reaction patterns acquired in the therapy.

Interruptions and Termination of Treatment

Many patients in this phase, having instinctively learned their therapist's predilections, bring seemingly interesting material to allay the analyst's impatience and give an impression of steady progress and deepening of analytic insight. While the analyst may believe that they are engaged in a thorough "working-through," in reality the procedure has become a farce, a clever technique of procrastination on the part of the patient. Or a patient may reach that place in treatment where he merely repeats material he has brought many times before, in order to avoid opening up other conflicts. Or again, a patient may make a "flight into health" in order to avoid painful insight. The genuineness of these attitudes is not always easy to divine. The therapist may take them for indications that the patient is ready to leave treatment and to meet life entirely on his own, or he may realize that the patient is employing unconscious subterfuge. In either case, an interruption will show whether the patient is able to lead a normal life without his regular interviews.

During an interruption the patient learns which of his previous difficulties he still retains, and the following interviews usually center around those emotional problems in which he needs further help. The author of this section has used the method of one or more preparatory interruptions almost exclusively during the last twelve years (the interruptions varying in length from one to eighteen months) and has found that the analysis after interruption has, without exception, become much more intensive, accomplishing more in the following few weeks than had been achieved in months before.

At first, the interruption may have to be imposed by decree and the patient forced to rely on his own strength and judgment. Soon, however, he may recognize that he actually does not need the therapist as much as before. This diminishes the resentment brought on by the patient's feeling of helplessness and increases his confidence in his own powers.

It is advisable to make the interruption not too short. The patient should have an opportunity to struggle with his problems alone and should not be encouraged to turn to the analyst at the first hint of relapse. On the other hand, he should have the assurance that if he really needs his therapist, he can always return to him. We thus avoid recrudescence of the patient's resistance to giving up his neurotic escape reactions and the panic reactions which have been observed in experiments with the termination technique developed by Ferenczi and Rank.

Termination of treatment, if the method of preparatory interruptions is used, will not be artificial but will become a natural ending to the therapy. Experience—how the patient actually reacted to previous interruptions—will determine when the therapy should be brought to a close, not such theoretical criteria as the filling in of memory gaps and complete understanding of the etiological factors, nor even the depth of intellectual insight. In some cases, the patient will be capable of completely changing the life situation in which he failed before and which precipitated his neurosis, adapting it to his needs and to his capacity for gratifying them. In all cases, the patient will have given actual, tested proof of his ability to find ego-syntonic gratification for his needs.

At the present state of our knowledge, it is difficult to make precise predictions concerning the length of a treatment or the number of interviews required in any given case. Our task is to make the patient self-reliant by exerting a constant but not excessive pressure, blocking the patient's neurotic retreat into fantasy and into the past, and urging him toward the actual difficulties of his current life situation. The intensity of this pressure—upon which the rate of progress, and thus the length of treatment, depends—can be determined only through repeated testing during the treatment, observing the patient's reactions as they manifest themselves either in recrudescence of resistance, or in progressive efforts in his everyday life.

How much preparatory experience in the transference relationship a patient needs before he becomes capable of handling the corresponding interpersonal situations in real life, depends upon the nature of the case. With patients whose ego's functional capacity is only temporarily impaired under trying life conditions, a few interviews to relieve acute anxiety may suffice. The intensity of the neurotic regressive trends in the different patients, however, is of such extreme variety that the length of treatment may be anything from a few isolated interviews to the standard technique of daily interviews extending over several years.

Extra-Therapeutic Experiences

The so-called normal individual, when he fails in a life situation and has suffered a serious setback, will make new attempts to solve his actual problem instead of having recourse to the substitutive solutions of neurotic regression. An essential feature of neurosis is the giving up of systematic efforts of trial and error to overcome those difficulties which precipitated the neurotic breakdown. This neurotic reaction to traumatic experiences appears in all degrees of intensity. In some cases, no more help is needed than temporary support to enable the patient's ego to make new attempts at finding gratifications for its needs, even in the new baffling situation. At the other extreme are patients who react to almost every change in their life situation with neurotic escapes into fantasy and regressive behavior. Between these two extremes there is a continuous gradation from the more acute to chronic types of neurosis.

The degree to which one should rely upon the therapeutic effect of the patient's experiences in life depends upon the nature of the case and the phase of the treatment. In general, a greater part of the therapy may take place outside the sessions with the less severe cases, in which an interview a week or every other week may have enough influence on the patient's daily life to insure progress. At the other extreme is the patient who must be hospitalized and under constant supervision. Another generalization of approximate validity is that, with the progress of treatment, one can rely more and more on the beneficent effect of actual experiences in life; these experiences, of course, have been made possible by the preparatory interviews in which the patient has learned to handle certain emotional situations in his relationship to the analyst.

It is important to keep in mind that the patient will finally have to solve his problems in actual life, in his relationships to his wife and his children, his superiors and his competitors, his friends and his enemies. The experiences in the transference relationship are only preparations, a training for the real battle. The sooner the patient can be led against those real obstacles in life from which he retreated and can be induced to engage in new experimentation, the more quickly can satisfactory therapeutic results be achieved.

In every psychotherapy, therefore, whether it takes the form of the standard technique or that of some briefer method, an integral part of the treatment consists in observing and systematically influencing the patient's experiences in life.

The attitude has been overstressed that a "real psycho-analyst"—in contrast to the "practical psychotherapist" who might give advice and directives to the patient—should not try to guide the patient in his daily life and should encourage or discourage his activities as little as possible. It was formerly felt (and sometimes still is) that during treatment the patient really need not do much concerning his practical problems, and that in any case to influence his daily activities was not the concern of the therapist. This assumption that the interviews will solve everything as if by magic has prolonged many treatments unduly. Freud himself came to the conclusion that in the treatment of some cases, phobias for example, a time arrives when the analyst must encourage the patient to engage in those activities he avoided in the past. (A patient who retreats into isolation, for instance, should in the different phases of the treatment try again and again to have human contacts.) This is a fundamental principle of every treatment, an intrinsic part of the therapy.

Even more generally accepted than the motto "As little interference in the patient's daily life as possible" is another rule all students of psychoanalysis were formerly taught: "No important changes in the life situation until after the completion of treatment." Back of this rule was the sound observation that some patients were inclined to act out in life their ever-changing trends as they became liberated during the treatment. For example, a formerly very cautious, intimidated patient, when he becomes aware of the dependent attitude responsible for his former habit of never standing up for his rights, may impulsively give up a good job just to prove his independence and courage. Or a patient whose sexual repressions have been relieved, may impulsively rush into promiscuous activities.

And yet, in a certain phase of the treatment the patient may be ready to marry, for instance, even though he still needs further treatment. Serious delay of therapeutic progress may result from adherence to the rule of "no important, irreversible changes during treatment." Marriage, change of occupation, even change of profession, may be indispensable to the therapeutic success of a case. and waiting for the end of treatment before such a change may destroy all possibility of success. The advice not to make important decisions during treatment, therefore, should be given the patient in a modified, more flexible form: "No important, irreversible changes in the life situation, *unless both therapist and patient agree.*"

First Attempts.—The therapeutic process must at no time be thought of as restricted to the emotional experiences within the transference relationship. Too often it is forgotten that transference experiences and life experiences take place simultaneously and parallel to each other. Having learned to handle hitherto-conflictful emotional constellations in the transference relationship, the patient must then be helped to experiment with the same type of constellation in real life.

Like the adage "Nothing succeeds like success," there is no more powerful therapeutic factor than the performance of activities which were formerly neurotically impaired or inhibited. No insight, no emotional discharge, no recollection can be as reassuring as accomplishment in the actual life situation in which the individual failed. Thus the ego regains that confidence which is the fundamental condition, the prerequisite, of mental health. Every success encourages new trials and decreases inferiority feelings, resentments, and their sequelae— fear, guilt, and resulting inhibitions. Successful attempts at productive work, love, self-assertion, or competition will change the vicious circle to a benign one; as they are repeated, they become habitual and thus eventually bring about a complete change in the personality.

The chief therapeutic value of the transference situation lies in the fact that it allows the patient to experience this feeling of success in rehearsal, a rehearsal which must then be followed by actual performance. And curbing the patient's tendency to procrastinate and to substitute analytic experience for reality (by careful manipulation of the transference relationship, by timely directives and encouragement) is one of the most effective means of shortening treatment. Fostering favorable experiences in the actual life situation at the right moment in the treatment tends to make for economical psychotherapy, bringing it to an earlier conclusion than otherwise. The therapist need not wait until the end of treatment but, at the right moment, should encourage the patient (or even require him) to do those things which he avoided in the past, to experiment in that activity in which he had failed before.

While it is important not to urge the patient prematurely, the therapist's fear that his patient will fail is usually stronger than it should be. The therapist must prepare the patient for failures, explaining that they are unavoidable and that the most important thing for him is to be always ready to try new experiments. Moreover, failures can be turned to advantage when they are carefully analyzed and their cause thoroughly understood by the patient.

Franz Alexander, M.D.

Manipulation of the Transference Relationship

We have repeatedly referred to the transference relationship as one of the most important tools with which the psychotherapist must work. Whatever the form of psychotherapy, be it a long-drawn-out psychoanalysis or the briefest of brief therapies, how the transference reactions are used determines the course of the treatment and may well decide whether or not it will be successful.

To make any tool serve our purpose most effectively, we must first understand its full potentialities—both to help and to hinder the work in hand. The intricate subject of the transference phenomenon itself is discussed in Chapter 5. Here we shall consider only the therapeutic importance of the transference relationship, why it should be controlled, and how to manipulate it in such a way as to facilitate a more economical and flexible therapy.

THE CHANGING CONCEPT.—In the early days of psychoanalytic practice, a great deal was written about the "handling of the transference." The choice of words is peculiarly apt here because, in the sense in which we use it as a therapeutic tool today, the transference relationship was not "manipulated" nor even "controlled." The importance of the repetition of the old conflict within the transference relationship received great emphasis and the development of a transference neurosis, in all negative as well as positive aspects, was therefore encouraged.

Until very recently, indeed, the belief was widespread among psychoanalysts that such a complete transference neurosis was unavoidable, that every improvement in the emotional life of a patient could be achieved only by solving his neurotic fixations as they were displaced onto the analyst, and that a patient inevitably involved his analyst in all his daydreams, desires, and emotions—a neurotic condition (the transference neurosis) of which he then had to be cured. Some analysts went so far as to interpret the patient's every dream during treatment in the light of the transference neurosis; whether or not he appeared in a dream, the analyst was found behind some figure the dream had produced. The transference neurosis was used by the therapist as a background, a basis of interpretation, to further the uncovering of unconscious material, to implement abreaction, and to assist the patient in working through his problems. It was regarded as the *sine qua non* of psychoanalytic therapy.

This practice accounts in part for the long span of many psychoanalytic treatments, the seemingly "interminable" cases, and for the negative therapeutic results in some instances. On the credit side, however, it also accounts for a vast body of data regarding both the etiology of psychoneurosis and the subtle relationship existing between the patient and the therapist.

With the expansion of knowledge and experience, this laissez-faire attitude toward the relationship of the patient to the analyst became greatly modified. Today, even in the standard psychoanalysis, it is recognized that the transference relationship can and must be controlled in certain situations. Psychoanalysts found that the transference neurosis could be used by a patient as resistance to insight and that, if it became a total retreat from life, the cure could be as bad as if not worse than the disease. Gradually psychoanalysts learned what pitfalls to expect and how to avoid them, and an effort therefore was made to keep the transference neurosis within workable limits.

In recent years, this tendency toward conscious control of the transference relationship has become more and more common as analysts pursued their research into certain disease syndromes and neurotic disturbances. As time went on, "types" of transference relationship were experimented with more and more. In studies of gastrointestinal disturbances, asthma, and hypertension, for example, having once isolated the conflict characteristic of the disease, they were able to anticipate the type and intensity of transference neurosis which would develop. Consequently, an attempt was made to restrict the growth of the transference relationship to those facets of the transference neurosis which reflected the conflict, avoiding a more extensive transference neurosis which would have been more difficult to resolve.

Now the concept of the inevitability of a complete transference neurosis has been abandoned by most psychiatrists. It is realized that frequently such a transference neurosis is not merely unnecessary or undesirable, it is sometimes almost impossible. While it is true that the transference situation has the most important role to play in overcoming the patient's neurotic reactions and undesirable emotional attitudes toward his fellowmen, and while most patients do become dependent on the analyst and tend to reenact in respect to him traumatic emotional situations of their past—not all neurotic conflicts can be easily transferred to the analyst for the simple reason that he may be an unsuitable object for that particular patient's particular emotions, he may not represent the person in the patient's past about whom his emotional disturbance is centered.

As has been suggested, the transference neurosis often complicates the therapy and impedes progress; by the nature of its repetitiveness, it becomes a focus of resistance to treatment. When it was realized that psychoanalytic treatment could be made both shorter and more effective by controlling this resistance, it was natural to try for even briefer methods and to develop techniques for an even more subtle manipulation of the transference relationship itself.

While a transference neurosis is a potentiality in any therapeutic relationship, today we watch its manifestations carefully, always ready to shape it to our therapeutic purpose. Instead of encouraging a repetition of the whole childhood situation with all its conflicts, we rather concentrate our interest on that phase of the transference situation around which the central conflict gathers. We use the positive attitudes of the patient toward the therapist to establish rapport and to keep the curative process in motion. When negative or hostile feelings appear, we do not ignore them but deal with them in a way to keep the patient from becoming so fearful that the process is blocked and the procedure prolonged. Likewise, when positive feelings become too intense, we must handle them lest the patient develop such a dependence on the therapist that he wishes never to give it up.

Emphasis is no longer on the transference neurosis but on the transference relationship as the axis of therapy. As a result of this change of attitude, we have even greater respect for the skill necessary so to manipulate the transference relationship that it can be made to serve our purposes without entailing the dangers of the old methods. To this end we have made conscious use of other techniques: the timing and frequency of interviews, guidance in everyday life, the choice and timing of interpretations, variations in the therapeutic set-up and in the attitude of the therapist, and the use of "extra-analytic transference" relationships.

As a result, we find a great variety of types and intensities in the transference relationships of our cases. In some a true transference neurosis has been inhibited completely (see Cases A, B, C, D, E, F, G_2, N, O, T); in some the transference neurosis has been allowed to develop but only along the path chosen by the therapist (see Cases G_1, K, L, M, P, Q, U); in some the transference neurosis has been encouraged to develop over a wide area but only to a certain degree of intensity (see Cases I, J, R); and in some not only has the type of transference neurosis been controlled by the therapist but also the intensity, keeping it even thus within bounds (see Cases H and S).

WHEN AND WHY CONTROL THE TRANSFERENCE RELA-
TIONSHIP.—One of the most important of our technical problems is to decide what kind and degree of transference relationship is the most useful for the production of the desired psychodynamic changes in a particular patient. Although an
initial transference relationship to the therapist establishes
itself spontaneously, we can encourage some types and hinder
others. This may be done not merely to avoid the growth
of an amount of dependence or resistance which would prolong the analytic process, but because there are some cases in
which a true transference neurosis may be dangerous.

There are other patients, however, who need a repetitive
experience which can be gained only through the transference
neurosis. These are people who have been greatly deprived in
the past, who had little of the normal affection which is the
birthright of every child and the foundation of normal development. These individuals may be able in intensive treatment to make up for this lack and to find a baseline from
which to build up normal relationships. The therapist, however, must take care to control this regression and not let
so great a dependence develop that it will be difficult to wean
the patient from treatment. In such a case, it is especially necessary that the therapist keep the patient aware of his relationships outside the analytic atmosphere, situations which he
must meet as a mature person (see Case H).

Another determining factor of the kind of transference
relationship which must be established is the type of conflict,
its severity and depth. If the conflict is deep and old and
centers about a parent figure, it is imperative that the analyst,
for a while at least, be able to represent that parent figure. If
the patient has lacked a proper pattern on which to build up
his character, due to the early loss or failure of a parent, then
it becomes highly desirable that the therapist supply this
pattern and thus help the patient set up for himself standards
of conduct he would normally have had in childhood. This is
particularly true of the delinquent or impulse-ridden character
whose super-ego has never been well developed. The intensive

reeducation necessary, incidentally, explains why this type of patient requires a long period of therapy.

Some kinds of transference relationship interfere with the primary function of the therapist to help and guide the patient honestly. The therapeutic relationship ceases to be favorable, for instance, when feelings of distrust or antipathy toward the analyst are so powerful that the patient becomes fearful and guilty, may even withdraw from treatment. The therapist can more easily guide and support his patient in his relationship to others when the patient is not so highly disturbed by antagonism toward the analyst.

Hostile attitudes toward the analyst, moreover, are often a needless complication of therapy. When the object of such a neurotic attitude can be a person in the patient's daily life, this complication is removed and the therapy thereby shortened. Thus, a patient whose disturbance is due to ambivalence to his father may displace onto the therapist only the role of the good father while he fears and hates his boss. It is not necessary for him to repeat these negative feelings against the therapist in order to overcome them. It is necessary, however, that he be aided and advised by his analyst in his relationship to the external object of his animosity and thus work through his earlier conflict.

In helping the patient to adjust himself to the external world and his fellow beings, it is thus not always desirable that the analyst be the object of *all* the patient's impulses and feelings. There are many disturbed emotional relationships which should be worked out in the daily life of the patient. Those disturbances which cannot be easily reproduced within the therapeutic situation should be worked out in "extra-analytic transference" relationships whenever possible.

Aside from the fact that the analyst may not be a suitable object for the patient's displacements, he will be able to guide the patient in his relationships to others more freely if he is not the target for all the patient's feelings. The role of guiding agent is too often neglected by those who hold that the paramount function of the analyst is to act as a screen on which the patient projects his feelings. It is true, however, that when the analyst himself becomes the object of all the patient's emotions, he can act toward the patient in the way he believes best suited to enable the patient to surmount his difficulties. Whereas, if there is an extra-analytic object dividing the patient's emotions, the analyst can seldom control the other person's reactions to the patient so as to preclude those that hinder the patient's progress—such as fostering an undue attachment or intimidating the patient.

In analytic work with children, the analyst usually chooses to have contact with the principal person in the child's environment, since the child is not a free agent like the adult but is under the domination of parental figures. In work with an adult, however—although it is frequently helpful to have the therapist in contact with the extra-analytic object of the patient's transference, as will be seen in Cases K, L, and M—this is not always necessary and may, indeed, be complicating to the treatment. It is advisable only when that outside person can enter into a wholehearted unambivalent cooperation with the therapist to make the patient well.

As we have said, while sometimes the therapist is the object of all the patient's displacements, sometimes another person in the patient's world can be the object with the therapist acting as the guiding agent. Let us consider an instance of such a case in which the main object of the patient's emotions was not the therapist, but some individual in his everyday life.

A 37-year-old woman during analysis revealed instances in which she had repeatedly reacted toward other women and girls according to a pattern she had acquired when a child as the result of deep resentment against her older sister. The patient felt that this sister had always been more admired by the parents and that she herself had been patronized and belittled by them. As a child, she had been teased and even physically mistreated by her sister. When, during the course of the treatment, the patient was obliged to take care of two little girls who (like the patient and her sister) were two years apart in age, she identified herself with the younger child and displaced to the older girl traits and behavior which her own sister had shown. This situation was worked through many times until the patient came to see her young charge not as the image of her own sister but as she really was.

Here the patient displaced her central conflict not on the male analyst but on persons in her everyday life. The therapist's task consisted of making her aware of this repeated reaction pattern—interpreting the situation over and over in its repeated variation, looking for new equivalents and derivatives and new implications, so that light from different angles and depths was thrown upon the problem—with the purpose of solving the negative sister transference. If we held to the belief that all emotional conflicts have to be worked out on the analyst, this patient should logically have been sent to a woman for treatment. In this instance, however, the analyst became the guiding agent who showed her the repeated neurotic attitude and helped her to more rational relationships with those persons in her extra-analytic life who were the objects of her conflicts.

In still other cases, as has been mentioned, the therapist may become the object of one part of the patient's displacement and an individual in his daily life the object of another.

A 32-year-old woman with severe general anxiety, who had become extremely dependent upon a somewhat older woman, was rebellious against the social order, feeling that it granted more rights to men than to women. Again the patient was the younger of two sisters. The father, who had hoped for a boy, rejected the second daughter. The child could not cope with the rivalry with her sister and, after futile attempts to win the father, gave up her longing for him altogether, repressed her femininity and adopted a masculine attitude. She considered herself equal to any boy and in fistfighting was so proficient that she was feared by boy playmates. When the patient was in her early twenties, her sister became ill with an incurable disease from which she died some years later.

It was at the time of the sister's illness that the patient's anxiety states developed. After the sister's death, and a few years before the patient began treatment, she became excessively dependent on the woman mentioned, with whom she shared an apartment. Whenever her friend left the house for any length of time or did not show her enough affection, the patient went into a panic. From various dreams and reactions, it became evident that while the childhood relationship with her sister had been completely forgotten, she must have nourished intense feelings of hostility and death wishes against her to which she later reacted with deep guilt and anxiety. Whenever the patient felt especially friendly toward the male therapist, her craving for dependence on the woman friend became much stronger; on such occasions she sometimes even acted as if she were afraid of him. Once he asked her abruptly, "Why are you afraid to admit your friendliness toward me?" Her response, unconsidered and immediate, was, "My sister has the priority."

Her dependence represented her need to be sure that the sister had not died and would not retaliate for her death wishes. Her fear of the analyst was a reflection of her early jealousy; she dared not be loved more than her sister. In order to straighten out the relationship to her father, the displacement onto the analyst was dealt with; and to enable her to overcome feelings of guilt and reactive dependence in respect to her sister, the relationship to her woman friend was worked through.

It has been noticed that in all cases in which the transference relationship is consciously controlled and directed, in which the therapy embraces both therapeutic and extra-therapeutic situations, progress tends to be more rapid, to require fewer interviews and to maintain a higher emotional participation on the part of the patient than is true in cases treated by the older method of a complete transference neurosis. Keeping the therapy close to the patient's real problems by a realistic counterbalancing of analytic and extra-analytic transference reactions and interpretations tends to give the patient awareness of his emotions, to make insight more realistic and convincing, and to support the integrative function of the ego. And furthermore, it is made a simple task for the patient to test the insight gained from an expert interpretation within the transference situation while still under the guidance of the therapist and, then, prepared for a real life experience in a protected atmosphere, to use the new insight in the extra-therapeutic situation.

How to Manipulate the Transference Relationship. —Since in the transference relationship two people are involved, two sets of factors must be considered. In the patient there are certain fixed patterns (his neurosis) which strive for expression. In the therapist lies the power not only to guide but to temper this relationship for the good of the patient.

The type of transference relationship in any particular instance depends on the patient's personality and the kind of conflict from which he is suffering, and on the therapist's personality and skill. It must be remembered that not all of the patient's reactions within the therapeutic situation are neurotic, many are normal. Thus the therapist's own realities may play an important part in determining what type of transference relationship will tend to develop.

The therapist's age, sex, personal characteristics, etc., make some types of transference onto him more probable than others. That a female patient who is very much attached to a father-figure finds contact with one therapist easier than with another is probably due to the first therapist's *real* personality—he can more readily represent the desired father-figure because of his own personal qualifications. The fact that an analyst is foreign-born may appeal to one patient and repel another, regardless of whether the patient is himself of American or foreign birth. If a therapist is highly intellectual, he may satisfy the intellectual needs of one patient while another patient may prefer to be understood intuitively, to have the analyst identify himself with his problems through empathy, not through intellect. And thus with all the other realities— sex, age, color, religious belief, social position and the more abstract qualities of mind and manner.

There are no set rules which determine which analyst should treat which patient. The original, overt reaction of the patient to the therapist—whether he consciously likes or dislikes his therapist—should not be the deciding factor. It is only after his first responses to the therapist—which will be revealed in his dreams and behavior—have been worked through that the therapist can say whether he should continue the case or refer it to a colleague.

Certain practical details within the therapeutic situation automatically affect the transference relationship. Is the patient coming to the therapist as a private patient? Is he a clinic patient? Does he belong to a research project, and, if so, does he know it? According to his personality pattern, each patient reacts to these situations in his own way. The private patient may feel more important, especially if he pays a large fee, and expect the therapist to be proportionately more interested in his case; or, contrariwise, he may feel the physician is interested only in his money. The clinic patient may be querulous in the fear that he is not a favored child, or he may feel pampered because he pays little or nothing for the same service wealthier patients receive. The research patient may take pleasure in the fact that he is making a contribution to science, or he may resent it and feel that he will be betrayed. And so on, in infinite variation according to the individual case.

And yet, in a properly manipulated transference relationship, these reality factors may become a help instead of a hindrance. The therapist may use this initial reaction in its present form to encourage or discourage the type of transference relationship he wishes to develop; or he may, through interpretation, change the form to one more benign to the treatment as a whole. It is in this handling and *manipulation* of the transference relationship that the power of the therapist lies. Every experienced therapist has learned how to use this sensitive instrument to help the patient. This is his art, its use differing with every therapist. The resultant relationship is determined not only by his skill but also by what he expects to be able to accomplish with that particular patient (the goal), and by the plan of therapy which he bases on the psychodynamics of the individual case.

The initial transference manifestations must be carefully weighed in every case, and cautiously encouraged until enough evidence is before the therapist to allow him to reconstruct the psychodynamics of the particular case before him. While extreme caution at the very beginning is unnecessary in most cases, in some instances an unwieldy transference neurosis or other disturbing complication can develop almost immediately if great care is not exercised (see Case T). When once the therapist has decided upon his successive goals and his general approach, he then attempts not only to guide but to temper the growing transference relationship so that it can be of the greatest possible service in the therapeutic process.

In order to use the transference relationship as a medium of corrective experience rather than merely a repetitive experience, we use all the techniques at our command—in a flexible manner, shifting our tactics to fit the needs of the patient in each phase of the treatment. Earlier in the chapter we have discussed variations in the frequency of interview and utilization of the patient's real life situation. There are many others; the very physical set-up of the therapeutic situation and the attitude adopted by the therapist can also be manipulated to further our plan.

The most frequently used means of controlling the transference relationship, however, is through interpretations of the patient's actions, attitudes, dreams, and fantasies. The degree to which such interpretations can be used varies greatly. In some of the cases reported in this book the therapist makes extensive use of interpretations in a way similar to that employed in the standard psychoanalysis; other cases show a tentative and limited use of interpretation, while still others have been carried on with almost no interpretation at all.

Skillful use of interpretations (in choice, timing and manner of presentation) is the most powerful means of regulating the type and intensity of the relationship at the therapist's command. The therapist may choose to refer to the infantile neurosis in his interpretations and thus encourage a dependent transference relationship; or he may eschew all mention of the infantile conflict and (using his own insight into the patient's past conflicts) base his interpretations solely upon the present situation. Unerring judgment and sureness of touch, in psychotherapy as in diplomacy, is a fine art and it is here that the accomplished therapist excels. This complex subject of interpretation is considered in a later chapter and is demonstrated on the case material itself.

The manner of conducting treatment, once bound to the convention of the couch, now varies widely. Today most patients sit opposite the therapist in direct conversation, the form of interview most commonly associated with medical consultations. But even this scene can be varied to suit the occasion. The feelings aroused in the patient when the therapist sits behind a desk are very different from those he has when the therapist sits near him in the manner of a drawing room, or beside him on the couch in an even less formal fashion. Some patients like to walk around; some ask to lie down when they cannot bear the direct gaze of the therapist. If the therapist smokes a cigarette with the patient, the atmosphere may change immediately from the formal one of the standard psychoanalytic interview to one of friendly cooperation, with therapist and patient on an equal plane. And so on. The therapist varies these factors according to the type of transference relationship he hopes to encourage.

The therapist's own attitude toward a particular patient also has a great effect on the type and depth of the transference relationship that will develop. For instance, to treat the patient as a dependent, helpless person by even the slightest intimation will encourage the development of a dependent neurotic transference relationship. The therapist must decide carefully what attitude he must take to best further his purpose. In Case A, for instance, this is well exemplified; here the therapist chose deliberately to act as differently as possible from the way the father had always treated the patient. This is frequently the therapist's best choice—to be unlike the forbidding, the punitive, the indifferent, or the too permissive parent, in order to let the patient see how much of his reaction is determined by the character of old relationships. In accordance with the theory of the phenomenon of transference, the patient tries to put the analyst in the position of the important parental figure; the therapist must decide how far he can allow the patient to follow this unconscious pattern and how soon to interpret the patient's attitudes in the light of the past. By his own attitude and by his interpretations, the therapist provides a corrective experience for the patient in a new relationship. A master of the treatment of adolescents in this respect was Aichhorn, watching the transference relationship like a hawk, changing his attitude to fit the current phase of the treatment.

The therapist must also decide to what extent he will attempt to influence the patient's environment. In the standard psychoanalysis, the tendency was for the patient and therapist to carry on their work in an "ivory tower" atmosphere of isolation. Our flexible approach has brought us to recognize the tremendous importance not only of the external happenings in a patient's life but also of giving active direction and help. This automatically alters the transference relationship, making the development of an unwieldy transference neurosis less probable because of the emphasis on the reality situation of the present.

Our experience has proved again and again that it is not necessary for the patient to go through a complete transference neurosis—complete in every detail, concerning every disturbed relationship—in order to overcome his neurotic conflicts and fixations. The therapist can accomplish his task by a carefully planned manipulation of the transference relationship.

Edoardo Weiss, M.D.

Demonstration of Flexibility

To illustrate more concretely what we mean by flexible therapy, let us assume that we are faced with an actual patient who has come to us because of symptoms which may or may not be psychogenic in origin and consider how we shall treat him. This hypothetical patient also has some idiosyncrasies, but he has come to us not because of his personality but because of physical distress from which he wishes release. Our first duty is obviously to determine conclusively whether or not there is some non-psychogenic organic difficulty. If there is not, then we must attempt to persuade him that his general personality may have contributed to his physical distress.

If this man were to be treated by the standard psychoanalytic method, the analyst would assume an understanding but impersonal attitude, waiting for the transference neurosis to develop and offering little or no suggestion or direction. As a result, the patient might easily transfer onto the analyst all the conflictful emotions from his past life and tend to become one of the "interminable" cases mentioned elsewhere; or, conversely, he might become disgusted with the entire therapeutic situation, feel that he was not receiving active help, and flee treatment after two or three interviews.

If this man were treated by a "common sense" approach, other results would be obtained. This is an approach frequently used by ministers, social workers or good friends who are often turned to in times of stress. Here one might hope to force insight upon the patient with the expectation that his own good sense would make him grasp the irrational aspects of his behavior. In such a method, irritation would soon lead to irritation, argument to argument, and soon the situation would be aggravated, not improved.

Or this man might be met in a purely supportive approach, with sympathy but with little or no effort to give him insight into the cause of his distress. This would serve merely to confirm the neurotic patterns and no solution of his difficulties would result.

Let us see how a therapist using a flexible approach to the problem would handle it.

Case A [2]

(Conversion Hysteria and Severe Personality Disturbance)

A neurologist referred a 42-year-old businessman for psychotherapy because of numerous complaints which indicated either a focal epilepsy or conversion hysteria; among other complaints were an uncontrollable jerking motion of his arms and three attacks of unconsciousness several years before, in

---

[2] For purposes of discretion, all cases reported in this book have been disguised.

one of which convulsions had been observed.[3] The patient had a long history of extreme irritability combined with a domineering, intolerant attitude—a picture which had been complicated a few months before he consulted the analyst by complete loss of potency. Treatment, consisting of 26 interviews over a ten-week period, brought satisfactory results. By the end of the sixth week, all symptoms had disappeared.

The patient seemed to have found a pattern for his overbearing attitude in that of his father. His whole early life had been spent under the shadow of a domineering father, a self-made man of violent temper and unlimited self-confidence, who tyrannized his family as well as his business subordinates. The inwardly rebellious child's mother-protector, to whom he had been very close, died when he was ten years old. One of his most dramatic memories was of the time when, on his return from college after his first long absence from home, he dared oppose his father for the first time in his life during a minor argument. They faced each other ready for actual physical combat, the patient feeling that since he was now physically the stronger he could certainly subdue his father. Yet he gave in at the last moment and accepted the role of an obedient son.

His marriage several years later, however, was without his father's consent; in fact, it was not until shortly before his death that the father was reconciled to the marriage. Upon the death of the father, the patient (then about thirty) took over the family business of manufacturing glassware. From that time on, his main desire was to prove that he could do better in business than his father, and, with stubborn determination, he succeeded in expanding the business very successfully.

But this was the only field in which he functioned satisfac-

---

[3] An electro-encephalogram, made for the purpose of a differential diagnosis at the time the patient came to psychotherapy, was inconclusive although it showed some features which would indicate focal injury. Although these features were explained on the basis of a severe concussion sustained by the patient three years before, no new clinical symptoms appeared nor was there any exaggeration of the symptoms, among them the jerking, which had existed for many years before the concussion.

torily. In all human relationships he failed. His imperious, aggressive behavior spread into his social and family relationships; gradually the social contacts of the family ceased almost completely and the home situation itself became intolerable. The patient's wife divorced him (taking the son with her) because of his intolerant behavior, but after a year and a half they were remarried. However, the situation in the home was as bad as ever. The patient continued to display extreme irritability toward his associates and especially toward his wife and son. His wife was again considering separation when treatment began.

The patient tried at once to impose the old father-son pattern on the therapeutic situation. His attitude toward his father had been one of rebellion mixed with an almost unlimited admiration and passive devotion. He made efforts to induce the analyst to impose strong rules on him, to dictate his behavior. He followed religiously the few suggestions that could not be avoided—such as abstinence from alcohol and sedatives, and temporary discontinuation of his work in the factory. At the same time, there were immediate signs of competition with, and rebellion against, the analyst. The patient began his treatment by producing material with which he tried to impress upon his therapist what an enterprising, masterful person he was. Whenever something concerning his emotional reactions was explained to him, he almost automatically responded by explaining to the therapist something about his business—or about sports, in which he was an expert. His unconscious tendency was to push the therapist into the role of the tyrannical father, against whom he could rebel and with whom he could compete without any sense of guilt. By rebelling openly, moreover, he saved his face and so could continue the treatment without shame.

After the second interview (by which time all this was evident to the therapist) the analyst made every effort to counteract this tendency, leaning over backward in an attempt to avoid the role into which the patient instinctively tried to inveigle him. Had the therapist followed rigid rules of technique, he would have remained passive, allowing the patient to make him the father of his childhood; he decided, however, to take just the opposite attitude in the hope of breaking up the patient's pattern of behavior more quickly. Instead of appearing to "conduct" the treatment firmly, he took pains not to be arbitrary in any way, letting the patient decide on the frequency of the interviews, allowing him to lie down, sit up, walk about, smoke, and generally act as he liked during the sessions. Further, the therapist emphasized repeatedly the limitations of psychiatry and of his own knowledge, making his suggestions and interpretations extremely tentative, encouraging the patient to express his disagreement and to accept only that which he himself judged correct.

An unusually tolerant attitude was maintained by the analyst. Where the father had been extremely critical of the patient, the analyst openly acknowledged admiration of certain of the patient's qualities—his quick mind, his physical skills, his sophistication. He also expressed interest in the patient's business and social activities. Of particular importance was the fact that the therapist's tolerance extended to sexual matters. It became apparent that the straitlaced father had had a very intimidating effect upon the patient concerning any sexual expression. The therapist had ample opportunity to display the opposite attitude, since the patient's sexual yearnings and attempted adventures took an important place in his associations.

In further interviews, the reason for the patient's need to make the analyst a tyrannical father-figure became evident. He displayed more and more competitiveness toward the analyst, he would accept interpretations grudgingly, constantly correct them and then suddenly make a remark such as, "Of course, I could never become an analyst; my mind doesn't work that way." The therapist's response was that, had the patient devoted himself to the profession, it was quite possible he might have become even more expert than the analyst.

It was fascinating to observe the patient's confusion in the face of the analyst's behavior. One could see that although he was not altogether satisfied with the lack of strict guidance, yet he began to thrive under the permissive and encouraging treatment. It was as if this man in his forties were, within a few days, going through the process of maturation normal during adolescence. He had spent his life learning how to deal with a father who, by his very violence and arbitrariness, had always put himself in the wrong. The patient had felt justified in rebelling against such a tyrant; his hostile competitive tendencies had not been blocked by guilt, and his hostility had been repressed only out of fear of his brutal father, not because there was any internal inhibition present. Now in the treatment situation he found himself opposite a person in authority who did not browbeat him, who assumed an objective, helpful attitude while minimizing his own role. When, in spite of this, the patient developed competitive feelings and realized that he could not justify them, he became confused. This gave the therapist an excellent opportunity to demonstrate to the patient his aggressive competitive impulses, not as reactions to a domineering father, but rather as manifestations of his own need to appear important and strong. This excessive need for self-assertion was' at the same time understood as having been reinforced by paternal subjugation.

As the patient gradually became more tolerant of the therapist's interpretations, the conditions in his home improved markedly. This started by his assuming a paternal attitude toward his son, with whom he had been competing as with a younger brother. The change showed itself in everyday contacts with the boy and was made vivid in a dream in which he took his son big-game hunting in Africa, something he had always wished his own father would do with him. He himself recognized that he could now act as a father toward his son because he had at last found in the treatment what he had always wanted—understanding and support from a person in authority. The benevolence toward his son, moreover, helped compensate for the injury done his pride by accepting aid from the analyst.

The patient's need to put the therapist in the role of a tyrannical father culminated in a dream reported in the eighteenth interview. In this dream the analyst smashed glassware the patient had manufactured; in immediate association, the patient remarked that it reminded him of the time his father, in a violent rage, had shattered a set of glassware because he had not liked the design.

During this interview the analyst asked the patient to describe his work more in detail. The patient responded eagerly and, in a distinctly didactic and condescending fashion, instructed the analyst in the mysteries of glass manufacture for the rest of the hour. Following this interview, the patient regained his potency. This sudden improvement is to be explained by the fact that his self-confidence had been tremendously increased by his assumption of authority with the therapist. Then too, under the encouraging atmosphere of the treatment, he had been rapidly emancipating himself from the protracted effects of paternal intimidation which had left him, through all these years, in the role of a now-rebelling, now-submitting son.

In the twentieth interview the patient reported he had dreamed he was a college boy who went home with his foil shattered and his father had returned it to him fully repaired. He thus gave credit to his father for restoring his manhood.

These two dreams illustrate the utter confusion in which the patient found himself. In the earlier dream he made the analyst a despotic smasher of glassware, in the latter he made the father the benevolent restorer of his potency. In reality the analyst was the benevolent person and the father the tyrant. He had never learned to deal with a person whose only interest was to help and encourage him, and so in the dreams he simply reversed the situation. In this way he could rid himself of the oppressive feeling of guilt toward the analyst and say to him, "It was not you but my father who helped me; I don't owe you anything." His feeling of inferiority was also relieved; after all, the analyst was merely a raging fool like his own father. Thus, without either guilt or inferiority, he could continue to compete with the analyst.

The dream reported in the twenty-first interview shows all this with simple clarity. The patient saw himself as presiding in court with a famous Chicago judge sitting beside him and assisting him. Before them came the case of a married couple,

Mr. and Mrs. N., who sought a divorce. The patient (as judge) succeeded in bringing them together and persuaded them to give up the idea of divorce. In passing, he advised the husband to have his wife wear a chastity belt. (In his associations, the patient described the N.'s; the wife was unfaithful and the husband was seeking divorce. The patient felt that the marriage might possibly be saved.)

Then the patient told of an occurrence on the day preceding the dream. His wife had met the neurologist who had originally referred the patient to the analyst. They had discussed the patient's condition and agreed that he had improved amazingly in the six weeks since psychotherapy began. The jerking of his arms had stopped entirely, his general irritability had disappeared and he now found it easier to get on with his friends, his attitude toward his son was good and the marital relations, both sexual and emotional, were better than ever before. The patient said that his wife had now completely dismissed the idea of separation.

It is obvious that in this dream the patient exchanges roles with the analyst. In the dream it is the patient, not the analyst, who saves a marriage; the analyst is identified as the famous judge who merely acts as his assistant. However, in the last detail of the dream the patient's insecurity finds a disguised expression. He tries to overcome his insecurity by turning the situation about again. In the dream he gives fatherly advice to Mr. N. on how to treat his wife, to protect himself against her potential infidelity by having her wear a chastity belt.

From the patient's conscious attitudes and behavior, and from the unconscious material provided by the dreams, the therapist now had ample data from which to discuss his emotional difficulty in its entirety. This difficulty lay in the fact that the patient could not accept help from the analyst—more precisely, could not admit that he was helped—without reacting by feeling inferior, and thus having the need to compete with him to prove that he was, after all, the better man. It was easy to understand why he had to assume this competitive attitude since his father had never missed an opportunity to make his son feel inferior.

After this interview the patient showed an increased emancipation from the effects of paternal intimidation. The first evidence appeared in quite adolescent form. He began to dream of extra-marital relations and in his associations recalled a series of attempts in that direction which he had never dared carry to completion.

About this time the treatment was interrupted with the plan to resume it at a later date. Two months later the patient continued in the same good condition, the home situation remained harmonious, the patient had no recurrence of his symptoms, his sexual potency remained undiminished. Treatment was therefore not resumed at that time but the patient was encouraged to return whenever he felt it advisable. After another nine months, the patient reported that his condition remained satisfactory.

Comments on Case A

The psychodynamic factors which brought about these rapid therapeutic results are easy to see. The main factor was that the patient was given an opportunity in his relationship to the analyst, first, to develop the same emotional conflict he had toward his father (the transference neurosis) and, second, to find a new, less neurotic solution for this conflict. The fact that the analyst's manner was directly opposite to that of the father demanded a new solution from the patient since his reaction to the analyst's behavior, dictated by the past, was illogical and anachronistic.

The patient's attitude was, in a sense, similar to that of an intimidated animal—a combination of rebellion and fearful, grudging submission. The jerking of his arms were abortive rage attacks, inhibited blows. The irritability toward his family and friends was a sign of his insecurity. Then too, his needs for dependence were frustrated because his inferiority feelings and hostility would not allow him to lean on anyone. His impotence was the expression of his adolescent insecurity, since all sexual expression was linked in his mind with "paternal veto."

The analyst, whom he immediately installed as a father-image, consistently refused this role and treated him as an equal, thus making rebellion pointless and fearful submission absurd. The patient was forced gradually to accept the role of an independent adult—into which he grew with amazing rapidity. Since he was a successful businessman, at the height of his mental and physical powers, it was not impossible for him to accomplish this belated emotional maturation in a brief period. Excessive paternal intimidation had barred him from reaching this maturation—or, more precisely, had perpetuated the insecure, partly competitive, partly submissive attitude of adolescence. This intimidation, however, had not become internalized completely and so a new, encouraging experience was capable of counteracting the inhibiting effects of the earlier family influences.

This case is an apt illustration of the value of corrective experience, which the therapeutic relationship makes possible. The patient had to experience a new father-son relationship before he could release the old. This cannot be done as an intellectual exercise; it has to be lived through, i.e., felt, by the patient and thus become an integral part of his emotional life. Only then can he change his attitudes.

This case is not claimed as a cure since only time will prove whether the patient can maintain the adult attitudes he learned in the therapy. The patient grew greatly in self-confidence after the intimidating influence of the father was replaced by the novel experience he had in the therapeutic situation. As soon as he accepted his responsibilities as a mature individual, he lost his impotence; he gave up his infantile rivalry with his son and became paternal. His manifest symptom, the jerking motion, ceased when he could give up hostile feelings engendered by his old feelings of inferiority. By the same token he gave up his general irritability and asocial inclination. With such a change in his own attitudes, he experienced new attitudes in those around him. A new emotional climate developed in his home which in turn will help him to maintain his emotional growth. The vicious circle of his neurosis was replaced by a benign circle.

It seemed wise to end the treatment at this point, not just because he had lost his symptoms but because he needed an opportunity to demonstrate his progress. How far the momentum of the treatment will reach is always an open question, since the therapist has no precise measure by which to gauge psychic change nor to see what events may come, bringing new demands on the patient's powers of adjustment. Therapeutic results are thus seen as an organic part of emotional growth rather than the magic effect of a few interpretations. The treatment may be the first step in this growth. In every treatment, however, a phase is reached when further progress may be blocked by the therapeutic relationship in that it tends to nurture dependence. Then it is time for the patient to continue growth on his own. At this moment in the case described, an interruption was made with the plan of resuming treatment should it be indicated at some later date.

This case is also an example of the importance of reaching an early psychodynamic formulation and of making a plan accordingly. The therapist purposely assumed an extremely conciliatory, laissez-faire attitude on the basis of the psychodynamic appraisal of the patient's specific emotional problem.

Merely supportive therapy in this case would probably have accomplished little, since the patient had to undo a conflict based on anachronistic attitudes. To do this, he had first to experience the conflict emotionally with the therapist (paternal image) and then to correct it in a new relationship. For the therapist to have taken a strong hand with the patient or to have argued with him would have played into his fixed patterns of behavior and, therefore, would hardly have relieved his symptoms. The so-called common-sense attitude toward such a boastful person—to meet him on his own ground—would never have given this patient an opportunity to appraise his own behavior. It would probably have turned the therapy into a series of argumentative conversations which might well have aggravated his symptoms.

On the basis of these conclusions, we might have felt in earlier times that only a prolonged psychoanalysis could reach the depths of this patient's emotional difficulties. What would have been the result? To have put this patient on the couch for a classical psychoanalysis would have prolonged the treatment unduly, since the depth of the father-son conflict would have entailed the development of an intense transference neurosis in which a long battle between rebellion and submission would have been played out. The therapist chose, however, to bring this conflict into focus directly by showing the patient immediately that he was not the father the patient's experience demanded. In this way he brought the patient to an earlier correction of his neurotic attitudes.

Finally, this case is given as an example of how flexible a therapy *can* be when the psychodynamics of the case are fully understood—flexible as to the timing and the manner of conducting interviews, as to the activity or passivity of the therapist, and as to the handling of the transference relationship.

Franz Alexander, M.D.

Chapter 4

THE PRINCIPLE OF CORRECTIVE
EMOTIONAL EXPERIENCE

In all forms of etiological psychotherapy, the basic therapeutic principle is the same: to reexpose the patient, under more favorable circumstances, to emotional situations which he could not handle in the past. The patient, in order to be helped, must undergo a corrective emotional experience suitable to repair the traumatic influence of previous experiences. It is of secondary importance whether this corrective experience takes place during treatment in the transference relationship, or parallel with the treatment in the daily life of the patient.

The simplest example of such a corrective experience is offered by the procedure called narcosynthesis. The patient in narcosis re-lives in fantasy the dangers of combat which he had been unable emotionally to master in reality. Because the narcotic and the presence of the therapist in whom he has confidence reduce the intensity of his anxiety, the patient becomes more capable of facing the situation to which he had succumbed.

The character of the transference relationship is unique in that the patient has an opportunity to display any of a great variety of behavior patterns. It is important to realize that the mastery of an unresolved conflict in this relationship becomes possible, not only because the transference conflict is less intense than the original one, but also because the analyst assumes an attitude different from that which the parent had assumed toward the child in the original conflict situation.

While the patient continues to act according to outdated patterns, the analyst's reaction conforms strictly to the actual therapeutic situation. This makes the patient's transference behavior a one-sided shadow-boxing, and thus the therapist has an opportunity to help the patient both to see intellectually and to *feel* the irrationality of his emotional reactions. At the same time, the analyst's objective, understanding attitude allows the patient to deal differently with his emotional reactions and thus to make a new settlement of the old problem. The old pattern was an attempt at adaptation on the part of the child to parental behavior. When one link (the parental response) in this interpersonal relationship is changed through the medium of the therapist, the patient's reaction becomes pointless.

In the formulation of the dynamics of treatment, the usual tendency is to stress the repetition of the old conflict in the transference relationship and to emphasize the similarity of the old conflict situation to the transference situation. The therapeutic significance of the *differences* between the original conflict situation and the present therapeutic situation is often overlooked. And in just this difference lies the secret of the therapeutic value of the analytic procedure. Because the therapist's attitude is different from that of the authoritative person of the past, he gives the patient an opportunity to face again and again, under more favorable circumstances, those emotional situations which were formerly unbearable and to deal with them in a manner different from the old.

This can be accomplished only through actual experience in the patient's relationship to the therapist; intellectual insight alone is not sufficient. It is, however, vitally necessary for the therapist to have a clear understanding of the genetic development of the patient's emotional difficulties so that he may revive for the patient the original conflict situations from which he has retreated. The patient's intellectual understanding of the genetics has only an accessory significance. The more precisely the therapist understands the dynamics and is thus able to reactivate the early attitudes, the more adequately can he provide, by his own attitude, the new experiences necessary to produce therapeutic results.

A completely neutral psychoanalyst does not exist in reality, nor would he be desirable. While it is necessary that the therapist maintain an objective, helpful attitude at all times, within this attitude lies the possibility of a great variety of responses to the patient. Spontaneous reactions to the patient's attitudes are frequently not desirable for the therapy, since they may repeat the parents' impatience or solicitude which caused the neurosis and cannot, therefore, constitute the corrective experience necessary for cure.

The Case of Jean Valjean

Every reader is familiar with the classic example of a corrective emotional experience in Victor Hugo's "Les Misérables." In his account of Jean Valjean's conversion, Hugo anticipated the fundamental principle of every psychotherapy which aims to establish a profound change in the patient's personality. It will be recalled that Jean Valjean, the ex-convict, underwent a dramatic change in his personality because of the overwhelming and unexpected kindness of the bishop whom he had tried to rob. While he was still stunned by being treated for the first time in his life better than he deserved, Valjean met little Gervais playing a hurdygurdy on the road. When the little boy's two-franc piece fell to the ground, the ex-convict put his foot on the coin and refused to give it back. Although the little boy cried and pleaded desperately, Valjean remained adamant. In a paralyzed and utterly confused state of mind he was unable to remove his foot from the coin. Only after Gervais left in despair did Valjean awake from his stupor. He ran after the boy in a frantic effort to make good his evil act, but could not find him. This was the beginning of his conversion.

Hugo writes: "He felt indistinctly that the priest's forgiveness was the most formidable assault by which he had yet been shaken; that his hardening would be permanent if he resisted this clemency; that if he yielded he must renounce that hatred with which the actions of other men had filled his soul during so many years, and which pleased him: that this time he must either conquer or be vanquished; and that the struggle, a colossal and final struggle, had begun between his wickedness and that man's goodness. One thing which he did not suspect is certain, however, that he was no longer the same man; all was changed in him, and it was no longer in his power to get rid of the fact that the bishop had spoken to him and taken his hand."

Jean Valjean did not know why he had robbed the boy. He felt clearly, however, that "if he were not henceforth the best of men he would be the worst, that he must now ascend higher than the bishop or sink lower than the galley-slave, that if he wished to be good he must become an angel, and if he wished to remain wicked that he must become a monster." Here the author interrupts his dramatic narration and goes into a psychodynamic discussion of Valjean's emotional processes in an attempt to explain his sudden conversion.

HUGO'S DYNAMIC PERCEPTION.—Were it not for the episode with Gervais and Hugo's psychological explanation of Valjean's emotional state, the story of Valjean's conversion would not deserve our attention. The scene with the bishop which demonstrates the effect of kindness upon unfortunate and maltreated pariahs is anything but novel. The encounter with the boy, however, shows not only that Hugo instinctively understood the emotional metamorphosis but also that he was acquainted with the dynamic process in all its details. Hugo shows us explicitly—and no better explanation could be given today—why Valjean behaved in such an inhuman manner toward little Gervais, robbing the helpless boy just after he had been overwhelmed by the bishop's generosity.

For Hugo the concept of disturbed emotional balance was not a mere phrase but a fully understood psychological reality. He raised the question why Valjean committed such a brutish act just at this moment and he answered it with another question, "Was it a final and, as it were, supreme effort of the evil thought he had brought from the Bagne, a remainder of impulse, a result of what is called in statics 'acquired force'?" Hugo understood that the bishop's act was a violent attack upon Valjean's precarious emotional equilibrium, which consisted in being cruel toward a cruel world, and Hugo saw that

Valjean in response had to reestablish his balance in a spiteful insistence upon being bad.

In this, Hugo describes an experience well known in psychoanalysis; that whenever a symptom or neurotic attitude is attacked by the treatment, a recrudescence of the symptom usually occurs before the patient is able to give it up altogether. The experienced psychoanalyst knows this storm before the calm, this exacerbation of the morbid condition which precedes improvement, and he watches with eager expectation for its occurrence.

MODEL OF BRIEF PSYCHOTHERAPY.—We might question that one favorable experience could undo the cumulative effects of lifelong maltreatment. We are justified, however, in assuming that Valjean, although a hardened criminal, had a conscience which was rendered ineffective only by the hardships of his emotional development. He had to emphasize to himself his adverse fate in order to feel free to act destructively. This equilibrium was disturbed by the bishop's unexpected and extraordinary kindness.

Valjean's conversion took place within a few hours; it is a model of brief psychotherapy. This masterpiece of psychodynamic analysis was written in 1862, about sixty years before Freud introduced his concept of the super-ego and its compelling influence upon human behavior.

That Hugo's story is no mere creation of fantasy has been proved by many clinical examples. Aichhorn's reports on his delinquent patients present similar occurrences. The author of this section has also observed the tremendous effect upon young delinquents of the mere fact that the therapist's attitude was not critical and moralistic but rather that of a benevolent and helpful friend. In some patients, the pronounced contrast between the patient's own self-critical super-ego reactions and the analyst's permissive attitude alone may produce profound results, as will be noted in the case material of later chapters.

Franz Alexander, M.D.

Chapter 5

THE TRANSFERENCE PHENOMENON

Although it is agreed that the central dynamic problem in psychoanalytic therapy is the handling of transference, there is a great deal of confusion as to what "transference" really means. The term, in psychoanalytic as well as in general literature, has undergone the fate of most popular terms and is often used to refer indiscriminately to many things not included in Freud's original concept. The sense of the word has been loosely extended to include everything from the "transference neurosis" proper, to the "emotional relationship existing between patient and analyst," to the "treatment situation as a whole."

As Freud originally used the term, however, its sense was much more restricted. By "transference" Freud meant reactions to the analyst as though he were not himself but some person in the patient's past. According to this definition, a patient's transference to the analyst is only that part of the patient's reaction to the analyst which repeats the patient's reactions to a person who has, at some previous time, played an important role in the patient's life.

REALITY TESTING.—It is important to distinguish between such transference reactions and reactions that are adequate to the present real situation. A patient does not react to the therapist only as though the therapist were somebody else, only as though he were some important figure in the patient's past. Sometimes he reacts quite naturally to what the therapist actually does or says, to the therapist's actual personality characteristics and behavior.

In actual therapeutic practice, this distinction is of the greatest practical importance. Especially in the later stages of

a psychoanalytic treatment, one of our most important therapeutic tasks is to help the patient distinguish neurotic transference reactions (that are based upon a repetition of earlier
stereotyped patterns) from normal reactions to the analyst and
to the therapeutic situation as a present reality. It is a fundamental part of all psychotherapy to teach the patient that his
neurotic reactions are in accord with old, outmoded patterns,
that they are anachronistic, and to help him acquire new ways
of reacting that conform more closely to the new situations.
This is the part of the therapy we call "reality testing."

This concept of reality testing seems to imply a contrast
between transference reactions and reality adjusted behavior,
that these terms are mutually exclusive. On the other hand, it
is clear that all behavior is patterned upon the past, is based
on experience. If we based our concept of transference on
this fact alone, it would have to include all of the patient's
emotional reactions to the therapist, for they are all presumably based upon some pattern from the past. The only
distinction left, then, is that in reality adjusted behavior the
patterns from the past have been modified to take adequate
account of the differences between present reality and the situations in the past upon which they are based.

When we use the word "transference" in this strict sense,
we mean an irrational repetition of stereotyped reaction patterns which have not been adjusted to conform to the present
situation. In the psychoanalytic literature we have another
term which has always been used in this more precise sense,
the "transference neurosis." In the transference neurosis we
include only such repetitions of earlier reaction patterns as
are neurotic, i.e., only those that are irrational or inappropriate
in the present real therapeutic situation. The concepts "transference neurosis" and "reality adjusted behavior" are truly,
therefore, mutually exclusive, just as the more general concept
"neurosis" is quite incompatible with that of reality adjusted
behavior.

DEFINITIONS.—We may summarize the preceding discussion
in the form of a few definitions:

In its *widest* sense, as we here use the word, transference is the exact repetition of *any* former reaction without adjusting it to fit the present situation. In a more specific sense, transference is the *neurotic* repetition *with relation to the analyst* of a stereotyped, unsuitable behavior pattern based on the patient's past. It is in this latter sense that the word is most frequently used in this book. The transference "relationship," then, is that relationship which obtains within the therapeutic situation wherein the therapist is indeed the representative of a figure of importance from out the patient's past.

When defined in this way, the transference relationship becomes identical with the transference "neurosis" except that transient neurotic transference reactions are not usually dignified with the name of "transference neurosis." Thus the transference "neurosis" may be defined as that mass of stereotyped neurotic behavior patterns (evidenced in the analytic situation) which are based on the past and do not take into account the differences between the past and the present. In contrast, we have "reality adjusted behavior," which we define as behavior in which patterns based upon past experience *have been corrected* to take adequate account of the differences between the present and the past.

If we wish to make our terminology more complete, it will be helpful to take account of still another possibility. Sometimes the real therapeutic situation is not significantly different from a situation in the past to which one of the patient's stereotyped transference patterns was adequate. For example, it is a quite adequate reaction to the therapy for the patient to turn to the therapist for help. Consequently, in the therapeutic situation, a stereotyped pattern of dependence upon parental figures may for a long time be a quite adequate reaction to the therapeutic situation. In such a case it will not be immediately evident that this reaction is a stereotyped one that cannot be modified to take adequate account of the differences between present and past.

If the therapeutic situation later changes, however, so that this reaction pattern is no longer adequate, its stereotyped character will immediately become evident. For example, if the therapeutic situation later requires that the therapist attempt to wean the patient from his dependence upon him, an energetic protest against this weaning process may reveal the fact that the patient's dependence is a stereotyped pattern that persists even after the therapeutic situation demands that he emancipate himself. Such an apparently adequate reaction to the therapeutic situation, that shows its inadequate and stereotyped character only when the situation changes, we may call a *"latent* transference reaction."

NEUROSIS THE RESULT OF INTERRUPTED LEARNING PROCESS.—In order to give explicit recognition to this distinction between normal and neurotic reactions, it is helpful to think of the function of therapy as one of facilitating a learning process. (This is in accord with a suggestion of Freud's who once referred to the psychoanalytic treatment as a process of reeducation.) Let us consider more in detail the nature of the difference between a neurosis and reality adjusted behavior.

We have pointed out that all behavior is based upon past experience. In normal development, however, patterns from the past undergo progressive modification. One learns from experience by correcting earlier patterns in the light of later events. When a problem becomes too disturbing to face, however, this learning process is interrupted and subsequent attempts to solve this problem must, therefore, assume the character of stereotyped repetitions of previous unsuccessful attempts to solve it. A neurosis may be defined as a series of such stereotyped reactions to problems that the patient has never solved in the past and is still unable to solve in the present. In other words, a neurosis is the result of an interrupted learning process.

This concept of a neurosis has obvious implications for our understanding of psychotherapy. It is the task of the therapy to help the patient resume and complete the learning process which was interrupted when his neurosis began.

Reactions to Therapy

Let us now apply these distinctions to the methods by which therapeutic effects are achieved, first considering that rational use of therapy which is motivated by the patient's desire for help.

RATIONAL UTILIZATION.—Sometimes a patient's symptoms disappear soon after he comes into treatment in a way which we call a "transference cure" (see page 133) and which we attribute to the fact that the patient gains emotional release and reassurance from having someone to whom he can talk freely— without danger of arousing the condemnation or other disturbing emotional reactions he might call forth if he told the same things to someone else. In the strictest sense, this is not "transference" but a rational and adequate reaction to the therapeutic situation.

This patient may perhaps find even permanent relief from his symptoms by such a rational use of the therapist as someone to whom he can turn for emotional support. The relief the patient derives from thus unburdening himself of his difficulties may, after a time, make possible a better adjustment to his real life situation; then, when his real situation has been improved, he may find the emotional support he has been receiving from the therapist no longer necessary. When the patient is able, after a period of such help, to achieve a better adjustment in his real life situation, we must admit that he has found a solution for his problem without developing a transference neurosis, that his use of the therapeutic situation has remained on a rational basis from beginning to end. After all, it is one of the therapist's most elementary functions to help people by listening sympathetically and without condemnation, and the patient has merely made intelligent use of the therapist in this role.

Not infrequently, however, even in supportive therapy, such a rational use of the therapy is blocked by the development of a transference neurosis. Even in purely supportive therapy where no attempt is made to give the patient insight into the motivations for his actions, the patient is likely to have neurotic reaction patterns which will cause him to react to *all* people upon whom he is dependent for help with guilt or injured pride or both.

RESISTANCE AND TRANSFERENCE IN INSIGHT THERAPY.— In insight or "uncovering" therapy, it is important to understand the dynamic relationship between transference and resistance.

To illustrate this relationship we cite the case of an attractive young woman who spent the greater part of one analytic interview talking in glowing terms of a minister with whom she was closely associated in church work. She concluded by remarking that it sounded as though she were in love with the minister. The therapist quietly agreed that she must indeed be in love with him, and the rest of the hour was spent in friendly discussion of the problem created by the fact that the minister was married. Two days later this patient had a violent temper tantrum; when she was seen by the analyst (before her anger had subsided), she was quite unaware of the cause of her outburst.

To the therapist, however, it was evident that, although disguised, this was a very natural, and indeed inevitable, reaction to the interpretation that had been made in the previous session. At that time the patient had been able to discuss her feelings for the minister because she had not yet fully sensed the conflict into which they must plunge her. She had thought of her feelings for the minister in terms of her pleasure in working with him professionally. Even after it occurred to her that she was talking as if she were in love with him, she did not take the idea very seriously. She was able to agree with the therapist that she must be in love with the minister because at the time she had no sense of the intensity of her feeling for him nor of the conflict and frustration in which these feelings involved her. Such an attachment to a married man was quite incompatible with her conscience, reinforced as it was by her religious training. Her love for the minister, therefore, faced her with frustration either of her forbidden love or of her devotion to her religious standards—both of which were very strong. Anyone who attempts to intervene in a quarrel between friends is likely to draw the anger of both upon him. Similarly, a therapist who attempts to make a patient aware of a conflict between two strong but incompatible wishes must inevitably stir up the resentment of both sides of the patient's conflict against himself. It was inevitable that this patient should react with anger to an interpretation that involved so much frustration for her.

In our psychotherapeutic thinking we often do not distinguish carefully enough between neurotic transference reactions and this kind of resistance to a disturbing interpretation. Frank opposition to an unwelcome interpretation may be a normal reaction in defense of the neurosis and irrational only in the sense that the neurosis itself is irrational. The patient's reaction in the case just cited differs from such a frank protest only in that, instead of being an open refusal of the proffered insight, it is unconsciously disguised as general ill-temper so that the patient is able to avoid full awareness of the conflict exposed by the new insight. A disturbing interpretation is a present reality, an attempt upon the part of the therapist to interfere with defenses necessary to the patient's peace of mind. When a patient reacts with anger to such an interpretation, therefore, his anger is not based upon a misunderstanding of the present situation as a repetition of a memory from the past. His anger is rather a direct reaction to the therapist as a real and present threat to the patient's peace of mind. Such a reaction is obviously a manifestation of the patient's resistance to treatment, but it cannot be looked upon as a manifestation of a transference neurosis.

The importance of this distinction must become clear as soon as we reflect upon the fact that, in insight therapy, the chief real contact between patient and therapist arises directly from the therapist's efforts to free the patient of his neurosis. Very often, however, not only does the patient wish (consciously) to be free of his neurosis, but he also clings (unconsciously) to his neurosis as a defense against conflicts which he is unwilling to face. As a result of this ambivalence toward his neurosis, the patient must inevitably develop a corresponding ambivalence toward the therapist who is trying to free him of his neurosis by making him aware of the underlying conflicts. In uncovering or insight therapy, the therapist becomes the representative or advocate of the repressed conflicts that he has interpreted to the patient, and very often also of emerging conflicts that the patient unconsciously expects the therapist to interpret. As a rule, in insight therapy this role of the therapist as representative and advocate of disturbing conflicts becomes for the patient the most important real aspect of the therapeutic situation.

Undisguised resistance reactions—frank protests against particular interpretations or against the therapist in his role as advocate of repressed tendencies—have a significance intermediate between that of a rational utilization of the therapy and that of a transference neurosis. They resemble reality adjusted behavior and differ from a transference neurosis in that they are reactions to an important real aspect of the therapeutic situation. They are irrational only in the sense that they are in defense of the patient's neurosis—which is by definition irrational.

One of the most frequent causes of a transference neurosis is the need to hide or cloak such frank resistance reactions. Frank resistance to an interpretation, or frank resentment of the therapist for having made it, is often tantamount to a confession that the interpretation has hit home; and if the therapist is quick to follow up such resistance reactions, he can usually utilize them very effectively to demonstrate the correctness of the original interpretation. The defense is much more efficacious, therefore, if the patient can distort his real resistance to the therapist's interpretation by substituting in its place a misinterpretation of the therapeutic situation as a repetition of some other situation from the patient's past.

As an example of such a regressive substitution of a neurotic transference pattern for a protest against the therapist in his real role as the author of an unwelcome interpretation, we cite the following incident. The therapist had interpreted a patient's conflict between his fear of the therapy and his shame at betraying his fear; to this the patient reacted with a dream in which a small boy urinated on him. In this dream the patient was protecting himself from a humiliating insight by reacting to the therapist's interpretation as being merely an insult. The symbolism by means of which the dream characterized this insult was based upon childhood fantasies of being urinated upon by the father, against which the patient's pride had reacted by substituting fantasies of being urinated upon by one of his younger brothers. Although this dream could have been interpreted as expressive of a homosexual wish toward the analyst (based upon a similar wish in his childhood toward the younger brother and toward the father), such an interpretation would have missed entirely the fantasy's real present significance—protest against the therapist's interpretation of the preceding day.

Thus upon careful analysis we find that the reactions of the patient toward the therapist fall into three categories: (1) a rational utilization of the therapy motivated by the patient's desire for help, (2) resistance reactions against the therapist in his role as advocate of the patient's disturbing conflicts, and (3) manifestations of the transference neurosis based upon a misinterpretation of the therapeutic situation as a repetition of some other situation from the patient's past.

Should the Transference Neurosis
Be Avoided or Utilized?

If we now attempt a more flexible approach to the problems of therapy, several questions suggest themselves. Is a transference neurosis inevitable? Or is it within the power of the therapist to determine to what extent the patient's neurosis shall become a transference neurosis? And—granting that the therapist can exert an influence—to what extent should he permit or encourage a tranference neurosis, and under what circumstances should he diminish the intensity of a transference neurosis that has already developed? We shall attempt to answer some of these questions here; other aspects are considered in Chapter 3 under the heading "Manipulation of the Transference Relationship."

THE TRANSFERENCE NEUROSIS IN SUPPORTIVE THERAPY. —In a therapy based upon emotional support, a transference neurosis is always a complication and has little positive value. If, for example, the patient reacts with guilt or shame to the therapist's efforts to help him, he may become completely unable to benefit further from a permissive and supportive attitude on the part of the therapist. In such a case, then, it may be necessary for the therapist to interpret (and thus help the patient to gain insight into) the motives of guilt and pride that underlie his transference neurosis in order that the patient may become capable of accepting further help.

Aichhorn has shown, however, that this kind of transference neurosis may be held back or very much diminished by decreasing the patient's sense of dependence on and obligation toward the therapist. Inducing such a patient to perform a service for the therapist, for instance, tends to relieve the patient's excessive guilt feelings and thus makes him more comfortable. Or better still, the therapist may use his influence to encourage healthy outside interests in the patient and thus lessen the patient's too intense absorption with his emotional relationship to the therapist.

Variations in the frequency of interviews may also be utilized to regulate the intensity of a patient's dependence upon a sympathetic therapist. Since the intensity of a patient's underlying dependence tends to increase with a greater frequency of interview, less frequent interviews will usually decrease the feelings of guilt and shame that may arise out of too intense dependent cravings.[1]

THE TRANSFERENCE NEUROSIS IN INSIGHT THERAPY.— As we know, these irrational reactions that react to the present only as a repetition of the past can be a very perplexing and

---

[1] While, as indicated on pages 32-3, the initial result of a reduction in the frequency of interview is to bring the patient's dependence into consciousness, once this first stage has been passed the patient's dependence may then be expected to decrease.

disturbing complication in the therapeutic process. It is, there-fore, one of Freud's most important discoveries that these reactions, disturbing as they are, can also be turned to thera-peutic account. As Freud once phrased it, one cannot overcome an enemy who is absent. By acting out his neurotic patterns in the analytic situation, the patient makes it possible for the therapist to observe them directly and to demonstrate to him their motivation.

Because of this double significance of the transference neurosis in insight therapy, it is evidently a matter of very great importance to inquire how to make maximum use of it to demonstrate to the patient the motives of his irrational reaction patterns while at the same time reducing to a minimum the complications that may result from it. We shall discuss first the principles involved in such an effort to make maximum use of the transference neurosis, and shall then apply these principles to some of the more important problems of thera-peutic strategy.

The principles that should guide us in our efforts to regulate and utilize the transference neurosis are well known and rela-tively simple. A transference neurosis of moderate intensity can be very profitably utilized to bring the patient's neurotic reaction patterns out into the open where they can be observed. To the end that the patient may gain insight into the motives for his neurotic behavior, irrational impulses inside the thera-peutic situation have certain advantages over their being carried out in real life, as the patient might otherwise be impelled to do. Not only can the patient's behavior in the analytic situation be more directly and more accurately observed but, what may seem even more important to the patient, many of the practical consequences of acting out disturbing impulses in real life may be avoided by giving voice to them within the therapeutic situation where the patient is expressly permitted to say any-thing and the therapist is trained to react to every utterance of the patient's with sympathetic, but otherwise dispassionate and scientific, interest and without praise or blame.

If the transference neurosis is allowed to exceed a certain optimum degree of intensity. however, its value for purposes of demonstration will be very greatly impaired. For purposes of therapy it is not enough to bring the patient's neurotic reaction patterns out into the open where the therapist can observe them. In insight therapy, the object of making the patient aware of his irrational impulses is to help the patient himself understand the motives for them, to help him become aware of the differences between the past situations which first gave rise to these impulses, and the present situation with which he is now confronted, so that he may modify his behavior accordingly. In order to help the patient to such an understanding, the therapist must appeal to the patient's good judgment. The therapist must work in cooperation with the patient's own ego. As soon as the patient's neurosis begins to affect his relation to the therapist, however, the patient's judgment will be impaired and this cooperation will become much more difficult.

The advantages of facilitating the transference of the patient's unsolved conflicts into the therapeutic situation must, therefore, be balanced against the danger of making impossible the cooperation between the therapist and the patient's ego that will be necessary if the patient is to be helped to an adequate understanding of his conflict. To this end it is important that the tranference neurosis not be permitted to exceed a certain degree of intensity.

IMPORTANCE OF THE THERAPIST'S ATTITUDE.—With these principles in mind, it will be of interest next to inquire what means the therapist has either to facilitate or to damp down the transference neurosis, and how he can best make use of these means to help the patient to an understanding of the motives of his behavior.

To induce a repetition of the patient's emerging neurotic mechanisms in the therapeutic situation is far from difficult. The most trivial accidents often provoke neurotic transference reactions of great intensity. For example, a young woman patient found on the couch a penny that had fallen out of the pocket of the patient who had preceded her and became so angry and reproachful that she could hardly be induced to speak to her analyst (a man) for several days. Later the thera-pist learned that when she was a child her mother had frequently sent her out to find the father when he failed to come home, and that the father—who was very promiscuous but to whom she was deeply attached—would often give her a penny for candy as a bribe not to disturb him when he was with another woman.

If the therapist knows what kind of problem is emerging into consciousness, he will find it simple to elicit such reactions deliberately. He may, for example, praise a patient for thera-peutic progress in order to bring out a latent guilt feeling about receiving the father's approval. Or he may express approval of a friend of the patient's in order to bring out latent jealousy reactions.

Therapists of experience know, however, that such devices must be used with the greatest caution and circumspection, for the reaction evoked may be one of such intensity that it is difficult to control. What is even more important, if the therapist has, in fact, deliberately provoked such a reaction, it may later be much more difficult to convince the patient that his reaction is really a repetition of an earlier pattern and not a quite natural reaction to the therapist's behavior.

To be able to control transference reactions and promote reality testing is, in most cases, much more difficult. It is for the very purpose of better understanding transference reactions that in a standard psychoanalysis the analyst strives to keep his own personality out of the picture. He sits behind the patient where the patient cannot see him, and avoids either telling the patient about his own private affairs or having social contacts with him. He tries to create, as far as possible, a controlled laboratory situation in which the individual peculiarities of the analyst shall play as little role as possible in stimulating the patient's reactions. Human behavior is complex enough in any case. The patient will be sure to react to what he discerns of the analyst's personal motivations and it simplifies the analyst's task enormously if he can reduce his own behavior, as far as possible, to a standard and well controlled pattern.

PSYCHOTHERAPEUTIC SITUATION.—The effect upon the patient, however, is likely to be just the opposite. Let us consider the patient's psychological situation when he first comes to the therapist for treatment.

Let us assume that the patient knows he is ill, that he is consulting the therapist as a physician, wanting to be cured of his illness. He has consulted physicians before and has some experience of being treated for physical ailments. Beyond this experience his impressions are very vague. He has little understanding of the concept that neurotic symptoms are motivated, or he may have picked up some rather bizarre notions about it; and as to psychotherapy or psychoanalysis, he either knows little or nothing or he may think of a psychoanalyst as a kind of wonder-worker who does, or claims to be able to, perform strange and incomprehensible feats of insight and therapy.

With this aura of mystery surrounding him the analyst, after one or two preliminary interviews, tries to behave in accordance with his professional ideal of suppressing his own personality as much as possible. He is supposed to listen sympathetically but not say very much and, after the first few sessions, he sits out of the patient's sight. He does not respond to what the patient says in the same way other people might be expected to respond. He neither praises nor blames. He encourages the patient to tell him everything and tries not to permit himself to become angry when he is insulted or to be pleased when the patient becomes fond of him. He answers questions only after he knows their motive. If he responds at all, it is with an interpretation of the patient's motives, with an interpretation that treats the patient's behavior not as something to be reacted to but as something to be studied with an unemotional technical interest.

It is easy for an analyst who has become accustomed to trying to live up to this ideal of impersonal behavior to underestimate the impression of unreality that it tends to make— especially upon an unsophisticated patient. (It is for this reason that in the psychotherapy of children and adolescents the therapist abandons this impersonal attitude for one of warm and sympathetic interest.) The impression of unreality that the standard technique fosters is beautifully caricatured by a dream one patient brought her analyst after she had been in analysis a long time. In the dream she pictured the analyst as in the hospital, in danger of dying from pneumonia; but when she visited him out of kindness of her heart, his only response was to reprove her for acting without analyzing the motives for her coming.

The effect of the aura of mystery resulting from the analyst's strangely impersonal behavior must evidently be to make reality testing more difficult for the patient. If the patient knows almost nothing about the analyst, it will be easier for him to become conscious of unreal fantasies about him. It is in the dark that one most often sees ghosts; a world in which the outlines of all objects are unclear is very easily peopled with figures out of one's own imagination. In other words, when the analyst sits where the patient cannot see his reactions and keeps the patient in the dark about what kind of person the analyst is, he makes it easier for the patient to develop a transference neurosis.

In a psychoanalysis, one of our most important aims is to make the patient aware of his unconscious irrational and ego-alien impulses. This process may often be facilitated by introducing the patient into a situation about which he knows almost nothing and by thus making the process of immediate reality testing more difficult for him. The advantages of facilitating a transference neurosis in this way, however, are short-lived. As we have already pointed out, in order to help the patient to an understanding of the motives of his irrational behavior, the therapist must appeal to the patient's good judgment and work in cooperation with the patient's own ego. By undermining the patient's capacity for reality testing, however, we make it much more difficult for the patient's ego to participate in the effort to gain insight. On this account it is desirable to damp down the patient's tendency to develop an unwieldy transference neurosis, and to facilitate the process of reality testing instead of making it more difficult.

To this end we must strive to make the therapy understandable to the patient, to rob the psychotherapeutic situation of its mystery. As we have already pointed out, many features of the psychotherapeutic procedure will seem strange to the unsophisticated patient. The therapist should therefore explain the reasons for any procedure that differs from what the patient might normally expect in such a situation.

In one very important respect, the psychotherapeutic situation is different from the ordinary relationship between doctor and patient. Ordinarily the patient expects the doctor to tell him what to do and, in return for doing as he is told, he expects the doctor to cure him. In psychotherapy the patient must be taught to play a more responsible role. In most cases it should be explained to the patient very early that he has two roles to play in the therapeutic situation: on the one hand it is the patient's thoughts, impulses, and behavior that are being studied, but on the other hand the patient must join with the therapist in trying to understand the motives for this behavior. Thus from the very beginning the therapist aims to take the patient into his confidence and to secure just as far as possible the cooperation of the patient's ego in the therapeutic task.

THE MODERN ATTITUDE.—To achieve this end, we must modify somewhat the above-described ideal of impersonal behavior on the part of the analyst. The therapist should not aim to be a blank screen upon which the patient is encouraged to project pictures out of his own imagination but, whenever possible, should endeavor rather to put the patient at his ease by behaving in the way the patient would normally expect from one to whom he has come for help and counsel. For instance, since the patient has come to the therapist hoping to be cured of a disturbing illness—or perhaps merely seeking advice and help in dealing with a disturbing problem in external adjustment—it will usually be quite in accordance with his expectations if he is asked to give an account of his problem and of the circumstances leading up to it. Then, as suggested in the chapter on planning psychotherapy, it will be well at first to accept the patient's own view of his problem. If he thinks he is suffering from an organic illness, we investigate this possibility objectively; if he feels that he is being unfairly treated on the job, we inquire sympathetically into the evidence for this belief.

In other words, we not only behave in such a way as to correspond to the patient's normal expectations, but we also tentatively treat the patient as a normal and rational human being and we continue to do so except when the patient himself proves the contrary. By so doing, we make it easier for him to behave toward us as a normal human being in the therapeutic situation and thus we lay the groundwork for the cooperation of the patient's ego in the task of understanding the motives for his less rational behavior.

When we assume this attitude, we also achieve even more effectively the aim of throwing irrational motivations into sharp relief, for just because we behave in a way the patient has a normal right to expect, and just because we proceed tentatively on the assumption that in his dealings with us he is a normal and rational human being, we thereby throw into sharper contrast any irrational tendencies that may develop in this relatively normal environment. We project the patient's behavior not against a blank screen but against a background of normal behavior, and the very fact that our behavior does not encourage the patient's irrational tendencies makes them all the more conspicuous when they do occur.

Advantages of Emphasizing External Reality

Considerations similar to those just discussed require that in the choice and timing of interpretations our guiding principles should be to keep the patient's as well as our own interest focused upon the patient's problem in adjusting to the present external reality.

At one time the real interest of psychoanalysts was concentrated chiefly upon reconstructing the patient's past history and, in particular, his infantile neurosis. After Freud pointed out the importance of repetition and working through in the therapeutic process, this interest in the past became focused upon helping the patient to work through his infantile neurosis in the transference relationship. We do not wish to minimize the importance of this interest in the infantile neurosis from the point of view of scientific investigation or for the therapist's orientation in planning the therapy, but we do wish to point out that when we make the working through of the infantile neurosis the center of therapeutic interest, it will in many cases have the effect of encouraging to a much greater extent than is necessary the tendency for the patient to misinterpret present situations as though they were identical with traumatic situations in the past.

In other words, by focusing interest on the infantile neurosis we tend to favor the compulsive repetition of memories from the past to the detriment of the reality testing function. Accordingly, insofar as it is our purpose to strengthen the reality testing function of the ego, our policy should be just the opposite: we should center the patient's attention rather upon his real present problems and should turn his attention to disturbing events in the past only for the purpose of throwing light upon the motives for irrational reactions in the present.

With this end in view, we should also try to keep the patient's attention focused upon his problems in the external world rather than upon his reactions to the therapist. We should, first of all, encourage the patient's rational cooperation in trying to understand his reactions to problems outside the therapeutic situation; then, when emotional reactions to the therapist occur, the therapist should pay close attention to the role of his own interpretations in provoking such reactions.

PROBLEM IS REAL.—The patient has come to us with a problem of adjustment to external reality that originated outside the therapeutic situation. In response to his request for help, we attempt to help him understand the conflicting motives that have prevented his finding a satisfactory solution for this problem. The patient's neurosis, however, has arisen as a defense against having to face insight into the nature of his conflicting motives. In spite of his desire for help, therefore, he will also resent the therapist's attempt to get him to face this disturbing insight. If the intensity of his conflict is not too great, he may be able to recognize frankly his resistance to the insight that the therapist has offered him; and he will then proceed, with the help of the therapist's emotional support, to struggle frankly with the conflict that the therapist's interpretation has reopened for him, until he has found a more reality adjusted and satisfactory solution for it. In such a case the reaction of the patient's ego to the therapist will remain, throughout his struggle with the reawakened conflict, a quite open and rational one.

If the interpretation is too disturbing, however, the patient may be unable to recognize his resentment of the interpretation frankly for what it is. As we have already pointed out, frank resistance to an interpretation is tantamount to a confession that the interpretation has hit home. Consequently, if the patient is quite unable to face what it is that he is resisting, he will attempt to rationalize his resistance by distorting his understanding of the nature of the relationship between himself and the therapist.

In searching for a basis for such a rationalization, the patient may unconsciously draw upon either one or both of two possible sources. The therapist must first consider the possibility that the rationalization may be true. Therapists, like patients, are very human and it may be that the patient is right when he says, for example, that the therapist was irritated or wished to depreciate him. In such a case we must admit that the patient's reaction is based in part upon reality and must wait for less ambiguous evidence that he is protesting against an unwelcome insight.

If the patient's resistance, however, is unable to find a fact in present reality upon which to base rationalizations, then he will be compelled to draw upon memories from the past upon which to base his misinterpretation of the therapeutic situation. To cite two very familiar examples, an interpretation of a sexual or of an aggressive impulse may be reacted to as a rebuke or as a threat of punishment from the father; or an interpretation of sexual impulses may be felt to be an attempt

on the part of the therapist to seduce the patient as some
father- or mother-figure once did.

In the handling of such a transference reaction, it is very
important for the therapist to be alert to the fact that it has
been precipitated by his recent interpretation and not allow
himself unwittingly to be diverted from the task of helping
the patient to gain insight into his present behavior. The
therapist will, of course, be interested in the memories upon
which the patient has based his misinterpretation of the therapeutic situation, but will also not lose sight of the ultimate
goal—to make the patient aware of the differences between
the memories he is re-living and the situation provoked by the
therapist's interpretation.

It is important to analyze carefully the form taken by the
patient's resistance to a particular interpretation. Such a reaction is a valuable indication both of the nature and of the
intensity of his resistance to that interpretation. The mere fact,
for instance, that the patient distorts his understanding of the
therapeutic situation by misinterpreting it in terms of the
past, must be regarded as a sign that the patient is not at
the moment able to assimilate the disturbing interpretation by
struggling openly either with the reactivated conflict or even
with his resistance against the interpretation. It is usually
better, therefore, for the therapist not to persist stubbornly in
reiterating his original interpretation but rather to follow closely
the patient's reactions to it.

An important interpretation is usually the beginning rather
than the end of a chapter in the therapy. The experienced
therapist does not expect the patient to accept an important
interpretation immediately, and knows that even an apparent
understanding and agreement on the part of the patient is not
equivalent to a real assimilation of the proffered insight. The
experienced therapist expects rather that the patient, by a
careful day-by-day study of his own reactions to the interpretation, will gradually gain insight into its full import for him
and will finally assimilate the interpretation completely by
finding a better solution for the conflict reopened by it. One
of the most frequent errors of an inexperienced therapist is

to fail to follow up in this way the impression he has made upon the patient by an initial, well-chosen interpretation.

ONE PROBLEM AT A TIME.—As soon as the therapist centers his therapeutic interest not upon the past but upon the patient's present problems, another very important principle becomes almost self-evident. This is the principle that it is best to choose and time interpretations in such a way as to focus the patient's attention upon only one problem at a time. Until a patient has utilized the insight contained in one interpretation by finding a better solution for the conflict that has been re-opened by it, it is better to keep his attention focused upon analyzing the resistance to it and not stir up quite new and unsolved problems. If this rule is not followed, the patient's resistance tends to take on much more complex forms, since the therapist becomes the representative or advocate of not one but a number of conflicts that the patient is unable to face and that may be very difficult to disentangle. On the other hand, by concentrating the patient's attention and resistance upon one problem at a time we tend to polarize his reactions about a single conflict and thus make them much easier for both therapist and patient to understand.

Ideally each therapeutic session should either help the patient toward a solution of a problem that has been stirred up in a previous session, or else leave the patient with a clearly defined problem to work upon until the next session. In a well-con-ducted therapy as much or more happens in the intervals be-tween interviews as in the interviews themselves. The patient should feel that every session brings him some gain, and each session should provide the patient with enough momentum to carry him to the next step in the treatment. This next step is, so to speak, the next lesson for which the patient does "homework" in the interval between. Here, again, keen aware-ness of the trend of the patient's thoughts and feelings is re-quired so that, not only can one time interpretations and the frequency of interviews carefully, one can also know on just what note to stop a particular interview. This is especially well illustrated by Case U, in which each session brings the patient to the very brink of the next bit of insight which the patient then discovers for himself.

Correct Therapeutic Orientation

The more attention is focused upon the patient's present problems, the more apparent becomes the value of Freud's concept of the therapy as a process of reeducation, a resumption of an interrupted learning process. This concept of psychotherapy should be the guiding principle of every therapist in his attempts to understand and direct the therapeutic process.

The patient's neurosis is an unsuccessful attempt to solve a problem in the present by means of behavior patterns that failed to solve it in the past. We are interested in the past as the source of these stereotyped behavior patterns, but our primary interest is in helping the patient find a solution for his present problem by correcting these unsuccessful patterns, by helping him to take account of the differences between present and past.

The great advantage of this kind of orientation toward our therapeutic problem lies in the fact that it centers our attention upon the dynamic potentialities of the patient's personality for healthy development, upon the forces that must be actually utilized in the therapeutic process rather than primarily upon the pathological mechanisms that are obstacles to the treatment.

Such an orientation is important because even the most disturbing symptoms are often manifestations of the very forces most essential for the therapeutic process. An outstanding example of this is to be found in the alcoholic, traditionally one of the most difficult of all cases in which to effect a permanent cure.

The aggressive protest of an alcoholic against his dependent cravings may take such disturbing forms that we are tempted to reject him as a hopeless case. If we overcome our irritation, however, and look for the rationale behind this disturbing behavior, we discover that this aggressive protest is only an excessive (but at the same time, a futile) manifestation of the very incentive that must be utilized in helping him learn to play a more independent role. At first he is so ashamed of his intense dependent cravings that he must use all his aggressive energy in attempts to deny them. If we can satisfy some of these dependent needs in the transference relationship and help him find satisfaction in his daily life (and thus diminish the intensity of his dependent cravings), he may become less ashamed of them and therefore able to accept some insight into the universality of the need for dependent gratification. When he no longer feels the necessity of denying his cravings, he will no longer have to overcompensate for them but will eventually turn his aggressive energies away from futile protest to constructive efforts at a more independent adjustment.

In making interpretations we often set up for ourselves the ideal neither to praise nor to condemn the motives that have activated the patient's behavior. We deceive ourselves, however, if we hope thereby to keep the patient from reading praise or blame into our interpretations. We are, of course, familiar with the tendency of a patient to attribute to the therapist attitudes similar to those of his parents and to that of his own conscience toward his unconscious impulses. But it is not only as a result of such transference mechanisms that the patient may get an impression as to how the therapist evaluates the motives he interprets.

If, for example, a young man has just formed an attachment for a young woman who in many ways resembles his mother, and if his therapist decides to call attention to this resemblance, it is by no means a matter of indifference just how he shall go about it. If he tells the patient that he is attracted to the young woman because she represents his mother, the implication will be that the patient should inhibit any sexual impulse toward the young woman as he would toward his mother. On the other hand, if the therapist waits until the patient has already begun to react with guilt to his sexual impulses toward the young woman and then points out to the patient that he feels guilty because he identifies the girl with the mother, the implication of this interpretation will tend to diminish the patient's guilt feelings because the patient will feel that the therapist is reminding him that the girl is really not his mother. It is evident, therefore, that it is a matter of great importance to the advancement of the therapeutic process in which way the therapist chooses to make this interpretation.

In order to decide correctly between the two alternatives, the therapist must first orient himself by forming some concept of the problem which the patient is at this time struggling to solve. It may be, for example, that the young woman resembles the mother not so much in her own personal characteristics as in the fact that the patient is attracted to her on account of his competitive urges toward another man. In such a case the problem with which the patient is struggling regards what to do with his competitive impulses and it will be necessary for the therapist to point out that the patient's competing for the young woman is leading him into the same kind of conflict that once resulted from competition with his father for the mother.

If, on the other hand, the young woman to whom the patient is attracted resembles the mother only in her physical features and personality traits and not in some way that would necessarily involve the patient in a repetition of his oedipal conflict, then the therapist must conclude that the patient's attraction to this girl is a step toward freeing himself from the mother by turning to another woman. If this conclusion is correct, then it must become immediately evident that telling the patient that this girl represents his mother will tend to inhibit his impulse to accept the girl as a substitute for the mother and will thus tend to keep the patient fixated upon his mother. The therapeutic indication in this case is just the opposite, to make the interpretation in such a way as to call attention to the fact that the girl is not the patient's mother and thus to facilitate the patient's attempts to solve his conflict by finding an innocent alternative to take the place of the forbidden sexual impulses.

Conclusion

The more we keep our attention focused upon the patient's immediate problem in life, the more clearly do we come to realize that the patient's neurosis is an unsuccessful attempt to solve a problem in the present by means of behavior patterns that failed to solve it in the past. We are interested in the past as the source of these stereotyped behavior patterns, but our primary interest is in helping the patient find a solution for his present problems by correcting these unsuccessful patterns, helping him take account of the differences between present and past, and giving him repeated opportunity for actual efforts at readjustment within the transference situation. Then, when the patient attempts to put his new attitudes into practice in outside life, he will find they have become second-nature. Thus does psychotherapy indeed become a process of emotional reeducation.

Thomas Morton French, M.D.

Chapter 6

INDICATIONS FOR THERAPY

Both prognosis, the estimation of treatability by psychotherapy, and choice of therapeutic approach must still rely on approximate criteria. Two sets of factors must be considered: the person's native-plus-acquired capability and the external circumstances confronting him; the modification possible in the individual to fit the situation, and in the situation to fit the individual. Mental disorders result from an inequality between the problem of adaptation and the capacity of the person to solve it; they are a failure in the adaptive function of the personality, an inability to find acceptable gratification for one's subjective needs.

EXTERNAL FACTORS.—External factors (sometimes almost unmodifiable) are of great importance in determining the chances of therapeutic success in a case and in choosing a suitable technique for treatment. Such physical defects, for instance, as sensory disturbances, severe neurological and orthopedic conditions, and chronic or crippling somatic conditions may play a causative role in any form of mental disease, or they may accompany it; a physical handicap, however, often need not constitute a psychological risk if properly handled and may indeed be turned to psychological advantage.

Constitutional low intelligence—not to be confused with emotionally conditioned intellectual blocking—will certainly play a role both in the evaluation of treatability and in the choice of technique. This is not to say that a high intelligence quotient means necessarily a better outlook for cure. Persons of limited intelligence can certainly be relieved of emotional distress by sympathetic handling. The deciding factor in such cases lies often in the amount of change possible in the life situation. Native abilities and talents should also be taken into consideration, as should education or training.

The possibility of introducing changes in the present life situation (such as in faulty family or work relationships) must be determined in every case. The life situation of an individual on whom a heavy responsibility falls—such as a family of many children and dependents—may not be easy to change and yet the burden itself may be a strong contributing cause to the mental disturbance. A person who is unable to get a divorce from a sick, neurotic, or psychotic partner will be in a less favorable condition to respond to treatment and will require a therapeutic technique adjusted to his needs.

Age must also be taken into consideration. Since treatment usually implies some change in life situation, advanced age may reduce this potentiality and make treatment more difficult. Advanced age is not an absolute contraindication; on the other hand, prognosis is better for the young who have a far greater opportunity for change and who, therefore, usually respond more readily to treatment. The treatability of children is greatly influenced by environmental conditions. Since the emotional difficulties of children are determined chiefly by parental attitudes, it is often imperative that the significant parent be brought into treatment also. When this is impossible or impractical, the child should be taken out of the home and placed in an environment favorable to the personality change he must achieve.

In every case, the external factors play an important role, either facilitating or impeding treatment. (Note particularly Cases L, K, and C.)

INTERNAL FACTORS.—Of even greater importance in determining either treatability or technique is a correct evaluation of the individual's adaptability. An indispensable guide in estimating this is a study of the patient's life history which should be considered a "performance test" and is, as such, superior to all performance tests known to psychiatry. How the individual has met typical life situations—weaning, excretory training, learning to walk and talk, first school experience, puberty, work situations, marriage—is indicative of the efficiency of his adaptability.

From an appraisal of the patient's adaptations in the past and of the way he is handling the present crisis which brought him to treatment, we can gauge the integrative capacity of the ego. The individual who had basic difficulties as a child—either constitutional or acquired early in life—will probably show a chronic deficiency in adaptability and will be less easily treated. In contrast, an individual who has made a fairly good adjustment to life in spite of early lacks and deprivations is obviously more adaptable and more readily helped.

The life history must be considered in its entirety. It is not enough to know merely the absence or presence of neurotic episodes; the actual life conditions under which such an episode occurred must also be comprehended. Under extreme difficulties even a well-functioning ego may crack. Repeated neurotic difficulties under favorable circumstances obviously have a less favorable prognostic significance than similar disturbances under unfavorable conditions. Thus we must consider (against the total background) the severity of breakdown, the frequency, the amount of provocation, and also the degree of mental health during intermissions.

Another helpful method of gauging the strength of the ego is to give careful trial interpretations as early as possible. The patient's reaction to such initial interpretations is an excellent guide in evaluating the patient's capacity for insight, as well as in indicating the character and the extent of his probable resistance and future cooperation.

"To Treat or Not to Treat"

In making decisions regarding the suitability of patients for treatment, we must bear in mind that sometimes a neurosis may be the only solution to the patient's difficulties. This is true when significant factors, both internal and external, are comparatively or perhaps completely unchangeable. The patient's reactions to initial trial interpretations are especially helpful in discovering these cases at the outset.

In Case T, for instance, any attempt to deprive the patient of the support offered by his neurosis at this stage might have precipitated a severe breakdown, possibly a psychosis—as his response to an early interpretation indicated. The extremely limited goal undertaken in the actual psychotherapy, however, enabled the patient to fit more comfortably into his present environment and to function even more efficiently in the intellectual sphere to which his activities were limited. This patient may gain enough satisfaction in his accomplishments to increase his emotional stability and allow adjustment to a more normal life situation later on. Here the patient is young enough to give hope of a future readjustment. In some cases, however, this hope is absent and anything but the most superficial emotional support contraindicated.

"NOT TO TREAT."—A businessman, nearly sixty years old, was brought to an analyst because of a phobia which prevented his going beyond the bounds of his own house and garden unless accompanied by his wife. The patient expressed great concern during the first (and only) interview because he was compelled to "neglect his business" as a result of this phobia, which he explained as the aftermath of an acute dermatitis following a sun bath—he called it "sunstroke."

Interrogation showed that the patient had a contract with his two younger business partners whereby his income continued even though he was no longer the active head of the organization. Refusing to share in the therapist's admiration of such an arrangement, the patient repeatedly expressed distrust of his partners' ability to carry on without him. When asked to give his reasons, he became confused and defensive, and contradicted himself repeatedly. It soon became obvious that for several years the aging patient, formerly a highly capable executive, had found it increasingly difficult to keep pace with his young partners and had become less and less active in the affairs of the company. Apparently, the partners felt that his complete retirement would serve the best interests of all and so did not in the least mind continuing to pay him a share of the profits. The patient had persuaded himself, however, that he was staying away from the office not because he was unable to face his changed status but because of a temporary illness.

To the doctor's cautious attempt to explain that the phobia might have an emotional and not a physical origin, the patient reacted with an immediate and massive resistance. The whole condition was a result of his "sunstroke." Any intimation that he might misjudge his partners' ability also met with rejection. Approaching the problem from another angle, the therapist began to discuss the emotional difficulties inherent in retirement and the acceptance of aging. Even though the analyst spoke in general terms to show that the problem was universal, the patient grew more and more restless when it was intimated that often a person finds it difficult to admit to himself that he has outgrown his usefulness and must surrender his place to the younger generation. No matter how tactfully it was presented, the patient could accept no hint that any part of his present situation might have such an explanation.

If the patient had possessed what we call "inner resources," his emotional impasse might still have admitted of a solution. A person who, during his life, has learned the art of leisure and has developed creative interests which do not require the same intense activity as business, or one who has learned to enjoy contemplation, will accept old age more easily than a man of action who has spent his life exclusively in a race for wealth and prestige. What could be learned about the patient's past did not offer much hope in this regard. A "self-made" man who had fought his way from poverty to financial success, he had only limited interests; his self-esteem was based exclusively on his accomplishments as a businessman.

There seemed little hope, therefore, that the patient would be able to adapt himself to a new way of thinking, a new way of life. The trial interpretations had uncovered a massive resistance; the history had shown no resources within him which might have been of help; his present business situation seemed to be unchangeable. Why, then, should he not retire believing that he was indispensable, instead of realizing that his partners considered him a nuisance? What compensation could be offered him in return for depriving him of the excuse of sickness?

Financially the patient was secure; going to the office was merely a matter of prestige with him. Giving up his phobia would have necessitated admitting not only that his mental and physical powers were steadily declining but (because of his contract) that he, the former leader, had become a parasite. The phobia resolved all these problems. The actual dependence upon his partners he displaced with a neurotic dependence upon his wife, regressing to the infantile insecurity he had known as a child when he first had to walk alone on the street. Since he was unaware of this and could blame everything on the "sunstroke," obviously this neurosis was a good bargain. He was "sick" and therefore entitled to his income without loss of face.

The therapist ended the interview, therefore, by saying that the patient had obviously done his share in life, he had accomplished great things, could he not now retire and enjoy his old age in quiet? Still firmly opposed to every suggestion, the patient called for his wife and departed. Although the patient himself was never heard from again, his wife telephoned a few weeks later to say that he no longer mentioned going down to the office but was content to stay at home.

"To Treat."—That the entire strategy would have been different if the patient had shown a less formidable resistance to the first interpretations is illustrated in a somewhat similar case.

Another businessman, sixty-six years old, had developed chronic alcoholism and spastic colitis after retiring from business. The initial trial interpretations concerning the emotional difficulties of retirement (involving hurt prestige and envy of youth) were met with considerable understanding and did not deter the patient from continuing the treatment. This was one of our early cases in brief psychotherapy. After 36 interviews—at first twice a week, later once a week—the treatment was successfully terminated.

Various factors made this patient more accessible to therapy than the first case described. This patient was not exposed to such a humiliating change in his role as a businessman; his retirement did not hurt his pride to the same extent because his prestige was not so closely connected with business success and had a broader basis. Furthermore, his wife had a fine understanding of his emotional problems and had an even less conventional outlook than the patient himself. This was a great help in the therapeutic task of changing the patient's prestige values and enabling him to accept his age without neurotic protest.

Not all these factors, of course, could be appraised in the first interview. The fact alone, however, that this patient did not shy away from the first trial interpretations but was capable of considering them with an open mind and a constructive curiosity—even though he did not accept them immediately—was a reliable indicator of a good therapeutic outlook. (See also Case B.)

Choice of Approach

Every form of psychotherapy must be based on a sound knowledge of psychodynamic principles. With this qualification in mind, we can easily distinguish two general types of psychotherapy—supportive and insight (uncovering) therapy. Supportive therapy is used primarily for the purpose of giving support to the patient's ego with no attempt to effect permanent ego changes; uncovering or insight therapy is used primarily for the purpose of achieving a permanent change in the ego by developing the patient's insight into his difficulties and increasing the ability of his ego to deal with them, through the emotional experiences in the transference situation. Since both types of approach are present in almost all treatments, however, this distinction is not absolute.

SUPPORTIVE THERAPY.—While supportive therapy is almost invariably present in treatment, the uncovering type of approach is contraindicated in two opposite types of cases and a purely supportive therapy used. In the first group, the acute, the ego's functional efficiency is only temporarily impaired. These are persons, previously well adjusted, who are suffering from an acute neurotic disturbance which developed under the pressure of unusually difficult external conditions. (See Case C.) In such cases, *no permanent change of the ego is needed* because the ego's functional capacity is only temporarily impaired by excessive emotional tensions. The therapeutic task consists in reducing the intensity of acute anxiety or other incapacitating emotions so that the patient's confidence in himself is restored and he is thus able to face the situation and make an adjustment to it.

Acute conditions if not treated are likely to become chronic, since the failure to meet actual life situations has a demoralizing effect upon the ego and may reactivate conflict situations of the past which have not been resolved. Once the ego fails, its mastery may break down. This explains why in a traumatic neurosis the patient may lose such basic faculties as walking or speaking—in fact, all coordinated movements—and regress to the helpless state of infancy. This tendency to return to the less responsible and more secure situations of childhood is latent in everyone and asserts itself when life conditions become difficult.

At the opposite end of the scale are those severe chronic patients in whose warped ego *there is little hope of effecting a permanent change.* In these cases of constitutional or acquired weakness of ego, supportive therapy attempts in the main to strengthen those spontaneous defenses which are characteristic of the patient, and to satisfy the patient's need for assistance by actual guidance. (See Cases T and E.) Inferiority feelings are not traced back to their origin but are combatted with reassurance; guilt feelings are not explained but are assuaged by permissive attitudes; anxiety is relieved by the physician's assuming a protective role. The effectiveness of purely supportive treatment in such cases is of necessity limited; moreover, it requires a long (although not necessarily frequent) contact with the patient and is, in a sense, interminable.

UNCOVERING THERAPY.—The range of cases in which uncovering therapy is applicable is extensive, including some acute types and a great variety of chronic cases. In this type of therapy, the aim is to improve the ego's integrative faculty and increase the ego span by substituting flexible adaptive behavior for fixed neurotic defense mechanisms. (See Cases P, M, and U.)

The main therapeutic factor in this type of therapy consists in exposing the patient's ego, during the transference situation, to the same emotional constellations (although of less intensity) which he could not handle in the past and against which he developed neurotic defenses. As the patient learns to handle conflictful emotional constellations in the therapeutic relationship, he is encouraged to experiment with the same emotional difficulties in actual life situations.

Choice of Technique

Having decided on the treatability of the patient and on the general type of therapy required, we have still the finer task of choosing the most suitable techniques. Shall we suggest that the patient come for daily interviews? weekly interviews? How much shall we try to change conditions in his daily life? Shall we encourage or limit the development of the transference relationship? And how much shall we try to accomplish in this case—what is our goal?

These questions are posed not in an effort to make an exhaustive list but rather to indicate the manifold considerations affecting the choice of technique in handling a specific problem. For instance, by limiting the therapeutic goal, we do not mean any artificial point at which the patient should stop his personality development. We do, however, set some limits on our anticipation of personality change *within* the treatment. At the same time we recognize that every change leads to new adaptations and new growth, so that, in a sense, there is no limit to our goal. When a patient is relieved of his conflict, the psychic energy formerly employed by his defenses is released and can be applied to new endeavor. This is what we have called "post-analytic improvement."

The particular technique best adjusted to each individual case is determined by so many factors that generalizations on the choice of specific techniques are useless. There are three outstanding variables in every therapy: (1) the psychodynamics of the case, (2) the actual circumstances in the patient's life affecting treatment, and (3) the therapist's experience and particular skills.

About the first much has been said; each problem contains its own clues. The second concerns practical considerations which enter every treatment, as illustrated in Case G (the patient was a businessman in a foreign country and had to interrupt treatment) and in Case S (the daughter refused to come to treatment and the problem was worked through with the mother).

About the third variable, much could be written. Every therapist's choice of method is dictated partly by his talents and his skills, and partly by his experience. Cognizance is taken of this fact in assigning cases within a clinic staff, and it is demonstrated also in the tendency of one psychiatrist to refer patients to another who has proved his aptitude for handling certain problems. Some therapists have a predilection for certain techniques which another might not use so freely in the same type of problem. For example, dreams are used extensively by some therapists, less by others. Some therapists are particularly skillful in the manipulation of the patient's environment for therapeutic purposes, as Cases K, L, and M show.

This does not mean that therapists do not change their technique from case to case. The therapist chooses the approach and techniques which, in view of the "total situation" of each patient, seems most applicable. In Case A, for example, the therapist chose deliberately an attitude which would be in sharp contrast to what the patient expected. It should be noted that while this ability to choose the appropriate attitude (out of the many possible) is based for the most part on the therapist's initial formulation of the psychodynamics of a particular case, it is also the result of training and long experience in psychotherapy. Indeed it is often this general background that enables a therapist to choose his approach with assurance long before a clear reconstruction of the patient's past can be made.

Because of the variables involved in every treatment, techniques are best demonstrated on the material itself. We shall make no attempt, therefore, to consider the indications for each specific technique but shall try to show in the case presentations of later chapters how interlocked are the psychodynamics and circumstances with the method of procedure necessary for each case, and how we have learned through experience to choose, modify, and combine techniques as the therapeutic process demands.

Franz Alexander, M.D.

Chapter 7

PLANNING PSYCHOTHERAPY

Consciously directed effort reaches its goal more easily and more rapidly than does random effort. This axiom is of such universal application that it is often forgotten, persistent effort and good intentions being made to compensate for haphazard direction. Whether the problem is one of international collaboration or of chess, a definite plan of action based on a full understanding of the problem and on knowledge of the materials and procedures necessary to solve it makes success surer, quicker, easier. Not only should the ultimate aim and the main subsidiary purposes of the entire strategy be clearly visualized, but the maneuvers or tactics necessary to further these ends in the varying stages of the procedure should be tentatively decided upon.

Need for a Planned Therapy

In the field of psychotherapy this is particularly true. Every treatment can be made more pertinent, efficient, and economical by intelligent direction and planning. An adequate plan of procedure is one which determines just what is to be accomplished with a patient and the general approach best adapted to this end, and also what chances there are for success, what difficulties stand in the way, and how the therapist expects to deal with them—always remembering the patient's actual everyday problems. Although the grand strategy, the main goals and approaches necessary for treatment of a particular case, may remain the same throughout, the second half of the plan, the tactics, should be considered "subject to change" at any point in the therapy, although complications and modifications (so far as possible) should be foreseen and allowed for. In standard psychoanalysis, such a complete plan of therapy reduces the number of unprofitable side-excursions (saving unnecessary expenditure of time and effort) and helps prevent "interminable" analyses. In any properly handled flexible psychotherapy, a comprehensive plan is a *sine qua non*— whether the therapy be one with a limited goal or an intensive analysis handled in a special way.

Drifting into therapeutic relationships, becoming deeply involved in therapeutic responsibilities without having formed such a plan promptly, is unfortunately common in psychotherapeutic practice. Working under pressure is one of the many reasons for this tendency. The need to accomplish as much as possible in the time available may make a careful examination of the patient's life seem impossible and may make it seem imperative to rely on quick intuitive impressions in an attempt to give the patient prompt relief from his most pressing difficulties. In such cases, lack of plan may seem to be merely a concession to external necessity. It is a curious fact, however, that in the practice of psychoanalysis—the form of psychotherapy in which the therapist is least pressed for time— there is also a tendency to put off this task of forming an adequate plan of procedure. Indeed, often the mere fact that the analyst anticipates a long treatment exercises an insidious influence upon him, tempting him to listen too passively to the patient's material and to postpone the preliminary step of formulating the dynamics involved.

The psychoanalyst may rationalize this passive approach to his patient's problem in one of several ways. He may invoke the maxim of scientific caution: One should be sure that evidence is adequate before drawing conclusions; since many times the clue to the genesis of a patient's neurosis is furnished by memories recovered only after prolonged analysis, is it not better to wait than to base one's actions on mere speculation? Or he may appeal to history for justification: Did not Freud himself warn against too much intellectual activity while listening to the patient and recommend free-floating attention to associations as the ideal attitude?

Anyone familiar with reports of Freud's analyses will, of course, realize how far from this was Freud's own practice.

Freud was never afraid to attempt a reconstruction and every one of his reported analyses shows how active and alert his mind was to all possible implications in the associative material to which he was listening. It is, of course, highly important that the analyst avoid one-sided and intellectual preoccupation with some one aspect of the patient's material; that he try to remain equally sensitive to all details of the material until gradually or suddenly many apparently disconnected details fit themselves together into a single picture, into a single connected whole. This, as we understand it, is what Freud meant by free-floating attention. But certainly it is not necessary to be intellectually inert in order to be open-minded, nor is a completely passive receptive intellectual attitude a particularly good one for psychoanalyst or psychotherapist.

NECESSITY FOR EARLY PSYCHODYNAMIC FORMULATION.—Especially in the first hours of an analysis, there are pressing considerations that should demand of the analyst a very active intellectual initiative toward the goal of arriving at an adequate dynamic formulation just as soon as possible. The considerations that point to this conclusion are of two kinds.

First of all, it is very often easier to get a clear picture of the patient's problem and life history as a whole during the first few hours of an analysis than it will be at any time later until the analysis is almost completed. It is preeminently during the period before the patient has become deeply involved emotionally in relation to the analyst that it is easiest for the analyst to gain an adequate perspective upon the patient's problem as a whole. The analyst during this period may be compared to a traveler standing on top a hill overlooking the country through which he is about to journey. At this time it may be possible for him to see his whole anticipated journey in perspective. When once he has descended into the valley, this perspective must be retained in his memory or else it will be gone. From this time on, he will be able to examine small parts of this landscape in much greater detail than was possible when he was viewing them from a distance, but the broad relations will no longer be so clear. So, in the analysis, the patient's emotional reactions to the therapist will later bring into focus one narrow aspect after another of the patient's dynamic pattern; but often it is only at the beginning, before the patient's emotions have focused intensely upon the therapist, that it will be possible to review the patient's life history as a whole and see these many reaction patterns in their correct relationship. If the opportunity for a comprehensive orientation concerning the patient's problems is not taken advantage of in the beginning, it will often be difficult to make good this omission later in the analysis after the patient's transference reactions have become more intense.

A still more important reason for attempting an early and comprehensive formulation, however, is the need, as soon as possible, to sketch out a therapeutic plan. Here again the temptation is very great merely to treat the patient's problems as he brings them to us and thus, as it were, to let the patient drift into an analysis. Such a planless therapy obviously entails the danger that the therapist may later find himself involved in unanticipated difficulties. It is highly important, therefore, to outline as soon as possible a comprehensive therapeutic plan, to attempt to visualize in advance (even if only tentatively) just what we shall attempt with our patient, what we hope to accomplish, and in particular what complications we expect and how we plan to deal with them—in other words, to outline a sort of grand strategy for our treatment instead of trusting to our therapeutic intuition on a day-to-day basis to deal with the patient's difficulties as they arise.

In order to do this, it is necessary first, of course, to make a dynamic formulation of the patient's problem. By surveying the patient's life history the therapist should attempt to discover why and how the patient's neurosis arose. Then after an early interview he should attempt to get a bird's-eye view not only of the immediate cause of the patient's disturbance but also of the possibilities for normal satisfaction open to him and the obstacles (both present and past) that prevent his obtaining such satisfactions. After evaluating all the possibilities and rejecting those that may be dangerous or impractical, he will outline plans for helping the patient achieve those that seem to be realizable.

It is highly important, in making our plans for therapy, that we anticipate as accurately as possible the difficulties that are likely or certain to be encountered in a particular course of treatment. Very often after the treatment is well under way, a therapist becomes discouraged and may even conclude that a case is hopeless because the patient becomes disturbed in ways that should have been anticipated as a necessary complication of a correctly planned therapy. If disturbing complications take us by surprise, there is always a tendency for us to evaluate them as more desperate than they are; but we must always regard it as a disturbing complication if a psychotherapist allows himself to become discouraged. If the outlook for the success of the treatment is not good, the therapist should have recognized this in advance. Periods in which the patient is disturbed must be expected in nearly every therapy, but these should as far as possible be planned for in advance and the therapist should not undertake the treatment unless, after surveying possible complications and estimating their severity, he feels reasonably confident that he can handle them and carry the patient through them. If the patient is accepted for treatment, then when disturbances do arise in the course of the treatment they must be evaluated, not emotionally in terms of discouragement, but intellectually and objectively, in terms of the precise mechanism and the therapeutic approach necessary to deal with this mechanism. This will be very much easier to do if the difficulty has already been anticipated before it occurs.

Problems of the Period of Preliminary Investigation

For practical purposes we may divide the therapy into two unequal phases. The first phase of a psychotherapeutic treatment must usually be a preliminary investigatory one, whose aim is, as quickly as possible, to arrive at a psychodynamic understanding of the patient's problem which will be adequate to serve as the basis for a more or less comprehensive though tentative plan for our subsequent therapeutic procedure. After such a plan has been formed we enter into the second and usually much the longer phase of the treatment which we shall call the phase of planned therapy.

The investigatory phase of the treatment varies greatly in character according to the emotional attitude which the patient first brings to the therapeutic situation. Patients who are able to give adequate histories often make the therapist's task of formulation a relatively easy one. It is necessary only that the therapist be properly alert to this task of quick formulation. Instead of just passively registering for future reference what the patient tells him, the therapist must have a good orientation as to what he wants to know and what material is most likely to be significant in evaluating the nature of the problem with which he has to deal.

DETERMINING MOTIVE FOR TREATMENT.—First of all, it is important to determine what is the motive that brings the patient to the therapist. This is in many cases not at all clear. As an example we cite the case of a middle-aged woman who sought treatment at the suggestion of her husband's analyst. When she herself came to another (male) therapist she spent most of her first hour telling why her husband was dissatisfied with her. The therapist pointed out to her that she had told him only what her husband hoped the therapist could do for her and had said nothing about what she herself wished to gain from the therapy. Then he added: "I would not undertake to make over any woman just to please her husband." After this the patient admitted that she herself was depressed, that she was unhappy in her marriage but unwilling to face separation from her husband.

In this case the effect of the therapist's comment was merely to make the patient realize that she did want treatment on her own account. Some weeks later, however, she told of earlier events that made it clear what complications might have ensued if the therapist had not made this explicit at the outset. Some years previously she had undergone a sterilization operation. The reason for this operation, she now stated, was her husband's desire to avoid the inconvenience of using contraceptives. Obviously if her psychotherapist had not taken the precaution to make clear to her that treatment would be undertaken only because she herself wanted something from it, he would immediately have been identified with the husband who, she felt, was willing to subject her to a painful treatment, not in her interest, but in his own.

Indeed, failure to determine the patient's real motive for seeking therapy sometimes leads to most absurdly unrealistic relationships between therapist and patient. Not infrequently the patient may not consider his a psychotherapeutic problem at all. For example, the patient may think of himself as suffering from a physical illness and expect medical or surgical treatment, or he may ascribe his emotional disturbance to a difficult external situation or to the behavior of others and be quite unaware that difficulties within himself may have contributed to his problem. An inexperienced therapist, however, quite ignoring the patient's attitude, may struggle for months to trace back into the patient's childhood the causes of emotional problems of whose existence the patient has never been convinced; and patient and therapist may continue indefinitely each to talk in terms that the other does not understand.

In order to avoid such unrealistic complications, it is important for the therapist to find out first just what it is that the patient wants. It is the patient who must furnish the incentive for whatever is to be accomplished in the treatment, and no amount of reforming zeal on the part of the therapist will be of any avail unless he can turn some strong motive of the patient's to therapeutic use. It follows that the therapist must first meet the patient on his own ground, tentatively accepting the patient's own view of the problem and seeking only secondarily, after orienting himself as to the patient's real motives, to utilize these actual motives to further such therapeutic aims as may then seem to be attainable.

Thus, for example, complaints suggestive of physical illness must, of course, be thoroughly investigated. Only after a thorough medical investigation has determined just what organic illness may be present or possible, are we in a position to propose psychotherapy to a patient who believes he is suffering from a physical illness. After we have explored his medical status, however, our next task then will be to explain to the patient, with suitable examples, how emotional conflicts may give rise to disturbances of bodily function or perhaps to point out to the patient that he is unduly disturbed by a minor organic illness or in some other way reacting irrationally to the organic illness that may be present.

DUAL ROLE OF INITIAL INTERVIEW.—Such explanations have a double value. In the first place, they are necessary in order to explain to the patient why we wish next to inquire systematically into facts about his emotional life which he may consider quite irrelevant. But in addition to serving the purpose of starting us on our inquiry into the patient's emotional life, such explanations also constitute our first psychotherapeutic attack upon the patient's problem. Psychosomatic symptoms usually serve the purpose of enabling the patient to avoid facing an emotional conflict. Demonstrating to the patient that his illness is not in the main an organic one but must be a cover for an emotional conflict is, therefore, the first step that we must take in helping the patient to get rid of his physical symptoms by facing frankly his emotional problem. If the disguise of the physical illness proves to be very important to the patient, then we shall find that this task of persuading him of the possibility of an emotional cause of his illness will arouse considerable protest; and we shall be compelled to deal with this protest before we can proceed with further investigation.

In the case of a person complaining of external difficulties, we may again tentatively accept the patient's assumption that he is dealing only with an external problem and proceed to explore with him both how this external problem has arisen and what possibilities there are of finding a satisfactory solution for it. While we discuss the problem with him, however, we also observe how rationally the patient is able to discuss his problem, whether he is able to face issues squarely, and how far he may be torn between alternatives that are quite incompatible with each other. As we listen we also attempt to gain an impression as to what may be the nature of the underlying conflict that makes it so difficult for the patient to deal with this particular external problem. The patient, for example, may find it impossible to decide whether to accept a rather attractive offer of a new position, and as we discuss it with him we may sense that the decision is difficult for him primarily because accepting the new position means leaving home for the first time and going to live in a distant city. In such a case, pointing out to the patient the reason for his excessive indecision or for other irrational or conflictful attitudes toward his external problem may constitute a first and essential step in therapy as well as an introduction to a more thorough and systematic investigation of emotionally significant events in the patient's life.

Moreover, even if the patient is from the beginning aware of the psychogenic origin of his difficulties, it is well, after listening to an account of his illness, to inquire whether the patient himself has any idea of the immediate emotional cause of his illness. In a few cases, even quite unsophisticated patients may give us a remarkably clear picture of the psychogenesis of their difficulties, a picture which sometimes needs only to be rounded out by one or two bits of insight which were too difficult for the patient to face. In other cases, while taking the history the therapist may already begin the therapeutic process by asking questions which call attention to gaps or inadequacies in the patient's historical account. As an example we may cite the case of a patient who felt it necessary to confess in detail to his wife an extra-marital affair in which he was at the time involved. It was obvious that the patient congratulated himself that his confession was an evidence of his honesty and frankness in relation to his wife. The therapist's question, "Why did you do that?" therefore came very much as a surprise but was in itself the beginning of a new insight, as was evidenced by a dream reported by the patient the next day in which the patient was defending himself against the charge that he wanted to hurt his wife.

ILLUSTRATIVE INITIAL INTERVIEWS.—In many cases the patient is able to give a history that enables us to reconstruct a fairly comprehensive picture not only of the emotionally significant events that precipitated his present illness but also of the conflictful situations in the past that predisposed him to such an illness. Other patients, in spite of the fact that they are able to give a quite rational account of the external events in their lives, nevertheless seem quite incapable of revealing anything as to the emotional importance of the events they relate. Such cases present the therapist with greater difficulties in his attempt to arrive at an adequate formulation than do patients who are much more openly resistive to the therapist's efforts to get an adequate history.

In order to gain a preliminary orientation in such cases, it is necessary for the therapist to train himself to evaluate clues that may seem rather insignificant. The guiding principle in such cases, as indeed in all attempts to reconstruct the emotional significance of a patient's material, is for the therapist to listen with his ears sensitized to any hints of the patient's affective attitudes toward the events that he is relating. For the purposes of tentative formulation, any hint as to how the patient feels is more important than a very considerable amount of merely factual data.

Case X

As an example, we cite the case of a man who had suffered from gastrointestinal symptoms for years. A thorough investigation had satisfied his physicians that a duodenal ulcer many years before was not the cause of his recent symptoms and the patient was forced to the conclusion that his present gastric distress must be of psychogenic origin.

Nevertheless, nearly half of the first interview was taken up with protests about how miserable the illness made him and a detailed account of his symptoms and medical examinations, punctuated by frequent demands to know whether the therapist could help him. Only persistent questioning as to possible causes of the attacks elicited the statement that his stomach became upset when he had to take care of friends who became "disgustingly drunk in public." When finally prevailed upon to give an account of the major events of his life, he prefaced his history with the remark, "Doctor, I don't have a goddam problem in the world."

The history itself was singularly unrevealing. He had a fine family, got along with them splendidly, did not have even the normal difficulties; he loved his wife and his adopted son, had money in the bank, and had been successful in business. His family in childhood had consisted of his father and mother, and one brother four years younger than himself. There had been some envy of wealthy families who lived in the neighborhood, but upon the mother's insistence the father had sent both boys to college. His father had at first been disappointed that the patient did not stay in the family business, but the patient had been very successful in his own business and the father was now proud of him. He reported that he and his brother had never had any difficulties although they did not think quite alike, since social prestige meant more to the brother than to the patient. He admitted that one of his troubles was that he had almost no interests other than his business. Before his illness of the last few years he had been the "life of the party," but recently he had had little inclination to go out socially; now he did not know whether to give up social life entirely or, in spite of his illness, to "let loose and have some fun."

Under pressure from the therapist (a man), who indicated that there must have been some problem of importance to account for such disturbing symptoms, the patient at length thought of a clue. He recalled that his gastrointestinal illness had started about six years before, and that it was just about that time that his son was adopted. The decision to adopt the boy had been made after the patient and his wife had concluded it would not be possible to have children of their own.

It will be noted that this patient was quite unaware of any emotional reactions to the events in his life. This is in accord with the fact that he dwelt so intensely upon his suffering from his physical symptoms. It was evident at the outset that this impatient preoccupation with his illness must be taking the place of any disturbing emotions he may have had in reaction either to the events of his childhood or to his present family situation. This conclusion, which we might already have inferred from the patient's intensive preoccupation with his illness, was immediately confirmed when we listened to his extremely colorless account of his life history. His account of the harmony in his own family sounded too good to be true and it was impossible to elicit from him any emotional reactions other than those that accorded with his ideals of a successful person in his social group.

If we follow our rule of focusing attention upon hints that might betray his emotional reaction, it is possible, however, to piece together a fairly good impression of what constitutes this man's most disturbing problem. Obviously, the central affect in this interview is the patient's demand that something be done immediately to relieve him of the suffering caused by his gastrointestinal illness. This, as we have already indicated, must take the place of other emotions that are disturbing to him. In the remainder of the hour we get one or two hints as to what these may be. First of all, he thinks of his illness as somehow related to the fact that he sometimes has to take care of friends when they are drunk. This, in conjunction with the fact that his main symptoms are gastrointestinal, makes one suspect that envy of other people enjoying food and drink must play an important role in his illness. We learn later that he has a brother four years younger, but he is unable to recall any emotional reaction toward him. His afterthought that his illness began about the time that his own son was adopted, however, confirms our impression that the root of this patient's illness must lie in rivalry with a younger child for the love of a mother.

It is evident, however, that this successful man is quite unable to face any hint of the intense underlying dependent cravings upon which his envy of a younger child must be based. When his friends get drunk he must take care of them instead of getting drunk with them. From the time of his brother's birth on, he has probably overcompensated for his dependent cravings by playing the role of the "big boy" instead of competing with the brother for the position of being the baby in

the family. This compensation has been continued in adult
life in his pride in being a successful man and in his happy
family. When a child comes into the family, however, his
dependent cravings again become too intense and since his pride
will not permit him to become aware of them, he must seek
outlet in his gastrointestinal neurosis. In further confirmation
of this formulation, we also recognize that it corresponds
closely to the pattern usually found in cases of duodenal ulcer.[1]

———

The patient, the initial interview of whose analysis was just
cited, was able to give a fairly good factual summary of his
life history but quite unable to tell us of his emotional reactions
to it. In other cases we encounter just the opposite difficulty.
Some patients come to us so disturbed and preoccupied with
their emotional reactions that they are unable for a considerable
time to tell us much about the facts either of their present
situation or their life history. In such cases the best guiding
rule is similar to the one that we have just proposed for getting
hints as to the significance of a colorless case history. Disturbed
patients, to be sure, show plenty of affect. Our problem here is
to sense the dominant trend and source of this affect.

Case Y

To illustrate this principle we cite the case of a young un-
married woman, six months pregnant, who had been referred
by the court to a social agency for financial assistance and
help in making plans for her prior to her confinement. From
the court the therapist, a woman, knew only that the patient
had been very insistent upon taking legal action against the
putative father, Mr. M.; that at the time when she became
aware of her pregnancy she had been living with her parents,
but that her father had since died and she was now living alone

---

[1] "The Influence of Psychologic Factors upon Gastro-Intestinal Disturbances: A Symposium," A Report upon Research Carried on at the Chicago
Institute for Psychoanalysis, *Psychoanalytic Quarterly*, Vol. III, pp. 501–588,
1934.

with her mother. It was also learned that she had very recently stopped work on account of her pregnancy. The court worker had suggested that the agency might help the patient to find a place to live away from home during the rest of her pregnancy.

It was with this theme that the patient opened the interview, assailing the therapist with questions: What maternity home and hospital could she go to? How many homes were there? What were the names of them? Where were they located? Were they sponsored by churches? These questions were asked one after another without a break. When the therapist suggested that she could answer the questions more intelligently if she could learn more about the patient's situation, the patient stated that she was living with her mother; that her father had just died; that she didn't wish to stay home because it was too unpleasant there. Her oldest sister (fifteen years older than patient) had just come to live with the mother, bringing her child. The patient and this sister had never got along. Although her own feeling made her *want* to leave, she *could* stay with her mother as long as she liked.

After giving this information, the patient immediately returned to her barrage of questions about maternity homes and medical resources in the city. In this new series of questions the additional fact was brought out that the patient was a member of a Lutheran church which she attended regularly. "Do the Lutherans have something?" she asked. She had thought of an arrangement by which she could get her hospital care and live there too. She was rather pressing in her demand for such an arrangement but also indicated a certain resistance to the idea. She wanted to be sure to look the place over; she had never lived away from home and this in itself would be new and different; she could still stay on in her mother's home or she could make arrangements to live with any one of her three other sisters with whom she got along well.

It will be of interest at this point to consider how the therapist should handle this situation. It is evident that the patient is at the moment too disturbed to be able to give a systematic history. Moreover, it is important to form some impression as to the cause of her agitation in order not to increase her disturbance unnecessarily by inappropriate questioning. If we try to sense the dominant motive back of her importunate questions, it seems evident that she is reacting somewhat aggressively to an intense anxiety. This patient has never lived away from home, and yet she feels now under pressure to leave home on account of her sister's unpleasantness. In addition, her pregnancy has presumably exposed her not only to the critical remarks of the sister but also to unknown dangers with which she surrounds the prospect of medical care and delivery of the child. She is afraid, she doesn't know exactly of what, and is struggling to relieve her anxiety by taking the offensive, by asking a long series of questions so rapidly that they cannot be answered.

Obviously our first task must be to give sympathetic recognition to this patient's anxiety, we must let her know sympathetically that we sense that she is frightened. This should tend to relieve her anxiety by giving her the sense that she is no longer alone but is talking with someone who has a keen understanding of her discomfort and is there to support her in her anxiety. We may anticipate further that as she senses that she has someone to whom she can turn when faced with mysterious dangers, she may experience greater relief in confiding further in the therapist. (Here again we note that what we must do in order to orient ourselves to this patient's situation coincides exactly with the requirements of good therapy.)

Before reporting further the course of this interview, it will be of interest also to inquire what impressions we can glean from this patient's behavior that may be of help to us in planning for later therapy. Now that we have sensed the anxiety back of this patient's opening avalanche of questions, we also have a clue to a probable motivation for her energetic efforts to take legal action against Mr. M. We have suspected that this patient has surrounded the prospect of going through pregnancy and delivery alone with a great deal of anxiety; and it seems quite probable, therefore, that her attempt to bring Mr. M. to court, like the volley of questions in the interview, is an aggressive reaction to her own anxiety. If this is the case, then anything that we can do to diminish the intensity of her anxiety will also tend to make her capable of a more reasonable and objective approach to the problem of Mr. M.'s legitimate responsibility to her.

We note also that the intensity of the patient's anxiety has polarized her picture of the world in which she lives about this one central affect. Her world is for the moment one of dangers and places of refuge. From the patient's account, we sense that she tends to turn to the mother for refuge but is driven away by her fear of her oldest sister. Maternity homes and medical clinics are possible places of shelter but to an even greater extent surrounded with mysterious dangers. The therapist is still an unknown quantity. Depending upon her handling of the situation, she may become either another danger or a much-needed haven of refuge.

The therapist did not proceed exactly as we have suggested, but did succeed in relieving the patient's anxiety considerably by assuring her that there was no imperative need for her to leave home immediately and that she and the patient would have time to consider alternative arrangements after they had thought things through a little more. In response to this reassurance, the patient was able to confide more about her situation. She had had no medical care with the exception of her first examination three months before. It was at that time that she had become aware that she was pregnant and the father of the child had taken her to the doctor with the idea of getting an abortion for her. She had refused and now he was holding this against her. She showed the therapist a picture of the child's father, whom she had met two and a half years before at a time when he was separated from his wife. She had maintained a constant relationship with him ever since, even though he had returned to his wife for a few months at one time. He had talked about a divorce for a year or more, but the patient had begun to wonder if he meant it. Even now she didn't know what to believe. He kept telling her that if she would drop the court case against him, he would get a divorce and marry her; but he had not done so before and she had no faith in his statements now.

The therapist inquired at this point how the patient happened to become pregnant at this time. The patient replied that in the last year she had felt that she did not care if she got pregnant. She thought that perhaps if she had his child he would have to take a definite stand. She thought he would have to go through with the divorce and marry her. She was very disappointed that this had not been so. She thought the wife would give him a divorce if she knew of the situation. But both Mr. M. and his wife had been to court and although the wife was quite angry about the situation she made no effort to grant him a divorce. Mr. M. employed his own private attorney and was angry that she had taken him to court. He pointed out that he would have been willing to give her the money he had to pay for a private attorney. He blamed her for her present predicament because she had refused the abortion he had tried to get for her. He had advised her to find an apartment and live by herself, so that he could keep in touch with her. She had seen him recently at church. He had rather encouraged her in coming to the agency to inquire about maternity homes. She just couldn't stay at home because of her conflict with her sister. When her father was alive things were different; he always stuck up for her.

After this burst of confidence, however, the patient returned to her rapid-fire questions about where she could get medical care.

In order to understand better just what gave rise to this second barrage of questions, let us now look back upon this series of confidences that the patient has been able to give to her therapist. We have already pointed out that the patient's anxiety was relieved considerably by the therapist's reassurance that it was not necessary to leave home immediately. Consequently, for a time, her thoughts cease to be polarized exclusively about her fears and she is able to confide in the therapist the fond hopes that had preceded her discovery that she was pregnant. Striking evidence of her increased confidence in the therapist is the fact that she is even able to confess her hope that by becoming pregnant she might put pressure upon Mr. M. to fulfill his promises to marry her. Her recital of these hopes, however, leads her back immediately to her disillusionment. Associated with her disillusionment, as we know, is an intense fear of being left alone to face unknown dangers. To this anxiety, as well as to her disillusionment, she had reacted by aggressive efforts to compel Mr. M. to fulfill his promises to her. These efforts to put pressure on Mr. M., however, only defeated her own purpose. From her account now it seems clear that Mr. M. has wished and is still quite willing to acknowledge much of his responsibilities toward her but her aggressive determination to bring him to court threatens only to estrange him from her. As she reaches this point in her recital she is again faced with anxiety at the possibility of being left alone without anyone to turn to. Her last association reveals how intensely she longs for someone to whom to cling. When her father was alive, she tells us, he always stuck up for her. But this reassuring thought is of little avail since the father is dead. Consequently, at this point a new series of questions betrays the reemergence of her anxiety.

In the light of this new insight it is now possible to map out what should probably be the next major step in the therapy. This patient is evidently clinging to an impossible goal in an attempt to compel Mr. M. to fulfill his promises to marry her. We do not know, to be sure, just what Mr. M.'s attitude is. It is even possible, if the patient should give up her attempt to force his hand, that he might ultimately decide to seek a divorce in order to marry her, but he has already shown that however willing he may be to accept his responsibility toward her he is only antagonized by her determination to take action against him. We might be impelled at this point to indicate to the patient how unrealistic her behavior is, but we have already noticed that as soon as the patient herself begins to realize how impossible it is for her to achieve her goal, her anxiety overwhelms her and drives her again to seek refuge in questions. It is evident, therefore, that her anxiety is too great to permit her to think rationally about this problem and that any attempt at this point in the therapy to point out the unrealistic character of her hopes would make her still less able to face her predicament.

The correct procedure, then, must be just the opposite: not to try to force upon her a reality she cannot yet face but rather to seek to diminish her anxiety by letting her know that she has at last found a friend in the therapist—someone who understands her hopes and her disillusionment, her anxiety when she discovered her hopes were not to be fulfilled, and her fears that she will be left without anyone to turn to for sympathy and understanding. By thus diminishing her anxiety, the therapist can hope ultimately to make her able of her own will to deal more realistically with the problems she must face.

Planning the Therapy

To illustrate the problems involved in therapeutic planning, let us return to *Case X* and attempt to formulate a plan of therapy upon the basis of our psychodynamic understanding at the end of the first interview.

From our discussion of this first interview we concluded that the patient's gastrointestinal symptoms had arisen in reaction to rivalry with a younger brother based upon intense dependent cravings for the mother; that the patient had already repressed these impulses and overcompensated for them by pride in being the big boy and later by pride in his business success; that the dependent cravings had been reactivated by the adoption of his child and were then compelled to seek outlet in his gastrointestinal neurosis.

We have already pointed out that this formulation corresponds closely to the formulation that has been found to hold true for many other cases of gastric neurosis and duodenal ulcer. In formulating our therapeutic plans, therefore, we have the advantage of being able also to draw upon experience with other similar cases.

Let us inquire, first, just what emotional readjustment is necessary in order that this patient may be relieved of his gastrointestinal symptoms. The dynamic basis of this type of psychosomatic neurosis may be described as a vicious circle. The patient's intense dependent cravings are in conflict with his pride and give rise, therefore, to a strong compensatory urge upon the part of the patient to deny all dependent cravings and to prove to himself and others his ability not only to achieve for himself but also to take responsibility for others. This compensatory need for the patient to prove that he is a big boy, however, and especially the need to deny to himself all dependent cravings, results in the frustration of these dependent cravings and thus tends only to intensify them further.

Obviously, in attempting to treat such a case our therapy must attempt to reverse this vicious circle. If we can succeed in making the patient more tolerant of his dependent cravings, then he will be able at least to indulge such of these cravings as are relatively harmless and thus diminish the intensity of his dependence. In order to make the patient more tolerant of his dependent cravings, however, it is necessary to avoid hurting his pride too much. It will be noticed that the gastrointestinal symptoms achieve both of these ends inasmuch as being ill gives the patient an excuse for dependent gratification. A sick child has a justified claim upon the parents' care and affection. Thus the illness succeeds in making dependent cravings compatible with the patient's pride. The aim of the therapy must be to help the patient to achieve these ends without the necessity of being ill. It will usually be desirable, therefore, for the therapist to help the patient find means of dependent gratification that can be made acceptable to him, and this task will often be made easier if it is possible also to make the patient realize that the therapist appreciates and values his positive achievements and pride in independence and success. This method of approach is beautifully illustrated in Case L (see page 244). A somewhat more cautious approach to a considerably more difficult therapeutic problem of the same kind is illustrated by Case F.

EMOTIONAL READJUSTMENT, NOT INSIGHT, THE GOAL.— In attempting to formulate a therapeutic plan for *Case X,* we began by asking ourselves what emotional readjustment was necessary in order that the patient might be relieved of his symptoms. In any intelligent attempt to formulate a therapeutic plan, this must always be our first question. Every therapeutic effect is an emotional readjustment. It follows, therefore, that in making our therapeutic plans we must formulate our goals in terms of the emotional readjustment that we hope to help the patient be able to make.

In a standard psychoanalysis, giving a patient insight into the nature of his repressed conflicts is our most effective means of bringing about the necessary emotional readjustments. Standard psychoanalysis, however, is a suitable method only for patients who are willing to cooperate in such an attempt to understand their unconscious conflicts. Attempting to give a patient insight has therapeutic value only for a patient who is capable of tolerating such insight; and, indeed, even in a standard psychoanalysis there are often periods of stubborn resistance in which a patient becomes incapable of tolerating insight into his conflicts. The principles that guide us in handling such periods of resistance are similar to those that must guide us in treating patients who from the beginning are incapable of tolerating much insight.

In such cases it is important to remember it is the emotional readjustment which may result from insight that is our real therapeutic goal, and not insight for its own sake. Indeed, not infrequently, the relationship between insight and emotional readjustment is just the opposite from the one we expect in a standard psychoanalysis. In many cases it is not a matter of insight stimulating or forcing the patient to an emotional reorientation, but rather one in which a very considerable preliminary emotional readjustment is necessary before insight is possible at all.

As a striking example of such a need for preliminary emotional readjustment in order to make insight possible, we may refer back to *Case Y*. In this case our therapeutic goal for the moment was to diminish the patient's anxiety by giving her a sense of the therapist's understanding of the conflicting emotions that so disturbed her. By thus diminishing her anxiety we hope to make it possible for her spontaneously to face the realities of her situation. Any attempt immediately to give her insight into the unreal character of her demands would have tended only to make her feel that the therapist was unsympathetic and would thus have increased her anxiety and made her less capable of facing her problem.

COMPLICATIONS RESULTING FROM ATTEMPTS TO FORCE INSIGHT.—We have already emphasized that in planning therapy it is important to take account in advance of probable difficulties and complications. Continuing our discussion of therapy in duodenal ulcer cases, we may illustrate this point by considering some of the complications that the therapist must anticipate if he is too eager to force insight upon the patient and forgets that insight is often possible to this group of patients only after a previous emotional readjustment has made them able to accept and assimilate it.

Therapists who have been fascinated by psychoanalysis but who have not yet had much practical experience with the difficulties involved in carrying through a psychoanalytic treatment to completion, often tremendously overvalue the therapeutic efficacy of insight. Once such a therapist has become aware of an important repressed trend in a patient's associations, the goal of therapy becomes one of giving the patient insight into this trend. Insight is expected to cure the patient as though it were a magic wand.

Insight, however, is no magic wand. If an emotional readjustment has not already taken place to make the patient able to tolerate an insight that previously could not be tolerated, then of course the patient will be quite unable to make use of the therapist's interpretation, and too persistent or energetic attempts to press an unwelcome interpretation upon the patient may sometimes lead to disturbing complications.

Let us now consider, for example, how our duodenal ulcer case (*Case X*) might look to us if we should forget the limitations of insight therapy and should proceed in the blind faith that insight can cure anything. Having concluded that the patient's gastrointestinal symptoms had arisen in reaction to rivalry with a younger brother based upon intense dependent cravings for the mother, we might, in terms of a blind faith in insight, think of the therapeutic problem in this and similar cases as one of giving the patient insight into his intense dependent cravings and perhaps also into his hostility toward the brother. In justification of this approach to the therapeutic problem, we might argue that the patient's whole personality has been built up upon his need to deny to himself his dependent cravings and that it seems to be predominantly this denial of dependent cravings that makes it necessary for him to divert these emotional tensions into physical symptoms. In the first interview in *Case X,* this mechanism was particularly clear.

In the light of our experience in attempts to analyze patients with duodenal ulcer, we now know, however, that too persistent and determined efforts to compel these patients to face their dependent cravings may lead to a rather distressing complication in the therapy. In a number of such cases the patient develops an intense dependent transference to the analyst. The attempts of the analyst to interpret this, however, are sensed as a frustration of the dependent cravings and lead to intense hostile impulses toward the analyst as a frustrating mother-figure or toward rivals corresponding to brother- and sister-figures. This involves the patient in a characteristic and very disturbing conflict, a conflict between hostile impulses and intense dependence upon the person who is the object of the hostile impulses. He is confronted with the problem: "How can I justify myself in accepting help from someone whom I wish to hurt?"

The logical defense against this conflict is to reject the proffered help and insight and then to reproach the analyst with the fact that he is not helping but rather harming the patient. This reproach seems to find a certain justification in the fact that the analyst has indeed mobilized this disturbing conflict which may drive the patient actually to suicidal impulses. Such suicidal impulses give the patient an apparent justification in protesting that the analyst not only is not helping him but is driving him to his own destruction. This reproach, of course, has a double value for the purpose of relieving the patient's conflict. If the analyst is really doing him harm instead of good, this not only justifies the patient's hostility but also relieves him of the obligation to feel grateful to the analyst. In accordance with this mechanism, a number of analyses of duodenal ulcer cases have succeeded in giving marked relief to the gastrointestinal symptoms but have resulted in substituting in its place a reaction of the type just described, which has proved very difficult to treat.

Let us now contrast the effect of such a blind reliance upon insight as a therapeutic agent with what we may anticipate as the result of a therapy based upon a more adequate appraisal of the emotional readjustment that the patient must make in order to be relieved of his symptoms.

In the former instance, placing his faith (without further analysis) in the therapeutic effect of insight, the therapist attempts to press upon the patient an insight that increases his frustration and thus drives him into paranoid defense. In the approach illustrated by Case L, on the other hand, the therapeutic goal is to help the patient find acceptable means of dependent gratification and at the same time to support his pride, thus diminishing the intensity of both sides of the patient's conflict. In the former approach, attempts to press upon the patient insight that he could not assimilate result in disturbing the patient to a quite unnecessary degree. This we may contrast with the approach illustrated by Case L in which diminishing the intensity of the patient's conflict first gave the patient very considerable relief before he had achieved much insight into the intensity of his dependent cravings, and then even made the patient capable of some insight into these dependent cravings and the reaction of his pride against them. Thus in this instance the insight, instead of being the cause of the therapeutic improvement, was one of the important results of a therapeutic improvement made possible by other means.

Although this insight was not the cause of the patient's initial relief, however, it is important for two reasons: first, because it registers the patient's newly acquired tolerance of his formerly repudiated dependent cravings; and, second, because this newly acquired insight will tend to stabilize and make more permanent this tolerance of his dependent cravings upon which his therapeutic improvement is based, even when less favorable external circumstances may later tend to reactivate his conflict.

THERAPEUTIC ORIENTATION TOWARD HOSTILE IMPULSES.
—Finally, it will be noticed that in Case L no attempt was
made to give the patient insight into his latent hostile impulses
toward analyst and mother and toward rivals. This illustrates
another point that is of considerable importance in planning
therapy. Therapy based upon the concept that our chief therapeutic tool is insight frequently proceeds upon the assumption
that every one of the disturbing unconscious impulses of which
the patient's material gives evidence should be brought to consciousness. Indeed, sometimes mobilizing the patient's aggressions is itself advocated as an important therapeutic goal.
When we formulate the therapeutic problem in terms of the
emotional readjustment it is necessary for the patient to make,
however, then the problem of dealing with repressed hostile
impulses is thrown into an entirely new perspective.

Hostile impulses are evidence of frustration, and frustration
is a sign of an unsolved problem. If the problem can be solved,
then frustration will cease and the resultant hostile impulses
should disappear. By digging in behind hostile impulses to the
problem that gave rise to them, therefore, it is often possible
to eliminate the hostile impulses without at any time focusing
the patient's attention directly upon them, merely by helping
the patient to find a solution to the underlying problem. It
will often simplify and accelerate the therapy considerably,
therefore, if we focus attention upon hostile impulses only when
the patient proves to be fixated upon a subsidiary problem arising out of the hostile impulses themselves. In the duodenal
ulcer cases, for example, the fundamental problem is to make
it possible for the patient to become more tolerant of his dependent cravings and thus to diminish their intensity. If this
can be achieved without mobilizing the hostile impulses that
have arisen from the frustration of these dependent cravings,
the therapy will be much accelerated. On the other hand, if the
patient is already fixated upon a subsidiary conflict about accepting help from the therapist while at the same time entertaining
hostile impulses towards him, the therapy will be much more
prolonged and difficult.

Thomas Morton French, M.D.

Chapter 8

THE DYNAMICS OF THE THERAPEUTIC
PROCESS

In the preceding chapter we pointed out that every therapeutic effect is an emotional readjustment, and that we should formulate our therapeutic plans in terms of the emotional readjustment we hope to help the patient make. Since, in order to formulate such a plan intelligently, we must base it upon a knowledge of the dynamics of therapy, we shall now attempt an analysis of the therapeutic process.

There are two main principles of therapeutic approach. We may attempt to make the patient's situation easier by adapting his environment to his needs, or we may make the more radical attempt to modify the patient's personality structure in order to bring it into harmony with the requirements of his environment. These two principles, far from being incompatible with each other, are employed in endless combination according to the requirements of each particular therapeutic problem.

Let us, therefore, consider these therapeutic approaches in turn, paying special consideration to the dynamic mechanisms upon which they depend.

Manipulation of Environment

Case L is a good illustration of the principle of modifying the environment to suit the patient. The recommendation to the wife to be more indulgent of the patient's dependent cravings, and the device of giving the patient the task of instructing other ulcer patients to be more tolerant of their dependent needs, are both modifications of the patient's environment—

designed, on the one hand, to relieve the intensity of his own dependent needs and, on the other, to make this consistent with his pride.

Supportive therapy may itself be placed in the category of environmental treatment. The therapist himself is, of course, one very important part of the patient's environment and his behavior toward the patient should be more under control than any other part of the environment. What we are accustomed to designate as "transference cures" may, therefore, best be grouped under the heading of environmental treatment.

Some patients experience great relief of symptoms as soon as they come into treatment. The effect often occurs too soon to be explained as the result of any insight that the patient might have obtained from the treatment, and is quite certainly to be attributed solely to the emotional release and reassurance that the patient derives from having someone to whom he can talk freely and without danger of condemnation.

The term "transference cure" was given to this type of quick relief of symptoms to signify "apparent cure" as a result of the satisfaction the patient received from his emotional relationship to the therapist and not of any more permanent modification of his personality such as new insight would have brought. In the early days of psychoanalysis, we looked upon such "transference cures" as exceedingly superficial and felt it our duty to urge the patient, in spite of his relief, to face his more deepseated problems in order to achieve a more radical and "permanent" mastery of his difficulties.

Sometimes, however, "transference cures" become permanent. Such a permanent improvement is usually to be explained by the fact that the relief the patient gets from unburdening his difficulties to the therapist makes possible a better adjustment in his real life situation; this, in turn, so improves that situation that the patient may, after a time, find he no longer needs the support of the therapist. One of the most instructive reports of a treatment according to this principle is to be found in Aichhorn's "Wayward Youth," in which Aichhorn tells how he first won the confidence and affection of a young patient and then used the boy's attachment to him to encourage interest in his work and in other healthy activities, until finally the boy no longer needed him.

The same principle applies to the therapeutic improvements achieved by putting the patient in an environment which suits his needs. The therapeutic effects achieved by a simple change of environment may, in some cases, persist after the patient has been compelled to return to his original situation. As in the case of the "transference cures," the relief experienced from a temporarily more indulgent environment may make it possible for the patient to adjust himself better to his original environment so that it may be no longer necessary to adapt the environment to his needs.

It is probably something like this that occurs when a patient receives a lasting relief from a vacation or from a prolonged period of rest. A tired mother, for example, may find her responsibilities in caring for her children extremely exasperating. Her irritation stirs up corresponding irritation in the children so that they become more difficult to handle, and the situation may go from bad to worse in a sort of vicious spiral. If the problem is not too deepseated, sending the mother on a prolonged vacation may restore her equanimity and enable her to face the usual annoyances involved in the care of any active child; in the meantime the secondary aggravation of the children's behavior—that was a reaction to the mother's tenseness and irritation—may also have disappeared.

Modification of Behavior Patterns

One of the common dynamic mechanisms found in practically every therapy, whether an attempt is made to modify the environment or the behavior patterns, is confession. In treatment aimed directly toward modifying the patient's reaction-patterns, the most elementary cases are those in which this mechanism—confession by the patient of matters about which he previously had been unable to speak to anyone—is the chief therapeutic device. As examples, we cite certain cases of bronchial asthma.

THERAPEUTIC VALUE OF CONFESSION.—From our studies on bronchial asthma [1] we have found that throughout the lives of patients subject to psychogenic asthma attacks there seems to run as a continuous undercurrent, sometimes deeply repressed, a fear of estrangement from the mother or a mother-substitute. (The mother-substitute may be of either sex, old or young, but it is a person to whom he is deeply attached, someone on whom he is dependent for love and who plays the role his mother used to have.) The basis of this fear is doubt about her reactions to certain thoughts and feelings which he realizes she may find offensive. To end this awful uncertainty he may try his mother out by confessing the disturbing impulses. If the mother accepts the confession as normal, then all is well for a time. If, however, the mother seems shocked, or if the patient is too uncertain of the mother's tolerance to dare make his confession, an asthma attack is likely to be precipitated.

This dynamic relationship between confession and asthma attacks has obvious implications for the specific psychotherapy for the disease. The psychotherapeutic situation offers, first of all, an opportunity for the patient to confess whatever it is that is disturbing him. If the asthmatic patient can gain confidence to confess fully and freely the impulses that are, at the moment, responsible for his fear of estrangement from some mother-substitute, then we may expect relief from his asthma attacks until some new forbidden impulse arises to disturb him. Sometimes such a period of relief may be quite prolonged. When attacks occur again, the therapist's problem is to discover the new disturbing impulse and encourage the patient again to find relief by confessing it.

The principle upon which this kind of therapy is based is a very simple one. As in every psychotherapy, the patient, by continued contact with the therapist, must gain confidence in the therapist's objective, noncondemning attitude. As the patient gains confidence that the therapist will not be offended by matters that might have offended the mother, he gradually

---

[1] T. M. French, F. Alexander, *et al.*: *Psychogenic Factors in Bronchial Asthma,* Psychosomatic Medicine Monographs, 1941.

becomes able to confess matters that he could not confess before and in this way obtains relief for shorter or longer periods
from his asthma attacks.

The effect of such a therapy is, of course, at first merely
symptomatic. By confessing what is disturbing him the patient
gets relief for a time from his asthma attacks. Often, however, symptomatic relief of this kind tends gradually to diminish the deep underlying insecurity and dependence of the patient. Having recovered from his fear of losing the mother-
figure because of his formerly hidden feelings, the patient
becomes more tolerant of himself, begins to feel greater security and independence, and so gradually loses his need for the
therapy as a testing ground.

It is important to note in these cases that the therapeutic
effect does not depend upon giving the patient insight to moti-
vate his telling his disturbing thoughts; the patient has the
need to confess. The purpose of interpretation in such cases
is to help the patient to confess rather than to clarify motives.
As a good illustration of a therapy based primarily upon the
relief that a patient can receive from confession of disturbing
impulses, we cite Case Q. In this case the interpretations
served, in the main, to *anticipate* and thereby facilitate the
patient's confessions.

THE DYNAMICS OF INSIGHT THERAPY.—In the therapeutic
approaches just described, interpretation and insight have
played a role subordinate to the main therapeutic goal—either
of giving the patient emotional support or of making it possible
for him to confess disturbing conflicts. When the therapist's
primary purpose is to give the patient emotional support or to
make it easier for him to confess, the content of the interpretation will usually be one that is reassuring rather than disturbing to the patient. Its purpose is to give the patient the sense
that the therapist is alert, sympathetic, and better able to understand the situation than the patient can, and that he realizes
how natural the patient's reactions are under the circumstances.
We may call this interpreting "with the current."

In many cases, however, it is necessary at times also to interpret "against the current." Insight into one's own motives may be very disturbing. The very insight the patient may need to free him from his neurosis may be one against which he has built up vigorous or complicated defenses to protect him from the impact of fully realizing the nature of his conflict. The neurosis itself is usually motivated by a need to remain ignorant of the true nature of the underlying conflict and serves as a solution of the patient's problem to the extent of relieving him, in part, from suffering the pain involved in facing his conflict frankly. In such cases, an important part of our therapeutic plan may well be to undermine the patient's defenses in order to mobilize the underlying conflict. Just as a surgeon must sometimes reopen a wound that has healed on top in order to permit it to heal from the bottom, so in psychotherapy it may be necessary to reactivate an imperfectly solved conflict in order to permit a new and better solution than his neurosis affords.

The dynamic problems involved in this kind of therapy may be best understood by comparing it to a learning process. Let us compare the patient's situation to that of a child just learning to walk. The child is clinging to a chair as a support. Several steps away is the mother holding out her arms invitingly, but to reach the mother the child must abandon the support to which he is clinging. For a few steps he will have neither the support of the chair nor the support of the mother's arms. Between the chair and the mother's arms is a blank space that is most difficult for him to negotiate. During this interval his problem will be not only more difficult than it was before he left the support of the chair, but also more difficult than it will be if he succeeds in reaching his mother's arms.

Similarly in psychotherapy, in order to reach a new and better solution of his conflict, the patient must give up the support of the partial solution offered by his neurosis; but after he has given up the support of his neurotic solution, he has not yet necessarily found a new and more healthy solution. During this interval he will usually be more disturbed than he was before he embarked on the venture of abandoning his neurotic defenses, and certainly more disturbed than he will be if he succeeds in finding a more normal solution. The therapist's problem before encouraging the patient to start upon such a therapeutic adventure must obviously be to estimate whether or not he will be able to carry the patient through this disturbing interval until the patient has succeeded in gaining the relief that will come from finding a new and better solution for his conflict.

Upon what will the success or failure of the therapist's attempts to encourage the patient in such a step in learning depend? The patient's neurosis is evidence of the fact that the patient himself has been unable to face his conflict alone. What can the therapist offer him now to make it possible for him to face a conflict that he has never faced before?

We must seek the answer to this question in the principle that accounts for the so-called "transference cure." We have already pointed out that the emotional reassurance and satisfaction which the patient derives from his relationship to the therapist may be sufficient to lead to a disappearance of his symptoms. The therapist must utilize this same ameliorating effect of the patient's bond to him in order to make it possible for the patient to face frankly conflicts from which he has previously shrunk away.

Before making an unwelcome interpretation, therefore, the therapist must estimate whether the patient's trust and confidence in him is sufficient to stand the strain. A disturbing interpretation tends to put the patient in conflict between his desire to repudiate the interpretation and his need to avoid controversy with the therapist. A disturbing interpretation, therefore, tends regularly to stir up hostility toward the therapist and correspondingly to weaken the positive emotional bond between patient and therapist. This is a point upon which Aichhorn has placed much stress. If the patient's bond to the therapist proves unable to stand the strain of the patient's need to repudiate an interpretation, the patient may find devices such as going to sleep or forgetting the interpretation to protect himself from the disturbing interpretation, or if such devices fail he may run away from treatment. In still other cases, self-destructive tendencies or other disturbing reactions may become extremely difficult to control.

Such considerations must obviously guide the therapist in determining how soon it is safe to attempt to face a patient with a particular disturbing insight. In terms of our analogy of the child learning to walk, the child may be quite unable to overcome his fear of walking all the way across the room, but if the mother comes closer he may be quite successful in walking two or three steps. Then after he has mastered this less difficult feat, he may be able to embark on the more dangerous venture of walking a longer distance. This is a principle of very great importance for the guidance of the therapist in estimating just how much insight a patient can face at any particular time.

No matter what the type of therapy nor how experienced or intuitive the therapist, he must be constantly on the alert for signs of the patient's readiness and capacity for insight into his emotional conflicts. Fortunately, when we learn to read them, the patient's behavior and associations give us precise indications as to just how much interpretation he can tolerate.

As an example, we cite an incident from the analysis of a male patient to whom a premature interpretation of a homosexual conflict was made. The next day the patient made no reference to this interpretation, but in his associations to a dream the theme of people going insane occurred repeatedly. It was obvious that the patient feared unconsciously that facing this interpretation would drive him crazy. The therapist, therefore, wisely refrained from pressing the interpretation and remarked only, "I think my interpretation yesterday must have frightened you." After thinking a moment, the patient said, "To tell you the truth, doctor, I can't remember what your interpretation was." Interpretation for a considerable period thereafter centered upon the patient's fear. After about a month, however, his fear had diminished sufficiently so that the interpretation could be repeated and this time the patient was much better able to discuss it.

At this point we should emphasize the great difference in the use of interpretation when the patient is seen daily (as

above) or almost daily, and when he is seen once or twice a
week or at even greater intervals. In the standard psychoanalytic
procedure, a therapist might risk a very unwelcome interpretation since he can see its effect the next day and protect the
patient against a mounting anxiety. If this same interpretation
were made in briefer psychotherapy, the anxiety might accumu-
late to such a degree that the patient is thrown into a panic.
An even greater alertness and an even greater agility are required of the therapist, therefore, in the type of psychotherapy
presented in this book.

Regulating the Intensity of Treatment

In order to illustrate the dynamic principles upon which our
therapeutic results depend, it will be of interest to apply them
to the problem of regulating the intensity of treatment.
Throughout the course of any treatment, the therapist must
make constant decisions on how intense the therapy should be
at any given moment. Careful use of interpretation is the
therapist's chief method of controlling this intensity; another
method, as mentioned earlier, is the regulation of the frequency
of interview.

It used to be frequently set down as a rule that in a psychoanalysis the patient should be seen daily five, or better six, times
a week. Any therapy at much less frequent intervals than this
was depreciated as "superficial therapy." A more important
objection to such a rule is that it focuses our attention upon
the quite unimportant question of what name we shall give to
our therapy, and diverts us from the really important question
of what considerations should guide us in deciding what is the
optimum frequency of therapeutic interviews for a particular
patient at a particular time. This is a question that should
obviously be considered in terms of our understanding of the
dynamics of the therapeutic process and along lines similar to
those that guide us in determining when to make important or
disturbing interpretations.

At those times when the therapist is relying primarily upon
giving emotional support to the patient in order to achieve

therapeutic results, there is little need of interviews more frequent than may be necessary to maintain in the patient this sense of emotional support and encouragement. Although in cases based on confession, psychogenic asthma for instance, fairly frequent interviews may be indicated for a period in order to give the patient enough reassurance to allow him to confess disturbing conflicts, in the following period relatively infrequent interviews are indicated. After he has obtained relief from his emotional disturbance, the patient may be free of symptoms for a prolonged period—months or even years—and need not return to the therapist until a recurrence of his asthmatic attacks indicates that some new disturbing impulse has arisen. (Many other patients also find it helpful, after the treatment proper has been terminated, to return thus to the therapist for reassurance, especially when unexpected strains develop in their life circumstances.)

Frequent interviews may, in some cases, make the patient too dependent on the therapist and thus actually aggravate the difficulties of therapy. In illustration of this principle, consider the therapeutic problem in many cases of phobia. Freud pointed out many years ago that such patients tend to become fixated upon their analytic treatment and are with difficulty induced to end it. He proposed encouraging them to act in defiance of their fears and so mobilize and bring into the analysis the emotional conflicts out of which the symptoms originally arose. He also experimented considerably with the device of setting a definite date for the termination of analyses in such cases.

The question arises whether the considerations upon which these suggestions are based ought not to be applied more systematically in the treatment of such cases. Since an intensive psychoanalytic therapy tends often to bring these phobic patients into a greater anxious dependence upon the analyst than is really necessary or desirable for the therapy, it follows that seeing the patient at less frequent intervals should accelerate rather than retard the therapeutic process.

The treatment of cases of anxiety hysteria will, therefore, usually resolve itself into two therapeutic tasks. The first is to wean the patient away from the dependent relationship by means of which he protects himself from the mobilization of his anxiety; the second is to work out with him the problem which originally gave rise to his anxiety—usually, as Freud showed in his earliest formulations, by getting the patient to accept responsibility for his sexual impulses. When the anxiety hysteria is of long standing, the first of these two tasks is usually much the more difficult. The therapist must first give the patient enough emotional support to make it possible for him to defy his fears, and then approach the problem of teaching him to deal with the sexual impulses from which his neurosis is a flight. Care must be taken, however, that the dependent relationship to the therapist is not allowed to become so great a source of gratification that it is an end in itself. Weaning from the therapist can then be facilitated by a gradual reduction of the frequency of interview.

Another point that must be considered in regulating the intensity of a treatment is the fact that the patient may not merely derive emotional support from seeing the therapist frequently; he may also find the therapeutic relationship seductive and therefore disturbing in that it stimulates erotic impulses within him. In such cases, too frequent interviews may complicate the therapy, especially if the therapist fails to interpret and discuss the conflicts arising out of this erotic transference. In more severe cases, this reaction to the therapy as a dangerous seduction may result in very undesirable consequences even if it is interpreted.

As an example of regulating the intensity of treatment in such a complication, we cite the case of a woman in late middle age who had actually developed a psychosis shortly after beginning intensive psychotherapy with a male therapist. After several months she had completely recovered from her psychosis and wished to resume therapy. The therapist, this time very much on guard, realized that refusing further therapy might itself precipitate another psychotic episode. As a test of the patient's latent anxiety, he therefore explained frankly to her that since the therapy had once precipitated a psychotic reaction there was danger it might do so again; but he then added, "If you are willing to take the risk, I am also."

The purpose of this statement was to determine how secure the patient's ego felt itself in the face of the possibility of another attack. Before challenging the patient in this way, it was essential, of course, that the therapist be sure that his question would not itself precipitate a recurrence of her psychosis by frightening her unduly. If the patient had still been on the verge of a psychosis, it would have been hazardous to pose such a question; but in this case the patient's recovery from her psychotic symptoms had been so complete that the therapist was sure it was safe to test her out in this way. If the therapist's challenge should result in an increase in the patient's defenses and a flight from further treatment, then her behavior could be taken as an indication that further treatment would be dangerous. On the other hand, if the patient, after this warning, should decide to resume therapy, this could be taken as an indication that the therapy, with proper safeguards, might be safely undertaken.

After thinking the matter over for several weeks, the patient decided to return to treatment. The problem was now to conduct the therapy in such a way as to prevent a recurrence of the psychotic episode. With this end in view, the therapist suggested several modifications of the earlier intensive psychoanalytic procedure.

First, he proposed that the patient sit where she could see his face. This permitted her to test the reality of her fantasies immediately by direct observation of the therapist. The standard technique of sitting out of sight of the patient (who reclines on a couch) in order to encourage free fantasy, is safe with neurotic patients because we know that the patient's ego is quite capable of distinguishing between fantasy and reality. With patients who we fear may develop a psychosis, however, it is desirable to give the patient the utmost facilities for testing the reality of his fantasies in order to safeguard him against the danger of their becoming delusions.

In the present case, two contrasting conflicts in regard to the treatment were revealed. On one day. dreams and association material would indicate that the patient was reacting to the therapeutic interviews as to a seduction and she would, for example, give expression to a wish that the analyst might burn in hell—as she feared she might, if she were seduced. On another day, however, the material would show that she was accusing the therapist of neglecting her and threatening that this neglect might result in her again developing a psychosis.

After recognizing this alternating transference reaction, the therapist attempted to deal with it by introducing a second modification in the earlier intensive psychotherapeutic procedure. This consisted in his supplementing his interpretations of the patient's transference reactions with variations in the length of intervals between interviews. Whenever the material indicated that the patient was reacting to the therapeutic situation as to a danger, the therapist would explain this to her and then suggest that he not see her again for a week. Whenever, on the other hand, the material accused the therapist of neglecting her, he would again interpret the reaction and set an appointment for the following day.

In this way, these alternating reactions to the therapeutic situation gradually diminished until it became safe to resume a more intensive therapy—with, ultimately, rather good therapeutic success.

Thomas Morton French, M.D.

Chapter 9

EFFICACY OF BRIEF CONTACT

Our research into techniques designed to make psychotherapy more flexible was begun under the title "Briefer Methods of Psychotherapy"—the word "brief" in contrast to the standard psychoanalysis, invariably a long process. Once our work in briefer methods became known, the question was often asked us, "How long is 'brief' psychotherapy?" The answer, we trust, is to be found in the cases presented in this book, which range in length of time from a single interview to a total of 65 interviews extending over a period of seventeen months. Whereas 65 sessions may seem long to those not trained in psychoanalysis, a treatment consisting of one, two, or three interviews would seem brief to anyone.

As a first chapter in our case presentations, we review three cases in which the treatment comprised no more than three interviews. That good results were achieved in such a short time was due, no doubt, to a favorable combination of circumstances in each case—the physician's ability to see at once the precipitating difficulty in relation to the patient's total personality; the capacity of the patient's ego for insight and his ability to use this insight to make changes in his life; and the ready confidence of the patient in the therapist who, for definite reasons in each case, seemed peculiarly fitted to help that particular patient. Such a favorable constellation of qualities in patient and physician is perhaps rare, but these three cases are deliberately chosen in order to show the *potentialities* of treatment based on a thorough knowledge of psychodynamic psychology.

The first of these three cases has an added historical interest in relation to our research and to this book. It was the striking therapeutic effect of two interviews in this case that first prompted the analyst to investigate the therapeutic possibilities of briefer procedures based on psychoanalytic knowledge and experience. From this time on, we have striven in each new case to reach a more and more precise understanding of the dynamics of therapy.

Case B

(Depression)

The patient, a 51-year-old scientist, had for the last three years devoted all his time and energy to a significant research, the results of which were to be presented at a national convention within a few weeks. He came to the therapist (a man) suffering from severe depression combined with actual antipathy for his work and dread of the coming national meeting. His emotional equilibrium was restored in two interviews.

In the first interview, the patient arrived in a state of extreme agitation, weeping and complaining of severe depressive symptoms. He said he was completely exhausted, he could not sleep, and he could not talk to anyone without crying. He had had three of these "nervous breakdowns" during the past three years, but this was the worst of all. He had been working with increasing intensity, renouncing all outside interests. For a period of six weeks, while concentrating on a highly complex mathematical problem, he had worked constantly with only three hours' sleep a night—and then he even dreamed about his work. He had made great progress on his research but had so far been unable to solve this final problem and now, worn out, he felt such a deep revulsion against his work that he could not even touch it. He did not want to read his paper at the coming convention and had decided to give it to his collaborators to read. He insisted that his name be not even mentioned.

The patient emphasized to the therapist that he worked not for fame but for "human welfare," stressing his unselfish interest in solving this problem which had puzzled workers in his field for a long time. The patient then recounted in some detail how his collaborators were urging him to finish and present his paper. He added with unmistakable satisfaction that no one else could fully master the mathematics of his discovery and that if he withdrew no one would be able to complete his work. He countered this immediately with the statement that, of course, he would be willing to help his collaborators if he became able to work again, but he wanted no fame or recognition. He had even considered retiring completely, but could not afford to do so.

The therapist called the patient's attention to contradictions in his attitudes. Whereas he had formerly been devoted to his work, he now had an extreme distaste for it. Although he avowedly wished to serve humanity, he obviously had some gratification in feeling that he alone could complete the present task. The therapist then explained that human actions are often "overdetermined," that they may have many different motives all active at the same time. Emphasis upon an acceptable motivation often serves to hide the unacceptable. The fact that he did not want recognition indicated the presence of intense guilt feelings—although unconscious—in connection with his work. Why did he have this exaggerated need to prove his complete unselfishness, if not to deny his very selfishness? This emphasis on his altruism, the therapist pointed out, was obviously a way of defending himself against self-accusation.

The therapist stressed his belief, however, that the patient's major motive was indeed to help humanity. He said authoritatively that the patient must also have selfish motives, probably unconscious, of which he did not approve but which are universal. Then the therapist spoke in general terms of the standards of our competitive culture, deploring the fact that a competitive spirit has unfortunately pervaded all fields of activity. He remarked that scientific advancement requires devotion to knowledge for its own sake, a quality which the patient obviously possessed to a high degree. The patient left the interview emotionally shaken and yet with apparent relief from his depression.

Since the patient's highly confused state of mind and his insistence on the fundamental nature of his discovery indicated the possibility of an acute paranoid condition, the therapist got in touch with scientists in the patient's field to establish the veracity of his statements. He learned that the patient had not exaggerated the significance of his present scientific discoveries and that he had, in the past, made highly important contributions to his field.

In the next interview the patient reported that after the first session he had gone through an intense emotional experience, but that his severe depression and confusion had immediately lifted. He had regained his self-confidence and now entertained the idea of participating in the convention. He said that as a scientist he had been impressed by the therapist's approach to emotional problems, that he had not realized they could be treated in such a rational manner. He had never suspected in himself the existence of unconscious irrational attitudes; for the first time, he recognized his self-deception.

Except in the field of sports, he had never thought of himself as a competitive person, and now quite suddenly he saw that his whole life seemed to center around competition. He added that the first interview had a peculiar effect upon him, that of a sudden revelation. So many things, the whole course of his life, became clear and meaningful to him. For the first time he had a glimpse into his self-assertive tendencies, but at the same time he had received absolution for them, since they were universal and could be ascribed to the culture of which he was a part.

The two interviews brought out the following data concerning his life. He had been married twice. His first marriage was very unhappy. He had suffered from premature ejaculation; his wife drank a great deal and was often unfaithful to him. After three years of marriage a son was born. When the child was two years old, his wife stole from the house one night, taking the boy with her. Later she wanted her husband to take her back, but he refused and insisted upon a divorce. He admitted that his failure in his first marriage had been a tremendous blow to his pride. His second marriage, however, was very happy. He and his wife were sexually well adjusted; they had two children of whom he was very proud.

At this point, after some hesitation, the patient admitted that in the last three years his sexual power had markedly declined. The therapist called his attention to the fact that his devotion to investigative work had become excessive in these three years. Was his work then a compensation, asked the patient in response. In reply, the therapist asked him to tell more about his earlier life.

Both his father and mother had been married twice; he was the son of their second marriage. Each had had six children from a first marriage and were old when the patient was born; the father was 68 and the mother 46. The patient found himself, therefore, in the emotionally trying situation of the late-comer. He felt that he had been spoiled by his parents. In early childhood he had suffered from a mild infantile paralysis and was small and puny. Treated as a weakling by the whole family, he had felt that only by some extraordinary achievement could he bridge the hopeless gap between himself and his older brothers. Even as a child he became a mathematical fan and when he reached school age he could solve arithmetic problems the teacher could not do. With a great deal of emotion he recalled a scene in which he had embarrassed the teacher before the whole class by solving a problem which the teacher had messed up on the blackboard. In high school he once solved in twenty minutes a geometrical problem which had never been solved before in that school.

At this point, the patient's attention was called to his statement that if he withdrew from his work no one of his collaborators could complete it, because of the complex mathematics involved. The patient replied that he had never thought of this remarkable congruence and, obviously impressed, added that he must have become the victim of a fixed behavior pattern. Then, with a sudden flash of insight, he made the significant confession that he had begun his present work possessed by the desire to prove the fallacy of an accepted theory in his field. To this the therapist remarked that the patient's work could not have been dictated exclusively by the wish to serve humanity.

It was pointed out to him that the old pattern, his need to prove his powers, had been reinforced by his sexual decline, an unavoidable part of the aging process. He was told that there is always a revival of the emotional problems of adolescence at his age. The therapist indicated also that he was especially sensitive about his sexual prestige because of the failure of his first marriage. The patient responded immediately by confessing a gnawing fear during the last three years lest he no longer be able to satisfy his wife and his marriage would go on the rocks.

Finally, the analyst ventured to expose him to the hardest fact of all to face, the fact which had obviously precipitated his present condition—that he was afraid of the younger generation, of his collaborators, afraid that he could no longer compete successfully with them. At this point the patient contradicted the physician for the first time. Of course he was not afraid; not one of the younger men nor even his contemporaries came near him in this field. His supremacy was unchallenged. Moreover, everyone admired and loved him because of his devotion to his research and teaching. His colleagues came and begged him to return to his work; they were all concerned about his condition. How could he be afraid of them? That would be pure insanity.

It took some time to convince the patient that he did not want to face this irrational fear of youth, the result of the competitiveness which had come with the insecurity of his advancing age. The therapist showed him that once in the remote past he had competed with his father—this went into complete oblivion. Later he had competed with his brothers— this he could still remember vividly. Then with his teacher— a few minutes ago he had felt an intense sense of guilt about showing him up. Still later he competed with the suitors of his first wife. Finally, at present, he was competing with the younger generation. But no matter with whom he vied for supremacy, the old guilt feelings attached themselves to every form of competition. This was his ingrained pattern. Did not his whole investigative work start with the desire to prove a current theory fallacious, to prove his own superiority? True, the strongest motive in his work was his pure scientific curiosity; true, he wanted to substitute for the old theory a new and better one, because of his deep devotion to science for its own sake. Added to this desire, however, was an admixture of destructive competitiveness, a desire to be the most successful.

This destructiveness created the feeling of guilt; this even made him afraid of his colleagues. Because his old insecurity had been revived, his research no longer served merely his scientific interest, it was also a means of proving his superiority at the cost of others. Wherefore he now made the sulking gesture of leaving his collaborators in the lurch at the last moment—as if to say, "Well, go ahead, you young giants. Do it without me, if you can. But you cannot. You need me!"

The analyst continued in a dramatic fashion, "And they come and beg you. But you remain adamant. You say, 'No. I am going to retire; I have had enough of fight and struggle. You do it yourself!' You are taking a malicious satisfaction in their impotence to solve the mathematical equations. In your own eyes you are fully rehabilitated. You can say, 'I may no longer be a great hero in the field of sexuality, but I am still better than the younger generation. I am better in what really counts.' All this you cannot permit yourself to feel frankly. You must have some alibi, and this you receive from your illness. You are depressed, you cannot sleep, you cannot stop weeping, you do not want any recognition. Why should you feel guilty? In this way you can have satisfaction and still not feel bad about it because at the same time that you hurt others you also hurt yourself. But would you be so generous if you were not sure they could not accomplish your work without you? sure that even if they could, they would certainly give you the credit? Your martyrdom is only a cover for a vindictive triumph over your colleagues—whose only crime is that they are younger than you."

As nearly as it can be reconstructed, this was the content and tone of the interpretation given. The patient's only reply was that all this opened up a new world for him; that this was the first time in his life he could talk about himself freely with someone. He said that he now felt quite different about the whole affair and would consult the therapist again whenever he felt the need.

The patient later described the two interviews to a friend as follows: "The analyst picked out of my life's history little pieces, assembled them in the same way that you put a jigsaw puzzle together and made a picture, a vivid picture which I could see plainly—namely, that I was exceedingly vain and yet at the same time that I hated vanity (and I do), that I often did things to punish that vanity without any recognition on my part of the motivating cause or compelling factor."

A few months after the second interview the patient informed the therapist that he had completed his work. He had presented the paper at the convention as he had originally planned. His depression had not returned and he now felt freer than he ever had before. Several times in the next few years, when the therapist had an opportunity to talk to him, the patient's reports remained favorable.

In two follow-up interviews eight years later, the therapist learned that although the patient had had a mild depression on several occasions, it had not seriously interfered with his work. He had inherited some money in this interim and had then become emotionally disturbed because, at the same time that he experienced great relief in having economic security, he had felt he was no longer needed. He still had an intense desire to rewrite his thesis so that people could derive more benefit from it, and he was about to retire to California to put the results of his investigations in final form.

From these two interviews it was evident that the patient had retained a clear understanding of his chief emotional problems and, although he was not "cured," he had derived lasting benefit from the original treatment. His later depressions had been of a transitory nature and were not introduced by the state of morbid hyperactivity which initiated his major breakdown.

Comments on Case B

It is difficult to account precisely for this favorable and rapid therapeutic result. At first the analyst was inclined to question its genuineness and thought that probably this was one of those "flights into health" sometimes observed in psychoanalyses when, because of some clear and successful reconstruction of repressed tendencies, the patient reacts by losing his symptoms in order to save himself from further unpleasant truths. The case of this scientist and later observations, however, no longer permitted of such a complacent explanation.

What would have happened if instead of going to the heart of the matter immediately, the therapist had followed the usual course? Would this 51-year-old patient have benefited more from a year or two of daily psychoanalytic treatment, in which slowly and methodically his pattern of competitiveness and guilt had been traced back to the Oedipus complex? Would he thus have gained more convincing insight into the source of his sickness? No doubt the therapist would have learned many details about the genesis of his emotional pattern. But was it necessary for the patient to know *all* the details of the beginnings of his neurotic difficulties?

If such results could be achieved—even exceptionally—in two interviews, how could an analyst know that he did not overlook such a possibility in a large number of cases? This case was the beginning of our decision to undertake a systematic study into the possibilities of briefer, not superficial and merely supportive, but deeply penetrating treatment.

The essence of these findings is that the therapeutic change is based on the increased capacity of the ego to deal with emotional constellations which were unbearable in the past. When the ego's synthesizing power is great, it is often sufficient that the therapist merely turn the spotlight upon old conflictful emotional situations which the weak infantile ego had not been able to face and from which it had therefore withdrawn. Obviously, this was the answer to the speedy recovery of the scientist. Such insight does not develop, however, unless the patient reexperiences intensively the once repressed emotions.

This scientist went through a revelation similar to that experienced by Jean Valjean in Victor Hugo's novel. He suddenly recognized the vicious competitive self-assertiveness of which he had been unaware. He saw suddenly his desperate effort to defend himself against the devastating feeling of his childhood, that he was hopelessly small and feeble. He could face this old feeling again only when he suddenly developed faith in the therapist's capacity to help him. Since he was a scientist, this faith could come only through his intellect. The precision of the psychodynamic formulations made by the analyst appealed to him as a physicist. Another patient with less intellectual inclinations might not have reacted so favorably to the opening interpretations; he might indeed have been repelled by them.

Only because of the patient's great confidence in the physician, which he confessed at the very beginning of the second interview, could he allow himself to face his intolerable insecurity. When he exclaimed that his fear of youth must be sheer insanity, a discriminatory judgment was set up by which he could distinguish between the old situation in which his insecurity was born and the present one in which he actually had nothing to fear—indeed, he was *hors concours*.

All this proves that in psychotherapy there remains an imponderable factor, which has been left to intuition or else to luck. How else could one find in the first interview the tone and the attitude which would create the emotional atmosphere needed for the patient to undergo revelatory experiences of this kind? In this instance it may have been luck. It is our premise, however, that luck can be replaced by a methodical procedure after a few interviews in which we obtain from the patient's story the necessary clues to such an approach. Then we can make an appraisal of the patient's problem in psychodynamic terms and plan our tactics accordingly. The technique of planned therapy, as described in Chapter 7, is an attempt to replace chance with prediction based on valid dynamic principles, applied to the peculiarities of each case. This does not mean that every case will respond to brief therapy. It can be hoped, however, that by astute and careful planning, treatment will become more economical of time and energy and therefore available to larger numbers of people.

Franz Alexander, M.D.

———

The second case to be discussed is another of those which first claimed our interest because of the satisfactory result achieved in a short time.

Case C

(Reactive Depression)

A physician, a German refugee 45 years old, came for psychotherapy because of an intense depression resulting from extreme irritation with his son. He was seen for a single consultation with excellent results. The therapist (a man) was also a recent immigrant.

The patient had had no serious neurotic difficulties before. He had been in this country for ten months, and his wife and only child, a nine-year-old boy, had only recently joined him. His chief complaint was that he felt extremely irritated by his son, that he could not concentrate on his work in the boy's presence, that he was annoyed by his demanding attitude and his constant need for attention. He was now so discouraged over his inability to adjust himself to the child that he had become exceedingly depressed and decided to consult a psychiatrist.

In the course of the discussion, the patient's attention was distracted from his complaints about his son with a few questions about the way he had lived before his family joined him. He then talked freely about the circumstances of his immigration and about his first attempts to reconstruct his life in the new environment. Although he had had a hard time in the beginning, he had been fairly successful in getting established in his profession.

As he talked it became clear to him that his son and wife had joined him "too soon," that they had come before he was ready to offer them the security they needed. With considerable emotion—at first hesitantly, then with conviction—he said he realized that life would be easier now if his son and wife were not with him. He saw that the demands of his son were really not exaggerated but seemed so because he himself felt insecure —not only within himself but also in his economic adjustment. He felt guilty and responsible, and even saw some justification for his son's behavior, since his own difficulties in the new environment did not allow him to be the ideal father his standards demanded. As he talked the whole situation over, he gained more and more insight into these feelings (which were not far under the surface) and with this insight he experienced marked relief.

But insight alone was not enough. It was necessary also to help this patient make some practical arrangement whereby he could adjust his way of working to the American style of life—chiefly through having an office outside the home. This made it possible for him to divide his energies; he could be a hardworking doctor part of the time, and an attentive father and husband the rest of the time.

When he was seen by the therapist two years later, the patient referred to himself as a "week-end father." He expressed his gratitude for the insight he had gained in this one interview, and added that not only his relationship to his son but his relationship to other aspects of his family life and to the American scene in general had greatly improved.

Comments on Case C

It might be argued that a confidential talk with a friend would have helped this patient as much as the psychiatric interview. The evidence, however, is against this assumption since the patient had often talked over his difficulties with his refugee friends, many of whom had had difficulty in adjusting themselves to new ways and conditions.

The therapeutic success in this case consisted mainly in bringing into consciousness conflicting emotions which were preconscious but still suppressed. This man had become rebellious against too much responsibility in a trying situation and was depressed as a result. Insight into his unconscious reaction to immigration in general, and to his family situation in particular, facilitated his emotional readjustment. He had a strong, efficient ego and its powers of integration were readily mobilized and set to work.

The fact that the patient was seen in only one interview precludes any analysis of the transference situation. We surmise, however, that the patient saw in this analyst who, he knew, had also gone through the trying experience of immigration a few years before, a good object for identification. This in itself speeded the rapport necessary for any successful therapy and served as a support of the patient's ego which had begun to fail under the heavy load of responsibility.

Another reason for this therapist's being especially suitable for this patient was the fact that he had already learned the ways of American doctors and could give the patient concrete advice and help in establishing himself in the medical profession.

Martin Grotjahn, M.D.

The third case to be presented in this group bears similarity to the other two, but is chosen for presentation for other reasons as well. It has a different setting from any other reported in the book: the patient was seen in the offices of a social agency by a consulting psychiatrist. As a part of the medical service of this agency, this physician made routine neurological examinations of the patients referred to him. This was not true of the other cases described, in all of which the reporting physician performed only psychiatric service. Furthermore, it was thought to be instructive to report one case from an agency, since in this setting the psychiatrist usually has an opportunity for only the briefest of treatment and must therefore learn to make the most economical use of his contact with the patient.

As in the first two cases reported in this chapter, the patient made a ready rapport to the therapist. She had a good ego and a capacity for insight which, although she is not to be compared intellectually with the others, was sufficient to enable her to accept interpretation and thereby change her neurotic attitudes. Perhaps it is pertinent to give an example to show that emotional insight has no direct relationship to intellectual endowment and advanced education.

The treatment was, in this case also, facilitated because the physician was able to offer practical help with the patient's problem. These two cases (Cases C and D) illustrate what a powerful adjunct to therapy practical advice and assistance can be.

Case D

(Frigidity)

The patient was a beautiful young Negro woman, nineteen years of age. She was married and the mother of a four-months-old infant. She came for treatment with the complaint that since the birth of her baby she had lost all sexual feeling for her husband, although she was still in love with him. Three psychotherapeutic interviews led to a complete sexual readjustment.

In the first interview, the patient complained a great deal about the housework and frankly admitted to the (male) therapist that she would prefer to work as a salesgirl if she did not have to take care of her child. She had been married for more than a year and had become pregnant almost immediately because she and her husband wanted to have a family. Sexual relations had been completely satisfactory until the baby was born. Since the sexual disturbance of the patient did not seem to be deeply rooted, a brief psychotherapy seemed promising.

The patient had been born in Chicago but her parents were West Indian Negroes who consider themselves an aristocracy among Negroes in general. Her mother, over thirty when she married, had been unhappy in her marriage and had obtained a divorce when the patient was two years old. From that time on, the mother took complete care of the girl. The father never assumed any responsibility nor did he show any interest in his child. The mother earned her living by working as a maid, usually keeping her daughter with her. The patient described her mother as a strict, demanding woman who had reared her daughter according to the West Indian moral tradition and seldom had time for any pleasure with her. The patient had not been allowed to mix with other children, nor, until she was sixteen, had she been permitted to go out with boys. As a young girl she had found her chief pleasure in reading; later she became very industrious, however, and when she was sixteen started to work, clerking at a soda fountain.

At this time the patient began going around with a young man two years her senior, whom she had first met in high school. He was considerate and kind and made a small income working for his father as a carpenter's helper. Her mother was not satisfied with this choice, however, because she considered him inferior to her daughter. Although she had often expressed the feeling that her daughter should marry early and avoid her own mistake of a late marriage, she had also repeatedly warned her daughter against men, teaching her to be suspicious of them all. In spite of these warnings, the patient grew very fond of the young man and, after a courtship of two years, they were married.

From the beginning, the young couple made a good sexual adjustment and planned to have a child as soon as possible. However, during the latter part of her pregnancy the patient began to show an increasing irritability toward her husband, and after the birth of the child she found, to her surprise, that she was unable to derive the former satisfaction from their sexual relations. This was the situation when the patient first saw the psychiatrist.

The patient was well poised and seemed quite aware of her stunning appearance; she evidently knew how to dress in an attractive manner with the simplest means. This secondary narcissism had apparently acted as a barrier against deeper damage which might easily have resulted from the many frustrations of her earlier life. The significance of this pride in her beauty was revealed when the patient was undergoing a routine examination. She had been examined previously by a gynecologist, but no unusual findings were reported. To the psychologically experienced therapist, however, it was immediately apparent that the patient was extremely self-conscious and disturbed over the deformity of her abdomen caused by childbirth. She had an umbilical hernia and the abdominal walls were collapsed. The patient had never mentioned this condition to anyone and had made no attempt to get treatment for it.

To the therapist it was obvious that there was a connection between her pregnancy, the resulting deformity, and her frigidity. It seemed apparent that unconsciously she blamed her husband for this condition and that her frigidity was an expression of hostility against him. To the patient the pregnancy, and even more the unfortunate aftermath, represented a narcissistic injury for which she held her husband responsible. It was a confirmation of her early teaching that nothing good was to be expected from a man. The patient had repressed her hostility against her husband and so was not aware of this connection.

The motivation of this repression was not altogether clear. The patient had transferred to her husband a great deal of her former dependence on her mother. In spite of this, however, she had maintained some superiority to him, according to the West Indian tradition of her parents. She said that she sometimes teased him for his shyness, especially in respect to exposing his body. She would jokingly ask him if he were afraid she would take his genitals from him. This was evidently a repression of the patient's anxiety lest she be damaged by him, an attitude which reflected her own hostility against him, a result, in part, of the mother's feeling about men. It is obvious that the patient's tendency to project onto her husband the role of the aggressor diminished as she became aware of her own aggression toward him.

The treatment consisted mainly in an attempt by the therapist to verbalize for the patient this resentment against her husband. It was explained to her in simple terms that she was really blaming her husband for the deformity of her body. Simultaneously, the therapist offered her practical help; he sent her to a gynecologist for proper treatment. It should be mentioned also that the patient had been encouraged to obtain contraceptives since she was conscious that her frigidity was due in part to her fear of having another child immediately.

It is significant, however, that the patient's emotional condition did not change with the use of contraceptives. It improved only after she had gained some insight into her hostility from the three interviews with the therapist. The therapist's attitude relieved her anxiety about men, whom unconsciously she regarded as aggressors. After she felt reassured and actively supported by the therapist, the patient's irritation against her husband disappeared and she was again able to enjoy sexual relations with him.

Comments on Case D

It should be noted that this patient had had no father after she was two years old; her attitude toward men had been fashioned by her mother. That she made a good heterosexual adjustment in spite of this bespoke her good ego capacity. Her ego strength failed her, however, in the narcissistic trauma for which she regarded her husband responsible. A new relationship to a man in the person of the therapist, one who wished to help her, not only made it possible for her to verbalize her resentment and hostility against her husband but also helped to undo her infantile conviction that men were vicious. In this connection, it should be remarked that racial difference apparently did not affect her relationship to the therapist.

In this case, deeper psychodynamic insight on the part of the patient did not seem indicated. The patient lost her symptom and was able to take advantage of practical advice.

A follow-up interview three years later gave the therapist assurance that treatment had been successful. The patient was well and happy and had no complaints. She felt that the therapist's assistance had been of such help to her, moreover, that she now came to ask his advice for a girl friend.

Rudolf A. Fuerst, M.D.

———

Discussion

Since in the minds of some there may be a reservation concerning the genuineness of therapeutic results based on such brief contacts, the following comments are added.

One common argument used to explain the long duration of psychoanalytic treatment is that a neurotic condition which required many years to develop can hardly be undone in a short time. Although this is true in many cases, this argument needs certain qualifications.

At the time Freud developed cathartic hypnosis as a curative measure, it was still unknown that most chronic disturbances have a long and insidious development. Experimental work convinced Freud and Breuer that hysteria had a traumatic origin. At first they attributed the disease to one major traumatic experience; later to a number of disturbing experiences. Only much later did Freud recognize the cumulative effect of the everyday experiences, beginning in infancy. Then he no longer sought one or more serious traumatic events but looked for the insidious influence of parental attitudes and family relationships as the source of emotional disturbances.

The daily interviews of the prolonged psychoanalytic treatment were expected to correct the cumulative effect of the many, sometimes seemingly trivial, experiences of daily life. However, many analysts remained under the influence of the hypnosis therapy which was designed to correct the effect of definite and significant emotional injuries. They believed the patient should recollect the innumerable small traumata which, woven together, fashioned the neurosis. It was, therefore, only logical to regard analytic treatment as necessarily long, since it was thought that the innumerable incidents had not only to be recalled but "worked through" if the neurosis were to be resolved.

It has since been proved, however, that it is not necessary to remember all the events which caused the neurotic reactions, and that, in any case, recollection is the result of improvement, not its cause. Moreover, in many (probably in most) chronic cases, the effect of a traumatic family atmosphere can be reduced to one specific emotional constellation. As soon as the therapist succeeds in reestablishing this constellation in the transference situation, the adult ego has the opportunity to grapple with it in a new attempt at mastery. The length of time necessary for any treatment, therefore, depends upon the degree of intensity the patient's ego can endure in the transference experience without resorting to regressive evasion.

The cases cited in this chapter demonstrate that the slow development of a neurosis does not necessarily exclude the possibility of a speedy, often dramatic, recovery—provided that the therapist is able to produce a replica of the traumatic situation with sufficient vividness to make it realistic, and provided that the ego can stand this reactivation. In the case of the scientist cited above (Case B), this was possible; such drastic interpretations given in the first two interviews might fail utterly in some cases, indeed might even precipitate a psychotic episode. The patient's emotional reaction to interpretations given in Cases C and D was less dramatic but equally effective.

Most simply stated, this means that a single drastic therapeutic experience can bring sudden relief or start one on the road to health. Every psychiatrist of long experience has had occasion to be surprised at an apparently sudden cure among his patients. And, what is most important, it makes no difference whether we deal with the effect of one acute traumatic situation or with the cumulative result of prolonged traumatic atmosphere of early family life. Under favorable conditions, the pathogenic emotional pattern of the past can be revived and its morbid results undone, sometimes in a comparatively brief treatment and occasionally in only a few interviews in which the patient undergoes a profound revelatory experience.

There is no logic in assuming that only a misfortune can have a permanent effect on one's personality. A single, equally intensive, beneficent experience can also leave its mark. If a treatment can provide such a restorative experience to counterbalance the misfortune, the effect of the trauma may be undone. The sudden recognition by the scientist in Case B of his destructive competitiveness, the immigrant physician's realization of his reaction to his own insecurity in Case C, and the young Negro woman's quickly aroused awareness that she was holding her husband responsible for her wounded narcissism in Case D —all are beneficial in this sense and therefore of curative value.

In the course of one interview the patient may react with violent anxiety, weeping, rage attacks, and all sorts of emotional upheavals together with an acute exacerbation of his symptoms—only to achieve a feeling of tremendous relief before the end of the interview. Such experiences, although curative in effect, are painful; they might be described as benign traumata.

In this fact is to be found the nucleus of the popular belief that in certain cases of mental disturbance some accidental and powerful experience may suddenly restore mental health. Perhaps this is the psychological explanation of the miracles of the Bible, the cures of Lourdes, indeed the magical cures of all cultures throughout the ages.

Both the theoretical survey of the psychodynamics of therapy and the impressive evidence gained from actual observations require us to abandon the old belief that permanent changes of the ego cannot be accomplished through shorter and more intensive methods. Since we have always believed in the sudden but permanent effect of "malign traumata" in certain instances, we have no reason to doubt the sudden but permanent effect of those "benign traumata" which occur occasionally in the form of intensive emotional experiences during treatment or by chance in ordinary life. Our task, our challenge, therefore, is to discover in just what cases is such intensive therapy possible, and to establish the techniques necessary to bring about beneficent results.

Franz Alexander, M.D.

Chapter 10

EMOTIONAL REEDUCATION IN SUPPORTIVE
THERAPY

In our research into the possibilities of briefer and more flexible techniques of procedure, we assumed an experimental attitude from the very beginning, taking all types of cases whether or not they looked promising. The following brief account of one of the first cases selected for our research is presented here to show that the initial impression is not always a reliable guide to the type of treatment required for a certain patient.

In this instance, the patient appeared in the first interview to be a borderline psychosis, a clinical picture for which prognosis is considered poor no matter what the method of psychotherapy, and certainly not one suitable for "brief" psychotherapy. The favorable results obtained show that the diagnostic classification is in itself an unsuitable criterion for deciding whether a case requires a prolonged, intensive treatment or can be helped by a briefer therapy. In all diagnostic groups there are milder and more severe cases, and it is not possible always to differentiate between them at first glance. The flexibility and the basic functional capacity of the ego necessary to effective psychotherapy must not be judged on superficial evidence alone; it can be accurately estimated only as one proceeds with the treatment.

It is of further interest to present this case since psychotherapists and case workers frequently encounter this type of patient and achieve, at times, surprisingly successful and, at other times, disconcertingly unsuccessful results. We shall endeavor to find, in the discussion of this case, some explanation for the outcome of this treatment.

Case E

(Schizoid Personality)

The patient, a very disturbed young man of twenty-one, came to treatment on the advice of the family psychiatrist. Recently transferred to a local university as a student of economics, this boy had been brought up in an extraordinarily unfavorable environment and had ample cause for a distorted personality development. Both parents were psychotic at intervals and under the constant care of a psychiatrist; occasionally one or the other had to be hospitalized. There were three children; the patient's older brother was an extremely schizoid (probably hebephrenic) personality; his younger sister seemed to be normal. Further family history is not needed to reconstruct the unhappy background of the patient's adolescence or to depict the highly disturbed interpersonal relationships which now existed within this small family group.

The university at which the patient had come to study was some distance from his own home. The stress of being away from home for the first time, as well as the morbid family background, led the family psychiatrist to suggest that the patient obtain help in adjusting to his new circumstances. The therapy, consisting of 33 interviews over a period of four months, produced good results.

In discussing this case, we shall concern ourselves less with the genetics of his difficulties than with the course of the treatment. It was obvious from the beginning that this case must be handled with the utmost attention to reality testing, rather than with any effort to unearth unconscious motivations in this anxiety-producing family constellation.

On his arrival at the therapist's office, the patient revealed strange mannerisms. He sang in the waiting room, imitated the noises of a bass viol, laughed in a silly manner, and poked his head into other rooms. He displayed tic-like twitchings of the facial muscles and occasionally grotesque movements of the right arm. Once in the therapist's office, he spoke little; in fact, the analyst found it difficult to make him talk at all. He would start a sentence, interrupt himself, begin to laugh, and then look appealingly at the therapist for help in getting started again. He insisted that he had not come to seek help of his own accord but only because the family psychiatrist urged it. In a spasmodic manner—and with constant help from the therapist—he gave a very few facts about his life. In a half amused fashion he spoke of his mother's "sex obsessions" and his father's "impotence." He also mentioned masturbation, then stated that he was not worried about it even though he revealed that he had kept a book on the subject for many years.

It was arranged that the patient should come twice a week for treatment. Throughout the four months of the therapy he appeared at the office with the regularity of an automaton. He said that he came because he had nothing else to do; it was with this same *laissez-faire* attitude that he attended his classes at the university.

Although he established a fairly good rapport to the therapist, it was based mainly on intellectual interest, amused curiosity, lassitude, and a sort of urbane condescension. The therapist accepted this attitude as satisfactory and did not try to push the patient toward any change. Instead, he maintained an attitude of sympathy, patience and tolerance, and made obvious his real interest in everything the patient told him. The analyst made no attempt to increase the rather tenuous transference relationship, but exerted himself to keep it on the level of a good but casual friendship, never letting it become negative in any sense.

Interpretations were chosen with unusual care. No symbolic interpretations were offered at any time. Instead, the emphasis was on the reality situation, both past and present. Interpretations were consistently aimed at making the patient aware of how extremely unfortunate and how abnormal his youth must have been with two psychotic parents, and how important it was now that he establish himself permanently outside the home environment and start living a more normal life. The therapist repeatedly expressed his sympathy with the patient in having had to grow up in such an atmosphere and encouraged him to talk about his mother: her profanity (even obscenity), her "brutal frankness," and her manic attacks on her husband in the presence of the three children.

A visit by the father and mother to the therapist provided more information. This was used by the therapist to stimulate further communication in an attempt to bring the patient to a freer expression of his carefully repressed feelings. The patient accepted everything from the therapist smilingly and without apparent affect. He insisted that no matter what happened at home he would remain indifferent; that nothing whatsoever could disturb his calm. Indeed, in this phase, the patient would smile in amused superiority at any evidence of emotional reactions in the therapist.

And then, slowly the patient started to react by himself; gradually he became more expressive. In the second month of treatment, the patient began to speak of his conflictful feelings for his father. (The father had just made a second visit to the therapist.) The patient could now discuss his emotions toward him—how much pity he actually felt for him, and yet what a hard fate it had been to have such a weak father. This conflict was worked through from a realistic point of view many times.

During the third month, it became obvious to everyone concerned that the boy had really changed a great deal. Indeed, the patient's family, the therapist, and the patient himself were all astonished at the amount of progress. He no longer displayed the absurd mannerisms noted at the initial interview; his manner of talking was more normal; and he spoke with more normal emotion about his father and mother. In his life at the university he had become much more independent; his school work had improved and he had passed some examinations. He began going out with girls and formed a good emotional relationship with one. He also became much more at ease, less restrained, in his relations with his friends in general, coming out of the complete isolation of frozen indifference in which he had lived before treatment started.

By the end of the fourth month, the therapist suggested terminating the treatment. The patient seemed now to be making a reasonably good adjustment to his environment. At the same time, it was arranged that the boy's parents should give him a car of his own. The therapist felt this was a necessary adjunct to the treatment, since the possession of an automobile would increase the radius of the patient's activities and bring him into easier and closer contact with his fellow students and other new friends.

Five months later—nine months after the first interview—the therapist saw the patient again for a brief, informal visit. He was still at the university. The patient said he "felt wonderful" and liked his work; he reported that he was "going steady" with a girl and, in general, was getting along well and had made many friends. After he finished school, he did not expect to return to his home but was planning on going into business in some other city. The therapist encouraged the patient to get in contact with him whenever it seemed wise to talk things over.

Comments on Case E

It is difficult to describe and evaluate what actually takes place in any psychotherapy. In this instance it seems particularly difficult to convey an accurate impression of the procedure.

The interviews were outwardly calm, often with such complete absence of true affect that they were boring. These hours with the psychiatrist, however dull on the surface, came to be of the utmost importance to the patient. Their appearance of superficiality was no indication of the depth of their meaning. There can be no doubt that extraordinary changes took place within the patient to account for the outward changes we have described. It seems probable that this emotional revolution occurred less on the level of consciousness than on a deeper level, the sphere of the unconscious. It is hoped that he will eventually become more able to face his repressed conflicts and be able to meet them, not with withdrawal but with consciously directed activity.

This patient was a highly schizoid personality who had lived in a family with several manifestly psychotic members, diag-

nosed and treated as such. He had found this mask of isolation an efficient defense against that dreadful reality—an extremely traumatic environment—and against anxiety lest he
become psychotic himself. He had repressed his feelings so
long that he had learned how not to show any emotion; it
was as if he had learned how not to feel at all. This defense
was an absolute necessity so long as he lived with his family.
Then he left home and entered the university. His defense
mechanisms had now become partly unnecessary and threatened
normal relationships opened to him in the university setting.
Yet he could not throw off his habits, his mask of indifference,
by himself. It was a strategic moment for him to come to
treatment.

The actual separation from the home environment was the
first major step in the patient's rehabilitation. The therapist
then entered the scene and (with constant emphasis on reality)
helped the patient to realize that not everyone is psychotic, that
the world can be a good place to live in, that there are
worthwhile people in the world—people whom he could love
and who would love him. With the support of his therapist,
the patient continued for some time to work on his external
and internal separation from home, comforting himself and,
for the first time in his life, realistically facing the environment of which until then he had been a part. Under the protection of the therapist, the patient experienced an emotional
reorientation toward his environment and toward his own part
in it, and could finally recognize his own home for the mad-
house it actually was, could see that this was the exception
rather than the rule, and could start new relationships in a
friendly world.

Most important of all the therapeutic changes effected during
treatment was that, once the patient dared discard his mask in
the presence of the therapist, he gradually lost his fear of his
own emotions; he learned that it was not necessarily traumatic
to have feelings and he gained the courage to express them, even
at the risk of having them misunderstood or repudiated.

The patient's experience within the therapy convinced him
that he need no longer protect himself from human contacts

and made it possible for him to extend them to new persons. The therapist encouraged these efforts not only by his emotional support but also by whatever practical means he could. The car, symbolizing both the family's blessing and a new personal freedom for the patient, helped the patient to a good start. The therapist was aware of the dangers of freedom to a personality so long isolated from normal relationships, but he knew that these dangers diminish with each successful new experience.

In cases of this type, continued contact with the therapist, however slight, is usually of great value to the patient. The relationship with the therapist remains, even in the background, an emotional slide rule. A retesting of the therapist's interest is often the balance required for continued improvement.

There is not much doubt that in this case the outstanding therapeutic factor was the emotional experience which the patient had in the transference relationship. This new experience —a new kind of relationship toward a person in authority (parent-image)—helped to correct the traumatic effect of the original experience in the family. The patient's semi-psychotic emotional withdrawal, a defense against the emotional climate of the family situation, became unnecessary in relation to the analyst. Then, when the patient dared discard this armor, he lost his fear of his own emotional responses and learned to deal with his feelings without repressing them. This initial therapeutic result was subsequently enhanced by his other human relationships. The therapeutic experience sufficed to give him a start and from then on his improvement was a natural result of his life experiences away from the traumatic home situation.

This case is an excellent example of the possibility of emotional reeducation within the transference relationship. It was the new emotional orientation—not intellectual insight or verbalization—that wrought the change in this patient's adjustment. Such an experience is not to be regarded as superficial; it is the beginning of a reeducation of the patient's affective life and, as such, will have a transforming effect on the whole personality.

The question arises why *this* patient responded so satisfactorily to a purely supportive relationship when so many similar cases prove disappointing even after a much longer contact. The answer is to be found in the strength of the patient's ego which, although not great, had somehow weathered the adverse conditions of an exceptionally traumatic family background, and in the therapist's ability to release the affect and then help the boy to a better adjustment.

Such a case as this also shows that psychotherapy and genetic research can no longer be considered to require parallel techniques. Not only was a complete reconstruction of the neurosis within the transference relationship not essential in this case, but it would have endangered therapeutic success and might well have forced the patient into a psychosis. It must be noted again, however, that it is only because of training (based on intensive research of forty or fifty years into the origins of mental disturbances) that a therapist is able to comprehend the meaning of the behavior of such patients as this, to command the techniques by which he can secure improvement, and to know when the moment arrives at which the treatment must be modified or terminated.

One last point should be considered: the question of whether this patient should have an intensive psychoanalysis in order to effect a thoroughgoing readjustment of his personality. It is immediately apparent that he could not have endured the searching procedure of a psychoanalysis at the time he came for treatment. Could not the "brief" psychotherapy have been followed with a standard psychoanalysis profitably? It is felt that in cases less closely related to psychosis this procedure would have been recommended at this point. In this instance, however, it was believed to be dangerous. It is an open question whether at some later time a more penetrating treatment will be indicated. This decision will have to be based on the patient's continued or expanded adjustment to reality.

Martin Grotjahn, M.D.

Chapter 11

CONTROL OF THE TRANSFERENCE RELATIONSHIP

The cases in this chapter are presented to show that therapeutic success can be achieved on the basis of a good transference relationship alone, one which is not allowed to develop into a transference neurosis but is kept at the lower level of a "working relationship."

In some cases, as has been indicated elsewhere, a well-developed transference neurosis is favorable to ultimate success. In the first two cases to be recounted, however, it seemed advisable to keep the negative aspects of the transference relationship out of the treatment entirely, using as the mainspring of the therapy the original confidence of the patient in the therapist—each, of course, with the transference colorings peculiar to the individual case.

As a general rule, the patient who comes for help voluntarily has this confidence, this expectation that the therapist is both able and willing to help him, before he comes to treatment; if not, if the patient is forced into treatment, the therapist must build up this feeling of rapport before any therapeutic change can be effected. The therapeutic relationship can be said to begin as soon as the patient makes contact with the therapist. The importance of this incipient relationship is well demonstrated in the first of the following cases.

Case F

(Peptic Ulcer)

The patient, a middle-aged lawyer, came to the psychiatrist originally for a differential diagnosis of symptoms indicating peptic ulcer. He remained in treatment for a total of twenty interviews over a year's time, with excellent therapeutic results.

The patient telephoned the Institute to request a consultation and was assigned to a woman therapist. When he arrived for the first interview, he did not know whether his therapist was to be a man or a woman; he had not bothered to ask when he was told an appointment had been made for him. This throwing himself on fate did not mean indifference to treatment but, as was seen later, an effort to show his independence of fate, his ability to master every situation.

He was well groomed and gave the impression of a successful, overcorrect businessman. His first statement was that he had come only to get a differential diagnosis. He suffered from symptoms which had been diagnosed by X-ray two years previously as peptic ulcer. Since then his symptoms had become increasingly severe in spite of careful diet. Now his doctors advised surgery. He had decided, however, to find out whether emotional factors were responsible for his suffering before he submitted to the operation. Although his underlying idea must have been that an operation would not be necessary if emotional factors *were* responsible for the ulcer, he approached the therapist with the greatest reserve, emphasizing repeatedly that he did not want psychotherapy, did not want to be psychoanalyzed.

The patient's very articulateness about his problems made it obvious that he could be approached only on his own terms. Realizing the patient's sensitivity and defensiveness, the therapist suggested he might prefer to talk with a male therapist. The patient refused, however, and continued the consultation with even greater eagerness—also with greater intellectual defensiveness.

Almost immediately it became obvious to the therapist that the patient did not want to go to a male therapist because of a strong competitive attitude toward men. If he had been forced to consult a man, the therapy would have taken a completely different course and a transference neurosis of great intensity would inevitably have developed. Later materia! showed still more clearly why he refused to be treated by a man and why it was a therapeutic necessity for this patient to be treated by a woman.

Underneath this defensive surface was a dependent need for help, enhanced by the desire to avoid an operation. The therapist saw that the patient felt intuitively that he could be helped more easily if he did not have to compete with anyone, as he might with a male therapist. It was also clear to the therapist that any hint to this effect or any interpretation of his need for dependence would increase his defensiveness and thus raise his emotional tension; he would then feel that he had not been helped by the consultation and then he would probably have submitted to the operation.

The therapist did not know whether an operation would be necessary or not but, understanding the patient's immediate need and realizing that he was highly sensitive to rejection (he had already told her of several severe setbacks in his professional life), she agreed to make a "differential diagnosis" and arranged another appointment with him for the next day. Thus she permitted the patient to satisfy his need for help without hurting his narcissism. Although the patient had said he did not want psychotherapy, it was obvious that he was eager to return.

During the next two consultations the patient recounted his past history and discussed his present conflicts. He had been the youngest child in a large family and had received more attention from his mother than had the other children. All the children idealized the mother but were in open rebellion against their ill-tempered father. The patient's ambition had been to live up to the ethical demands of his mother, who died during his adolescence. He developed strong intellectual and social ambitions, he was given to severe self-criticism, he became a "compulsive neurotic character," constantly fighting all tendencies in himself which he thought inferior.

His sexual development had been slow but normal. When he was about 26 years old, he had married the girl he loved, in many ways what the patient himself wanted to be—an outgoing personality, a social and professional success. They had had a satisfactory marital life for more than twenty years.

In the last few years, the patient had suffered from what he called "emotional hypersensitivity." He was upset by a decline in his business, the result of general economic changes and not due to any failure on his part. Although he freely admitted his worries and his irritability, he could not admit that he had ever envied another person success. While he withdrew in many ways from competition, he became quarrelsome and exaggeratedly self-assertive. He blamed his moodiness on his business situation and was unaware that much of his emotional tension was caused by the success of his wife. Nor did he permit himself to recognize that he felt forced into competition with the men whom his wife met in her professional career.

When these attitudes were pointed out to him, the patient responded with keen insight. He admitted with genuine surprise that he could sense the reaction in his stomach; he suddenly realized that when the names of certain of these men were mentioned he could actually feel his gastric juice flow. With this realization—although the therapist did not call this fact to the patient's attention at the time—the differential diagnosis demanded by the patient was achieved.

At the beginning of the fourth session, the therapist encouraged the patient to let his present problems rest while they tried to find out from his past experiences why he responded to his present problems in this particular way. During this interview the patient recalled several experiences of his childhood and (in short flashes) saw various neurotic aspects of his personality. He recalled his fear of boys toward whom he had felt inferior, and his effort to overcompensate for his timidity by hostile and daring acts. He recognized the feeling of guilt arising from his hostility and came to understand that his aggressive tendencies were responsible for his hypersensitive super-ego. Although this newly gained insight was far from being integrated into his personality, it permitted him to see that his emotions might be responsible for his present worry, for his character disturbance as well as for his physical distress.

Following this session, the patient decided to throw away all his diet regulations. "After all, I am just a nut," he said the next time. In this way he was acting on his original concept: If emotions caused his ulcer, the ulcer was not real, since emotions are not real. He accepted the effect of emotions, yet he denied them at the same time. This attitude he had expressed by giving up his diet but he did not put it into words. The therapist did not discuss the fallacy of this attitude; she deliberately avoided everything which the patient would have felt as criticism. Instead, she led the patient into a discussion of his relationship to his mother.

As he left this interview, the patient said to the therapist, "I won't worry any more. I'm your worry now." This statement was the first and only admission of any emotional dependence on the therapist. It was only after he had recalled how much he had been loved by his mother that he could express his desire to be taken care of by the therapist. She made no direct reply but nodded in a friendly fashion and arranged for the next appointment.

This expression of the patient's dependent needs was not interpreted at the time, nor was it referred to during the whole course of the treatment. The attitude of the therapist throughout was as carefully undemanding and unobtrusively commendatory as during the first consultation. Pointing out to the patient that he was dependent would have meant to him, "You have to learn to master your dependence, not try to satisfy it by turning childishly to a woman for help." This would have constituted a rejection which he could not have tolerated. The omission of interpretation meant, "You may relax and feel dependent," and it was thus the patient took it.

Two days later, in the sixth session, the patient told the therapist that he now felt completely relaxed; he had discarded all his medicine, had given up his diet, and was without distress. Although the therapist could not be certain that the patient would not overtax his stomach, she indicated no concern. The rest of the session was taken up by discussion of problems within his office and of his dependence on his partners. While he was able to recognize how the protected emotional situation of the office kept him from making new ventures, he also realized that he often behaved aggressively and was over-critical of the others in an attempt to compensate for his hidden dependence.

Initial Comments on Case F

At this point, after six sessions, one could say that the immediate goal of the therapy had been achieved. The patient was convinced that emotional factors were causing his stomach symptoms; and the symptoms, temporarily at least, had disappeared. What brought about this therapeutic result, similar to the so-called transference cure? The most obvious answer is that the patient was forced to realize that his physical condition was affected by his emotions and he felt he could, of course, control these emotions. In this sense, the therapeutic result was paradoxical. When the patient realized that emotions were responsible for his trouble he consciously "mastered" them, thus proving his original concept that he was stronger than his emotions. It must be noted, however, that this ego-success was made possible only because his dependence had been satisfied by his relationship to the therapist.

Was it not necessary for the patient to gain insight into, and mastery of, the psychodynamic conflict which caused his symptoms in order to get relief? Some therapists would hold that the entire conflict should have been interpreted; that the patient should have been given insight by interpretation into how the conflict between his dependent needs and overcompensatory strivings affected his personality. This therapist, however, had the impression that such an interpretation would have increased, rather than lessened, his emotional tension. She chose, therefore, to satisfy the dependent needs of the patient, as well as his ego-demand for mastery of his own problems, within the therapeutic situation. Thus his sense of frustration was diminished and at the same time the emotional charge of the conflict between his active strivings and his dependent needs was relieved. This was the main therapeutic factor.

This "relaxation" of the conflict, however, could not have been achieved if the therapeutic situation had not repeated in some degree the undisturbed infantile relationship of the patient to his mother. In this sense the patient's confidence in the analyst was a transference repetition, such as is found in a transference neurosis. This transference relationship, however, was manipulated so as to avoid repetition of the childhood situation, thus furthering the therapeutic process. If the patient had been an excessively passive dependent person, the situation might have needed another approach, since there would have been danger of his sinking into an "interminable" transference neurosis. In this case, however, it was clear that the patient would not cling to the therapeutic situation. In almost every consultation he reiterated his plea not to have a long analysis.

At this point, therefore, the therapist had to decide whether she should give in to the verbal demands of the patient and dismiss him with a symptom cure, or whether she should continue the therapy—and, if so, with what goal. In the usual psychoanalytic procedure, the therapeutic process would have been continued in order to get at the roots of the patient's neurotic personality. The patient's age, his occupation (which kept him out of town for several weeks at a time) and the nature of his character disturbance, which indicated that only a long and difficult therapeutic procedure would achieve a personality change, were against more intensive treatment. The patient's stormy emotional environment at home and his dependence on the therapist, however, indicated his need for continuation of the psychotherapy.

Although his emotional tension was probably caused, fundamentally, by the conflict between his dependent needs and his competitive strivings, this tension was constantly aggravated by his fear of losing his wife and by the competition with the men whom his wife met professionally and the consequent hostility he felt against them. He felt that he should "be above" such emotions as jealousy and he was afraid to do or say anything which would disturb the *status quo*. Because the therapist felt there was a better chance for a lasting therapeutic result if the patient could admit those feelings and discharge some of his hostility, she decided to continue the therapy for a while longer.

———

While the first six sessions took place in two and a half weeks, the following fourteen sessions were spread out over a year, chiefly because the patient was often out of town.

This was the stormier part of the treatment. During this time his confidence in the therapist often had to outweigh his anger and fear that the therapeutic procedure might endanger his marriage by making him realize his resentment and hostility toward his wife.

It should be noted here that these emotions, although expressed toward the therapist, did not indicate a transference neurosis and were not treated as such. The therapist did not attempt to represent any person beyond the therapeutic reality. Since in the course of treatment the patient gave up many of his illusions about his marriage, his emotional reactions toward the analyst were taken as understandable defenses against the disappointment which reality had forced him to face. For the therapeutic purpose, only the actual conflict had to be understood and its emotional content experienced.

In accord with the therapist's intentions regarding the handling of the transference relationship, it was left to the patient to conclude the therapy. After the twentieth session, the patient felt that he did not "have much to say any more"; that he was now able to handle his marital problem. He knew from experience now that when his emotional tension in this sphere diminished, his ulcer symptoms also disappeared.

Two months later the patient came for three more consultations. His progress had continued and he was now firmly convinced that his gastric distress had been due to emotional, not organic, difficulties. He had become able to admit to himself his competitiveness and hostility, and so had had little or no distress. Another follow-up interview two years later showed that the patient was still well and almost entirely free from the ulcer symptoms.

Further Comments on Case F

In reviewing this case, it should be pointed out that the patient reported no dreams during the whole therapy and that the interviews were conducted in an informal, face-to-face position, a situation which gave the patient a feeling of being able to control the part he played in the procedure. His train of thought was for the most part intellectual. In spite of this, he gained insight into the motivations of his feelings and their effect on his physical and psychological well-being. The therapist was aware that the method of treatment selected did not work through all phases of the patient's personality difficulties. She approached the presenting problem by deliberately selecting from the manifold motivations those which were the closest to the consciousness of the patient.

In this case, the therapist employed an approach based only on the handling of the positive aspects of the transference relationship. The therapeutic result was achieved by diminishing the patient's emotional tension. This, in turn, was accomplished by allowing him just enough dependence on the therapist to allay antagonism and by giving him insight into his hostile tendencies toward his competitors and allowing him to abreact this hostility in the therapeutic situation. The therapist was convinced that this result could not have been achieved so quickly if the transference relationship had not been kept positive all this time.

It should be emphasized that the therapist deliberately chose this course in order to relieve the patient's acute symptoms as quickly as possible. If she had felt that these symptoms could be relieved only with a more intensive therapy, she would have permitted the negative side of the transference relationship to develop and a transference neurosis would have ensued. She would then have had to anticipate a much longer period of treatment.

———

In the next case we see another instance of a carefully controlled transference relationship. In the earlier period of treatment with this patient a transference neurosis was allowed to develop to a very low intensity; in the psychotherapy five years later no appreciable transference neurosis can be discerned.

Case G

(Acute Reactive Depression)

The patient, a self-sufficient South American businessman of middle age, came to the therapist for two separate periods of psychotherapy. On the first occasion he was advised to come in the hope of relaxing his inhibitions and thus improving his relationship to his wife, then under the care of another psychiatrist. He had intensive psychoanalytic therapy for three months, with a sequel six months later consisting of four interviews. The therapeutic results were good.

Five years later, he returned to the therapist because of an acute reactive depression. This second treatment was carried on in four weeks of daily interviews, with satisfactory results.

The life history of this patient can be summarized briefly. He had been born in Central Europe, the oldest son of an upper-middle-class family. He adored his father—a self-made man, highly successful in business, conscientious and ambitious. His mother was a passive, spoiled, somewhat childish woman who dominated the family, not by her strength of character but by her demands and illnesses. The patient was five years old when the second child (a boy) was born. The patient thought he remembered the birth of this child and his protective attitude toward his little brother. Even as a small boy, the patient's main achievement had been in the intellectual field and his father had been very proud of him. When he was twenty years old, his father had sent him to Paris to study sociology at the Sorbonne. This experience became the turning point of his life.

In Paris he lived the active, cultured life of a financially independent student, and it was then that he experienced the great love of his life. Suddenly, however, this happy period was brutally terminated when the first World War broke out. He was interned in France as an enemy alien and, with several compatriots, had to spend four years in prison in great deprivation. When the war ended and he returned home, he found a completely changed world. The girl he had loved was married;

his father had died; his family was almost completely impoverished. He himself was no longer the strong, the idealistic young man who had lived in Paris; he had become shy and frightened; he doubted all his capacities and felt especially insecure with women. His morale might have broken completely if he had not had an almost fanatical belief that he must fulfill his father's expectations. But he did not know how. He worked in law offices on a very low salary for some years, and then he followed his younger brother to South America where, with his brother's help, he started in business.

Driven by the great desire to reestablish the family standards and to be the head of the family, he worked day and night and exceeded even his own expectations in gaining financial success. Early in his business career, he married a woman of his own nationality; they had two children. His unconscious yearning for dependence on his wife, and on his mother and brother, was overshadowed by his tremendous need to succeed. He demanded the utmost from himself and from those around him. Although he now lived in a different social and economic milieu, he followed unconsciously the culture of his early environment. His way of living, however, gave satisfaction only to his driving ambitious ego; emotionally he was compulsively inhibited and starved. His wife suffered a great deal from the tension in this marriage. About two years before the patient first came to the therapist, she broke down and was finally brought to this country for psychiatric treatment.

(1)

While visiting his wife during her treatment here in the United States, the patient was advised to undergo psychoanalytic treatment at least for a short period in order to understand his relationship to his wife better and thus be able to improve the marital adjustment. At first he was reluctant and defensive; soon, however, his genuine ambition to do well everything he attempted, to get the most out of every situation, overcame his resistance. In the treatment he abandoned himself to free associations which opened a flood of feelings he had not suspected in himself, at least not for a long time. With the intensity of a hallucination, he re-lived the emotions of his great love in Paris and realized what this love and its loss had meant to his whole emotional life.

After this experience in the therapeutic situation, there was no further need to convince him of the efficacy of psychoanalysis. He threw himself into it with avidity, searching for trends through the intricate details of the development of his personality. He was preoccupied with his thoughts and feelings day and night. His dreams were meaningful and his keen interest in them gave an emotional coloring even to those interpretations which were chiefly intellectual. He could be described as having a "drive" for self-analysis. The pressure of this drive was enhanced by the limitations of time, since his business demanded his return.

This period of therapy could be characterized as a narcissistic orgy. The patient's emotions were released and he re-lived his life with more feeling than he had in reality. The intensity of this emotional experience was comparable only to the great love of his youth; the difference was that then his feelings were shared with another. Since the transference situation was instrumental in precipitating this process, it became highly charged emotionally. The analyst represented not the mother, nor the father, but the beloved woman of the past. At the same time, she was also the observer and the teacher. The patient's emotional relationship to the analyst remained positive throughout this period.

The patient's memories of the repeated subjugation of his personal freedom to the will and mood of his mother, his brother and his wife, awakened great rebellion in him, as time went on, until he came to feel (he said) like a "serf." The negative aspects of the transference relationship, which would have turned this rebellion against the analyst, were blocked because his emotional attitude toward her was colored by his involving her in his recollection of his "great experience." Under her guidance, he therefore had to express his rebellion against the actual objects of his feelings. If the analyst had tried in any way to prohibit this expression of hostility—that is, if she had played the role of father or mother—the patient would have turned his aggression against himself, since he could not have expressed it against the analyst.

The time now came when, in both a practical and a psychological sense, it was advisable for the patient to leave the treatment and go home. The therapist had avoided the repetition of the infantile neurosis in the transference relationship simply by not forcing her authority on the patient. Had she urged him to stay, his conflicting emotions would have led him into an unwieldy transference neurosis. Instead of forcing him to continue the analysis and "fight out" his rebellion on the couch, therefore, the therapist took the chance that the new emotional freedom which he cherished so would enable him to find the satisfactions he needed without endangering his relationships to those about him.

It would be erroneous to assume that such a therapeutic attitude would be wise in every case. In this instance, the therapist felt it was safe for the patient to discontinue treatment because she knew he would be deterred from any untoward behavior, from acting out his impulses too freely, by his excellent ego, his highly developed social sense and the fact that he had been compulsively inhibited in his emotional life. (In the case of impulse-ridden personalities, the therapist would take the role of authority and try to keep all the acting out within the transference relationship.)

In spite of this, the patient's rebellion against his way of life did cause him enough trouble that six months later he returned to the therapist for a supplementary treatment. He now blamed the therapist for his rebellion and its subsequent emotional complications. The negative aspects of the transference relationship originated in the guilt feeling that he could manage his life more satisfactorily; he was angry because he felt dependent. This time the therapist interpreted the total situation to him and showed him that he found it humiliating to seek satisfaction for his dependent longings, to be "protected." The fear of this humiliation made him choose independence again, but this time for different reasons. He saw now that it had been an illusion that the analyst, whom he had identified with his early love, could produce an adequate substitute for the past. He had to find a balance between his desires and reality.

After four interviews he left, no longer anxious to continue the therapy. It was as if he had returned to an old love and found it disappointing. He could not revive any enthusiasm for the treatment; the insight gained in these interviews was more painful than gratifying. The therapeutic effect, however, was satisfactory. His rebellion was over; he settled down to a socially and economically successful career. That his relationship with his wife and children was good was confirmed by the fact that his wife was well and had no return of her neurotic symptoms.

This earlier analytic procedure and its brief extension have been described as an introduction to the psychotherapy which the patient experienced five years later.

(2)

When the patient now returned to the analyst, it was because of an acute depression accompanied by fatigue and decline of potency. In this depression he had not been able to free himself from the feeling that his life had been an endless series of irrevocable mistakes. He felt unable to face a future in which he saw nothing but the weakness of old age and death. He had recently become very restless, especially when alone in a room, and was sometimes surprised and disturbed by an urge to end his life.

His arrangements to come to Chicago were delayed for business reasons. It was during this period that an event which seemed peculiarly significant to him occurred. While sipping his coffee and reading his newspaper one morning, he discovered that he had won the state lottery. This was a great shock and seemed to demonstrate to him the planlessness of fate—he had bought the lottery ticket by chance from a street vendor while he was waiting for a traffic light to change. Such good fortune fifteen years before would have filled him with elation and he would probably have taken it as a sign that he had been chosen for success, since the money at that time would have changed the course of his life. Now, however, when his sense of security was already undermined by his depressed state, this incident appeared to him as proof of the stupidity of any effort and it filled him with fear.

The character of the relationship between doctor and patient was this time greatly changed from that of either of their previous contacts. The patient's need for help was much greater; the glamor and gratification of sudden insight that he knew in the first therapy was gone; in spite of himself, the therapeutic sessions were characterized by his depressed mood which he described as a decrease of vitality.

The patient complained that fear, disgust, and self-criticism were the dominant emotions of his life. He gave a great deal of thought to whether he should withdraw from business entirely and live the leisurely life of an elderly gentleman. He was aware that this would not be a solution for his present condition, since withdrawal from business would mean the acceptance of old age. And he knew not only that he was not as old as he felt, but that he wanted to be even younger than he actually was.

The patient's first dream after therapy began was a combination of depression and thoughts of homosexuality. He not only hoped for help from the analyst but despaired of receiving it. This hopelessness had occurred at other times in his life, notably when he was a prisoner of war, and the homosexual atmosphere prevailing in the prison was indicated in the dream. The patient felt that his present sexual troubles were due to his observation in the prison of homosexual practices (from which he had refrained rigidly) and to the long period of sexual frustration at that time. The patient was now preoccupied with sexual fantasies. While he feared that he was becoming old and that his sexual life would soon be over, he fantasied all sorts of escapades and adventures to prove to himself that he was still attractive to women.

Another dream showed his dependence on his wife, who represented his mother, and the frustration of his dependent needs because of their own dependence on him. He wanted to withdraw from it all, which would not only bring him relief but would also serve as an expression of his hostility toward his family, a way of punishing them. Although the patient dwelt on this problem of hostility and punishment, he gained no relief. Finally the therapist saw that his present depression could not be explained on this basis. He had had these feelings before going into the depression and, furthermore, he was now conscious of them. Since it was improbable, therefore, that they could throw him into such anxiety and depression, it seemed likely that the hostility as a conscious emotion was being used to cover up other feelings responsible for his present condition.

As if groping for new topics of discussion, the patient began to talk about his children. He spoke of his older daughter, now fourteen years of age. He described in great detail her attitude toward him, the obvious adoration of a shy adolescent toward her father. He recounted several little incidents showing how the girl, in the absence of the mother, tried to do pleasant things for him which were usually done by his wife. The patient talked about this with resistance and embarrassment. The cause could be seen in the attitude of the patient toward his daughter; he did not accept her ministrations graciously but was defensive and irritable toward her. The patient gained insight into this conflict with his daughter through a dream in which the girl was represented as a stone statue in his garden. The patient's own interpretation was that he wished his daughter were a stone statue (a woman without genitals) so that he would not be threatened by his impulses toward her.

The realization of his repressed sexual impulses toward his daughter now became the center of the treatment.

In a dream the patient returned as a traveler to the city of his birth and found the home of a friend of his mother, the woman who had represented the ideal mother to him during his childhood and adolescence. He entered the house, but it was early morning and everybody was asleep; he lay down on a couch in the living room and felt as if he were a young boy again. When the woman's husband walked through the room on his way to his wife's bedroom, the patient lay there feeling like a spy and not daring to move. Then the daughter of the house came into the room; in the dream she was still a child (actually she was only five years younger than the patient) and he felt like an adolescent boy. The girl began to chat with him, then took him by the hand and led him to another room. The patient repeated, "And she led me." This dream explains in the language of the past the problems of the present. The patient felt as if his own daughter seduced him to sexual thoughts and impulses as the other little girl had 35 years ago. But at that time he himself had been a child and knew no more of sexuality than a tense curiosity about the sexual life of his parents.

In this dream, as in the previous ones and in his conscious discussion, the patient drew a parallel between his repressed impulses toward his daughter and the impulses he used to have spying on his parents. His defensive attitude toward his daughter was a defense against "double incest," as he termed this conflict when he became aware that in his relationship to his daughter he was re-living his oedipal conflict "in reverse." Working through this conflict he analyzed in detail his fear of women, especially of the female genitals. The dream just mentioned and several others had expressed the desire to be adolescent again in order to start life anew. His repetition of adolescent emotional feelings (which come in the climacteric to both male and female) was motivated by the patient's emotional insecurity caused by his realization of decreasing sexual power.

This fear of impotence and old age made him repeat the earlier conflict. Instead of understanding his adolescent daughter's emotional needs, the patient had responded to them with the old adolescent impulses. While suppressing these impulses, he suppressed all or a great part of his normal sexuality, thus creating an emotional panic not unlike the panic of the adolescent.

The patient's fatigue and depression disappeared almost immediately after he realized the significance of this emotional attitude toward his daughter. The cause of the other symptoms—his sexual restlessness and desire for promiscuity—now became clear to him. In his fantasies he looked for a depreciated sexual object as a reaction to the repression of his impulses toward his daughter who represented the untouchable woman, just as his mother and his little friend had represented her when he was a child. Thus the "double incest" forced him to repress his sexuality and become old. However, because he was afraid of being old, he had a neurotically increased desire. (The structure of the symptomatology of this climacteric depression is the same as in the female climacteric.)

The analysis of these problems was often interrupted by the patient's resorting to discussion of the insecurity of his business on account of the war. Whenever the sexual problems became too painful to face, he used this source of insecurity as a defense. In fantasy, he tried to find ways of retiring from business with the rationalization that retiring now would save him from later trouble. He knew that such a step would be no solution for his problem, because he would feel old and humiliated if he gave up the activity which brought him so much gratification.

When the patient left treatment, he had decided to remain in business. His feeling was that in the future, as in the past, he must create his environment according to his needs and wishes. He was reassured that the conflict with his daughter, which he now understood, need not disturb him.

Comments on Case G

The most important therapeutic factor in the resolution of this acute reactive depression was the intensity of the emotional charge in his acute conflict—the suppressed sexual impulses toward his daughter. These impulses brought the patient's whole psychosexual development close to the surface and therefore accessible to insight and abreaction. While usually it takes a long time to reach the unconscious motives of psychosexual development, the pressure of the actual conflict was instrumental in making four weeks a productive period of therapy.

The transference neurosis played no role in this last period of treatment. The patient came with confidence to the therapist, and with eagerness to be helped. The actual conflict, the sexual feelings for his daughter, was not transferred to the analyst; the emotional charge of this conflict, however, acted as a motor in reactivating the early conflicts of the patient. These were interpreted directly, so that the patient gained insight into their influence on his present life without having to repeat them in the transference relationship with the analyst.

———

Comparing Cases F and G, we cannot help asking what personality factors of these two patients were responsible for the course taken by the therapy. What similarities enabled the therapist to keep a clear course to the therapeutic goal without the complications of a transference neurosis? Both of these patients were hard-driven men with strongly developed egos, used to mastering situations; both needed the feeling of adequacy in handling their emotional problems. The therapist did not interfere with this narcissistic need. However, this alone would not have been enough. The strong ego and the capacity for insight, in each case, made it possible for the patient to respond to the slightest hint of the therapist with a flow of material. This "talent for insight" was what enabled the patients and the therapist to hold the transference repetition to a minimum, to avoid the development of a transference neurosis. Relying on this capacity, the therapist was able to select from the total content of the therapeutic situation that which furthered the insight most directly, thus bringing the therapy to an early conclusion.

———

The third case to be presented is an example of a therapeutic process in which the emotional pattern of the patient was worked through by means of a transference neurosis which was carefully guided and controlled so that no regression was allowed in the transference relationship.

Case H

(Premenstrual Depression)

The patient, a 32-year-old married woman, sought help because of severe premenstrual depression. The symptom had developed about three years before; she would fall into tense, depressive moods which began about a week before the onset of the menstrual flow; then her hostility would "boil over" and she would remain in a continual temper tantrum until the second or third day of the period when her mood would return to normal. This depressed, hostile mood had recently become more generalized so that, although she felt somewhat less desperate, it lasted longer, starting in the middle of the cycle and continuing through the menstrual period. In addition, she had recently developed severe dysmenorrhea.

The treatment of about ten months comprised 67 interviews which were held at regular intervals—twice a week for the first eight months and at less frequent intervals during the last two months as treatment was tapered off. The regularity of interviews was essential because this case was one of an endocrine research in which the sexual cycles of the patient were tabulated.

The patient's early life had been greatly influenced by the fact that her parents had never lived happily together. Their essential incompatibility had been aggravated by their disappointment in their first child, a son, who became delinquent as an adolescent and was for many years the black sheep of the family. The patient, the only other child and three years younger than her brother, was a good child and the favorite of the larger family as well as of the parents. She reported to the therapist, a woman, "I've been told I was so contented as a little baby, and I have wanted to be contented throughout my life."

However, her contentment was short-lived. In spite of all the love and attention which she must have received as a little child, in preadolescence she became a demanding, rebellious girl and very tomboyish in her attitudes. She got along badly with her mother, an erratic, demanding person who resented the fact that she had given up her profession for marriage. The mother had concentrated all her attention on her daughter and rejected her son from the very beginning. The patient suffered from an early age from the hostility of this rejected brother; they were always in competition for parental attention and for scholastic achievement. Although she envied all boys their "masculinity," she constantly tried to prove that she was the superior person in every respect.

At seventeen, the patient eloped with a student and at eighteen gave birth to her daughter, Dorothy. The patient was aware that she rejected this pregnancy which was early and unplanned, and that she had very little motherly feeling for her child, whom she turned over to her own mother's care while she and her husband continued their education. She divorced her husband when the child was two years old and married again five years later. She had been married to the second husband for seven years when she came for treatment.

The second husband was compulsive and sexually inhibited, and she had become so frustrated that she felt it impossible to continue the marriage. Although he had a good relationship with his stepdaughter, he did not want children of his own. Thus the patient was frustrated in both aspects of her sexual life—her need for gratification and her desire to have children. She took pride in her pretty, talented daughter and sided with her whenever her husband tried to discipline her. At the same time, the patient became very jealous when the daughter turned to the stepfather. It was obvious that she identified herself partly with her daughter and was often more the adolescent rival to her daughter than a real mother to her.

On the surface it might seem that the patient's premenstrual depression and severe dysmenorrhea were direct consequences of her sexual starvation and of her consequent resentment toward her husband. Since the marriage seemed incompatible for many reasons, the immediate question was why this young and attractive woman did not divorce her husband and give herself a chance for better sexual and emotional adjustment. She was unable to do this because of her fear that she might repeat in another marriage the mistakes which were motivated by her basic emotional pattern. Her neurotic personality drove her into this impasse which expressed itself in her recurring agitated depression.

While the patient was convinced that she "loved men," she always surrounded herself with those toward whom she felt superior. This attitude toward men was in part a result of her hostility toward her brother whom she had always tried to humiliate. It was determined further by her identification with her neurotic mother; she did to men what her mother had done to her brother. It was probably fortunate that the patient's child was not a boy.

The patient thought she "hated women" and constantly expected them to return her hostility. Because she felt that her mother had suffered from her antagonism, she feared her daughter would become hostile to her. There were reasons to assume that the patient's mother really had been afraid of her daughter's hostility. She developed a severe nervous asthma after the patient eloped with her first husband, an illness which became chronic and finally led to her death. The patient was afraid of repeating her mother's fate and lived with the image of her mother constantly before her, tormenting herself in self-sacrificing masochistic love.

The patient's two outstanding problems, hostility toward her brother and hostility toward her mother, interrelated as they were in her development, presented the axis around which her emotional pattern was formed.

The aim of this presentation, however, is a discussion not of the patient's symptom-complex but of the psychotherapeutic procedure. Since it is never possible to reproduce any therapy in all its details, and since our intention is to follow the therapy chiefly in its transference aspects, we shall endeavor to show only how these two main problems were reflected and handled in the transference relationship.

The patient responded very strongly to the therapist's research interest in her case; she felt she was important to the therapist, a sort of exceptional patient. This was a manifestation of her old need to be the "exceptionally loved child." The transference relationship was motivated not only by her infantile dependent need but also by her great admiration for the therapist. The patient saw in the therapist the successful professional woman who could also be a wife and a mother, a realization of all those ambitions in which she felt frustrated. The therapist became both the good mother and the ego ideal of the patient—ways in which her own mother had failed.

Such a transference relationship carried with it the possibilities of a severe transference neurosis. Since all the emotional relationships of this patient were ambivalent, the transference relationship was sure to develop negative aspects also. Her hostility toward her mother was a potent warning. The therapist therefore chose to use only the positive feelings of the patient as the motive for the therapy. Since the patient was not made self-conscious about her childishly dependent feelings on the therapist, she could therefore relax in her confidence in the therapist.

The first result of this relaxed attitude was that she could face and realize her hostility toward her brother. Until this time the patient had no insight into the real nature of her relationship to her brother. She assumed that he was the bad boy and she the victim of his delinquent behavior. She had no idea what she did to him passively, because of her exceptional position in the family, and actively, by her hostile competition with him. The repetition of her infantile confidence in being loved and accepted made it possible for her to realize her destructive hostility toward her brother.

Her first dream during treatment was that she and her brother were wiping dishes. He got mad at her and started chasing her around and around the apartment. Finally he caught up with her and kicked her. She turned around and kicked him in the testicles. She was very distressed and felt she had done something very wrong. When she woke up she was still upset. This dream prompted the patient to say, "My hatred of him is the most fundamental of all the hatred I have in me." The patient was deeply stirred by the recognition of this fact and became depressed.

The chief aim of the therapy at this phase was to analyze her hostility toward the brother and make her realize how this affected her life in the past and in the present. In the following session the patient reported how badly she had felt after the previous visit. While going home she had thought, "I am like my mother. I have a martyr-like attitude. I used to tell my mother I never wanted to be like her; now I know that I am like her." She wept profusely. She wept from guilt toward her brother and from anger toward her mother with whom she identified herself in the hostility toward the brother.

Further analytic material gave confirmation of this identification with her mother and her realization of what it meant. She hated her brother as the mother had hated him; actually she had been "serving" her mother by becoming aggressive toward the brother. But the mother's hatred for the brother had made it impossible for the patient to have confidence in her mother. In spite of her mother's indulgence and adoration, the patient had never been able to believe wholeheartedly that her mother loved her. Her demanding attitude toward her mother had been motivated by this insecurity. By her demands, she had tried to reassure herself of her mother's love and at the same time have revenge on her mother. (This was brought out clearly in the transference relationship.) Her hatred for her mother had originated in this basic insecurity and in the conviction that her mother was responsible for her aggression and guilt in respect to her brother.

She came to realize that she had chosen her husband on the basis of her unconscious need to identify men with the depreciated brother. As a consequence of this insight, she slowly became aware of her own responsibility in her present sexual frustration—it was the result not just of her husband's neurosis but also of hers. The honesty of this insight made her feel she could not therefore be the lovable child, the "exceptionally deserving patient" of the therapist. She was afraid that the analyst would condemn her as she condemned herself. "I would like to hate you because you brought me to this," she said expressing a regret about the lost satisfaction in the therapeutic relationship.

Although the transference neurosis was now obvious, it had not yet showed its negative aspects. Her insecurity reactivated the childhood situation, however, and she began to make demands on the analyst. She was quite conscientious in speaking of the intensity of her old demands and how jealous she used to be of Dorothy for her own mother's love and care. She had wanted not only attention but material things; she had wanted to be the only one to whom her mother gave anything. Although it was easy for her to see that she repeated these original demands on the mother in her relationship to her husband (through her jealousy of Dorothy) and in the transference relationship, she continued to make regressive demands. During this period she said, "I want to see my mother and have her comfort me. I envy people who have mothers. I don't have anybody."

When such demands become repetitious, they usually indicate the necessity for reassurance to the patient that she is still loved and at the same time they constitute a warning that the patient's hostility is growing. Underneath this insatiable need to be loved the patient was saying to the analyst, "You are unable to give me what I need. You cannot do even as much as my mother. How can I achieve anything in this relationship? And why should I?" This hostile demanding attitude is the core of the negative side of the transference neurosis.

The therapeutic process thus far is clear. First the patient's hostility toward the brother was unfolded, then the hostility toward men in general, and finally the hostility toward the mother and her identification with the mother. In this phase, the material was dominated by a sort of homosexual panic.

Unconsciously the patient wanted to be loved by a woman, consciously she was afraid of being loved by a woman. This resulted in a flight into masculinity, a flight from everything womanhood represented to her at that time—childish dependence on the mother, responsibilities as a mother. The therapist's task in such a situation is to direct the analytic material. In this case, the underlying masculine identification was interpreted as a defense against the responsibility of becoming a real mother. The following dream shows the patient's insight into her emotional conflict:

"I was in the kitchen at home (my childhood home) with my mother and grandmother. I was telling them about my analysis and said that my being unable to give to my daughter could be traced back to my mother's relationship with me and her relationship to my grandmother. My mother was interested and asked me for further explanation. My grandmother, however, became more and more upset. My mother was working busily in the kitchen; she had to leave to get something. She had been speaking sadly of how she had been unable to give to her children, and how she needed psychoanalytic treatment. I said quickly to her, 'And mother, you probably never would have had asthma either.' My grandmother, on the contrary, became more and more angry and attacked me angrily for having applied this theory to her. She asked for proof and I retorted angrily that my proof was that she and mother and I had not chosen to have children but instead all of them were born by accident."

This dream is obviously an intellectualized rebellion against the treatment. The patient identifies herself with both the grandmother and the mother. In this way she admits understanding her conflict, but at the same time she is rebellious against the insight and especially against the responsibilities which it implies.

The therapist's task now was to rescue the analysis from the impasse of intellectualization. She asked the patient directly, "What sort of Christmas are you preparing for Dorothy?" The patient responded with a surprised, resentful glance and for a while was speechless. The problem of being a mother was taken from the level of theory into her everyday life. But the analyst's interest in the daughter brought to the fore once more the patient's childish competition with her daughter, her fear that the daughter might take something away from her. Thus not only in the dream but in the repetition of her conflict within the analytic situation, she was forced to recognize how she avoided the maturity of motherhood and acted as a child toward the analyst as well as toward her daughter. Her response was an even greater desire to escape responsibilities, as is evidenced by her next dream:

"I was visiting in a girl friend's house when a friend of hers arrived with her baby girl. The woman with the baby was an attractive, outgoing young person. I fell in love immediately with the baby girl who was about a year and a half old. She was attracted to me too, and came to me and I took off her outdoor things. I was gentle with her and she was adorable. The mother was calmly and placidly enjoying herself while I was engrossed with the baby. I said to the mother that I imagined the baby's father was crazy about her. The mother said quickly and with much hostility that he had left them. I was aghast. I could not understand how a man could leave such a lovely baby and wife. At first I thought something must have befallen him and I asked if he had amnesia. She replied that she herself could have thought so if she hadn't seen him leave when she was looking in the mirror. I gathered from this that there had been a quarrel and I asked no further questions."

In spite of the conspicuously staged motherly behavior, the importance of this dream is the patient's identification with the husband—the father who left the child. The therapist showed the patient her desire to leave her child as she had done in the past and fantasied doing again. This interpretation, which made impossible her escape from the responsibilities of motherhood into the freedom of her fantasy, let loose her hostility toward the analyst. She was angry, and felt herself criticized and punished. "You demand more from me than my husband ever did," she said desperately. This anger might have had its roots in the past or it might have been an adequate emotional response to the feeling of being caught in the conflict, since instead of getting satisfaction for her own dependent needs she was pushed more and more into the realization of her responsibility. The therapist chose to overlook the transference meaning of her anger and handled it as an adequate response to the therapeutic situation, thus blocking the patient's escape into the past.

This provoked the patient even more than before. She could not handle her anger; she became depressed and had a severe cold which enabled her to stay away from treatment. After this interruption, the hostility toward the therapist became even more obvious. The patient realized that she had escaped into illness because she could face neither her hatred for the therapist, nor her fear of losing the therapist on account of this hatred. This was a repetition of her old pattern—she could not get along with women, she could not endure what she called their domination. Now it became clear to her that the "domination" of the therapist forced her to grow up, to give up her childish demands and to become a woman, a mother. "My grandmother forced my mother, my mother forced me halfway, and now you want to force me all the way." Her emotional response to this crucial therapeutic situation was a repetition of all her rebellion against womanhood.

The positive aspects of the transference, her desire to identify herself with the therapist, her confidence in the therapist, were called upon now to help her work through this rebellion. She had to realize that her masculine professional efficiency could not cover up her lack of maturity, that her infantile demands could not give her any gratification. This was not an easy task for her for she suffered from her hostility. "I am crystallized hatred; everything else is veneer."

During this period of hostile transference reaction, manifestations of the transference neurosis were clear—her homosexual panic, her jealous competition with her daughter, her escape into illness. However, these forms of resistance did not last unduly long. The therapist handled the transference neurosis not by verbal interpretation of the underlying hostility but by provoking this hostility into expression.

It was the 37th session of this treatment, not much past the half-way mark, when the patient felt that her hostility was mastered. She felt a sense of achievement in having recognized the intensity of her struggle against womanhood, motherhood and motherliness, and asked, "Where are we going from here?"

It is unnecessary to describe in detail the further process of the analysis in order to show how the transference neurosis was handled. In the first half of the treatment her dependent needs and competition with her daughter for the mother's love were repeated in the transference neurosis; during the latter part the central problem was competition with women (also with her daughter) for the attention of men, for sexual gratification.

This right to sexual gratification, the right to have more children in spite of her growing daughter, now dominated the material. This problem was worked through in the repetition of her oedipal conflict. It was expressed in intensive jealousy toward her daughter and was repeated in the transference relationship. She dreamed and made fantasies of being a member of the therapist's family and being loved by the therapist's husband. She was afraid of the therapist's jealousy and punishment in the same sense that she had once been afraid of punishment by her mother.

This fear seemed to her to be justified when she realized the intensity of her desire to punish her own daughter for her attachment to the stepfather. These threats of the "negative transference" would not have seemed so realistic had it not been for her actual life situation. Before treatment, the patient could blame her husband for her frustrations, but she did not have the courage to seek a divorce because she was entangled in her neurotic fear and guilt toward men. Now she had the feeling that in order to "grow up" as a woman, she must be permitted to have a normal sex life and children. However, she was afraid that the therapist would side with her husband and would take the attitude that after a successful analysis she should be able to live with her husband; that is, she expected that the therapist (like many mothers) would not permit her any real gratification but would only hold out some promise for the future when both she and her husband had been successfully analyzed.

The patient felt guilty also because she wanted to take her life into her own hands, just as she had defied her parents when she eloped with her first husband as a seventeen-year-old girl. The therapist interpreted her fear of being restrained and punished in the sense of the past *and* the present; at no time did she suggest that she would interfere with her plan for a divorce.

In spite of all this, it was a surprise to the therapist when the patient in the fifty-second interview confessed with tears that she had completed preparations for a separation from her husband. (She secured the divorce shortly after treatment was terminated.)

It is a question whether this was a sort of "acting out" of her impulses or whether it was the mature consequence of the therapy. We assume that it was both. The patient was afraid of being forced to stay in the marriage, not so much by the therapist as by her own conscience and by her daughter. The more she felt that her daughter wanted her to remain in this marriage, the greater became her jealousy of the daughter. In this way the daughter came again into the role of the prohibitive mother. Further conflict with her daughter the patient wanted to avoid by separating the daughter from her husband; she was sure that if she could live with her daughter alone, their relationship would be happy. Thus the patient acted out her need for separation and avoided the interference or postponement which she feared from the analysis. The therapist accepted the *fait accompli* with the observation that only her future would show how much real change in her personality was accomplished.

The therapy was continued in an atmosphere of confidence. Now that the actual fear of the analyst as a prohibitive power was eliminated, the source of conflict within the transference relationship was abolished. This last part of the therapy—fifteen sessions covering a period of three months—showed none of the intensity of the previous struggle. The continuation of the treatment in this case was important for the research project, but therapeutically it consisted chiefly in guiding the patient during the period of reestablishment of herself both emotionally and professionally.

Comments on Case H

Although this case has been presented chiefly to show how the transference relationship was handled, an evaluation of the therapeutic result should be made. At first it seems that the only actual change effected by the therapy was the divorce. Was this divorce a justifiable step in the patient's emotional development, or was it chiefly a repetition of the infantile personality pattern which prompted her to run away from disagreeable situations and thus gave not only herself but others the illusion that she was independent? The answer to this question cannot yet be given; it depends on the long-term emotional adjustment of the patient.

The premenstrual depression and dysmenorrhea disappeared during the first month of the analytic therapy. This result could be directly related to the relief the patient experienced from an overflow of emotions and to a sense of security which came with the beginning of the analysis. Later her premenstrual symptoms recurred as an expression of her frustration. It may be assumed that a satisfactory sexual adjustment would not only decrease the actual sense of frustration but would also improve the hormonal function and thus do away with the internal somatic causes of frustration.

The future of such a development depends on the patient's chances of finding an adequate husband and on her capacity to adjust herself to him. The therapy freed the patient to make another trial. Any further result can be proved only by a long-time characterological adjustment of the patient. The insight gained during the treatment may be sufficient to enable her to change her behavior toward men and to live more comfortably with her daughter. If the patient's attitude toward her adolescent daughter becomes such that she does not disturb her daughter through jealousy, if she is able to give her daughter support and security in her relationship to boys without pushing her into promiscuity, the therapist will feel satisfied with the results of the therapy.

Discussion

Therapeutic situations in which the complete dynamism of the transference neurosis develops and has to be worked through in all its ambivalent aspects are like the classical analysis, whether the treatment is carried on in daily or weekly interviews. One difference between the standard psychoanalysis and the shortened, more flexible procedure lies in the type of transference relationship which develops during the treatment. The manipulation of the transference relationship does not depend alone on mechanical arrangements, although certain external modifications have been found useful in holding the transference relationship within desirable bounds. It depends chiefly on the deliberate plan of the therapist to use those aspects of the relationship which will best further the therapeutic purpose.

It is not always within the therapist's power to choose immediately which type of transference relationship he will have to work with, since this is determined in part by the emotional needs of the patient. It is in his power, however, to guide and control its course during treatment.

In the cases of this chapter we were fortunate enough to have a good rapport as the basis of the therapeutic relationship. A good rapport based on the patient's confidence in the therapist enables the patient to tell his life story, to make his confessions, and to tell of his relationships with other people in a way which permits him insight into the motivations of his own behavior and the behavior of others close to him. When the rapport is not good in the beginning, therapeutic results can be achieved only by a gradual working through of the negative feelings toward the therapist.

The first rapport represents, however, only a beginning of the transference relationship, although in some cases the insight gained in the early interviews may carry the therapeutic process quite far, as all three of these cases show. When the positive aspects of the transference relationship take on an erotic or highly dependent character, the situation may become unmanageable since the patient's main goal will be to hold on to the relationship to the therapist, and a transference neurosis will develop, as illustrated by the third case. The first and second cases show that if the conflict for which the patient seeks therapy is acute and highly charged with emotion, his feelings can be relieved just as in a transference neurosis.

This therapist thinks it a mistake, however, to interfere with the direct abreaction of such emotion by interpreting it as if it were a transference neurosis—that is, by relating it to himself—since this can only create resistance. In this, the therapist follows strictly the rule of Freud not to interpret the positive transference, but rather to use it for a long period as a source of valuable insight and emotional abreaction. As soon as we interpret any phase of the transference relationship in the light of the past, we open up the original ambivalence toward that person whom the therapist represents and thereby reactivate the negative as well as the positive attitudes.

In Case F, the positive side of the transference relationship was used as the dynamic motor of the analysis throughout. The therapist was aided not only by immediately good rapport but also by the intensity of the patient's conflict. Although positive attitudes toward the therapist dominated the treatment in Case G, the therapy in this case was more complex. Every psychoanalytic procedure will reach a point (probably sooner if interviews are frequent, than otherwise) when the negative side of the transference relationship becomes more and more obvious and the therapist must decide just when and how it is to be handled. In some cases it may be necessary to interpret the oncoming negative transference as soon as it is perceived by the therapist. In others, the therapist may wait and deal with the hostility or anxiety only after they have become strong enough to give the patient a new emotional experience. This was the course chosen by the therapist in Case G, based on the patient's total situation—a combination of reality and the psychoanalytic situation. When this patient, who suffered from a tyrannical super-ego, became aware of the dangers which might come from acting out his repressed aggressive impulses, he realized the intensity of his hostility. Thus a new balance in his emotional life became imperative. He could accept this balance, because the restraint which would have been imposed earlier by his super-ego, now became his own free choice.

It is not always in the power of the therapist, however, to avoid or delay the negative transference or the repetition of the neurotic conflict in the transference relationship, as we see in Case H in which a transference neurosis developed. The positive side of the relationship was stronger and more erotized in this case than in either of the other two; its roots were in the patient's identification with the analyst as the ideal mother and in the gratification of being accepted (loved) by her. Since such a relationship leads necessarily to frustration, which again increases demands, the negative transference has to develop—as it did in this case. While the patient longed to be loved by the therapist and to be dependent on her, she at the same time felt cheated and deprived because of the infantile conflict with her own mother, the core of her developmental disturbance. The negative transference attitudes, however, were not interpreted verbally. The therapist avoided all such statements as, "You are resistant," or "You hate me as you used to hate your mother," or "You make demands on me as if I were your mother." She chose rather to allow the unconscious motives which determined the patient's behavior to become so intense that they constituted a conscious emotional experience, since the aim was to make the patient recognize the actuality of those motives in her past and present life.

The transference relationship is the instrument of the psychoanalytic therapist. Our study shows that our greater knowledge through experience has helped us achieve a greater skill in handling this relationship of patient to therapist within the analytic situation. For data on which to base our use of this relationship, we survey the total emotional constellation of the patient in the therapeutic situation and in the environment. We do not expect that every phase of the patient's personality will evolve in the transference situation step by step. We select, therefore, from the problems of the patient those which are most intimately related to his complaints and to his actual disturbance, and we concentrate our therapeutic concern on them. Since the motivations of each one of these problems are manifold, we choose those to work with which will be most effective in giving the patient a new emotional balance and in enabling him to find new and better solutions for his problems.

Our ability to select pertinent material will become sharpened with greater experience. In this respect, we are working out not a new psychotherapy but, we hope, a shortened and more flexible method, specific to the emotional constellation presented by the individual patient.

Therese Benedek, M.D.

Chapter 12

ANALYSIS OF CHARACTER DISTURBANCE

Following the principle of adapting psychodynamic therapy to the structure of the individual case, we find that we can, in a relatively brief period, produce therapeutic changes previously considered possible only when the time-consuming technique of standard psychoanalysis was used. The two cases in this chapter demonstrate that a real change of character can be accomplished in a treatment, comparable to the standard analytic technique but one in which the patient is seen *only at weekly intervals,* the total number of interviews being relatively few.

It is not claimed that this abbreviated form of psychoanalysis is possible in all cases. Certain patients need prolonged treatment with frequent interviews. But, as this book shows, there are many instances in which more intensive but less frequent interviews—or even a less intensive treatment—than would have been prescribed in the past, will produce the desired therapeutic changes in an equally dependable but accelerated fashion. It is important, therefore, to determine whether the psychological factors involved in the case favor this more flexible approach. It is on this element, then, that we shall lay our stress in the cases which follow.

The social significance of this therapeutic approach cannot be overrated. It is obvious that this more flexible approach in psychoanalytic therapy allows us to treat many persons who, for lack of time or money, could not take advantage of the standard psychoanalysis. Psychotherapeutic techniques must not, however, fall prey to opportunistic expedience which would base shortness of treatment on the time and money available. In the long run, only that psychotherapy which is based on sound psychodynamic principles can produce those changes in a patient which will again make his life valuable to himself and to others. This may require a long time or a short, but any shortening of treatment must be based on the results of expert investigation and practice and not merely on the convenience of either patient or doctor.

The cases which follow show that certain types of cases can be treated by this method without loss of understanding of the dynamic structure and with therapeutic results comparable to those achieved in an orthodox psychoanalysis. Both cases are of young women with depressive, inhibited characters and a deep sense of inferiority. Although the basic conflict in each instance is a character disturbance, there are several points of contrast. The most striking is in their cultural background: one is the daughter of intellectual, thoroughly American parents, and the other is an immigrant, the daughter of a Polish peasant. In one the therapist is a man, in the other a woman. In the first (Case I) there is an elaborate overlay of the central problem, which explains in part the difference in time required to obtain therapeutic results—42 interviews, in contrast to the 15 interviews necessary for Case J. In both cases, a real character change was achieved by the treatment.

Case I

(Depressive Type)

This case was taken for modified psychoanalysis because the patient, a thirty-year-old woman, was in an acute depression over her pregnancy (then in the seventh month) and needed immediate, direct help before the baby was born. Moreover, she at that time expected to move to another city within a few months so that the standard psychoanalytic procedure seemed impractical. She remained for a little over a year, however, and had a total of 42 interviews. Although it had been decided to have weekly interviews until the birth of the child and then to start a more intensive treatment, the patient did so well with weekly interviews that this change was never made.

The patient had a seven-year-old daughter and had thought she wanted another child, but this pregnancy had been neither planned nor desired, and caused her great distress. She complained of confusion and said that all her life she had suffered from repeated neurotic depressions. She had always felt she should have had a career, not a family. Pregnancy made her feel inferior and dirty. She felt that she was inadequate as a mother and should become adequate and secure before she had more children.

The treatment in this case consisted largely of analysis of certain traumatic episodes and their effect on the patient's present behavior and feelings. Dreams, fantasies, and memories of childhood were used much as in the standard procedure. Unlike the standard analysis, this therapy evoked little spontaneous material involving the therapist (a woman), who made no attempt to produce more. The patient struggled directly with her present conflicts and cooperated well with the therapist, not only in trying to see how they originated in her childhood but also in making a deliberate effort to undo the effect of these early patterns in her present life. The most common reaction to the therapist was the expressed fear that she would consider the case hopeless; this was always interpreted in relation to the total material. This therapy also, therefore, involved a great amount of direct reassurance (unlike the standard psychoanalysis), with an effort at the end of every interview to make the patient feel her problem was soluble. Only a part of the voluminous material disclosed will be presented here.

The patient had been the second of seven children—four boys and three girls. The father, a professor of philosophy, had moved from one small denominational college to another, earning very little so that the family was constantly living very close to actual poverty. Many times the mother took courses at the college or taught school, and so was often away from home during the day. The patient recalled that she had begun to act as mother to the younger children at a very early age. The children had been brought up very strictly and religiously, and were taught that they were superior to their schoolmates. The patient was allowed little freedom of activity and was subjected to constant prohibitions and threats of punishment. Her earliest memory of her father was of his shaking a finger at her as he tried to teach her something, and of how she became anxious and could not understand him. Her mother was intellectually ambitious for her children as well as for herself, and the patient felt that her mother had always wanted her to have a career rather than to marry. The next younger sister had been the father's favorite, and the patient had repeatedly shoved her into first place by calling attention to her superiority. Instead of going to college when she finished high school, the patient had stayed at home to care for the younger children; then when this sister was ready to go to college, the patient went out and worked for two years to help finance her. Only when the sister protested vehemently did the patient turn her efforts toward putting herself through college.

All these facts were recounted by the patient in the first consultation.

Taking her cue from the patient's attitude toward her pregnancy and from the historical data given, the analyst decided not to wait for further significant material and told the patient at once that quite probably she felt guilty at being pregnant because as a child she had thought it wrong for her mother to be pregnant. The therapist explained that children usually object to the mother's pregnancy on two grounds: the fear of being thrown out of the infantile position by a rival (the new baby) and the feeling that the mother has done something wrong in getting herself pregnant. The patient said that her mother had always been reserved with her children and had never voluntarily told her anything about sex. In fact, all matters pertaining to the body were taboo. Even at sixteen, the patient could not believe that a certain nice woman teacher ever went to the bathroom. She refused to believe how babies were born when a friend told her, and was disgusted with her mother for confirming it. She would not admit, even to herself, that the sexual act could occur.

In the second interview, the patient insisted that she had never known when her mother was pregnant. In spite of the fact that there were five younger children, the patient seemed to have repressed all memory of the pregnancies. However, she remembered vividly the actual birth (when she was seven) of a younger sister. She recalled that her mother had told her father to call the doctor and that he answered, "You've had false alarms before." The patient did not know what was wrong with her mother. The doctor and a nurse came, however, and went into the mother's room, closing the door. Meanwhile, a friend of her father's had dropped in and the two men were deep in philosophical discussion when moans began to come from the mother's room. She heard the visitor ask what was wrong and her father reply, "It's all right, she is just having a baby." The patient said that after the baby was born she went into her mother's room and hit the doctor with her fists because she thought he had been hurting her mother.

Another event recalled in this same interview occurred shortly after this child was born. On a Sunday morning she had run over to a fire station near her home and played with the firemen who gave her candy. When her father asked her later what she had been doing, she lied, thinking he would disapprove of such frivolity on Sunday. He found out, however, and beat her both for the lie and for the deed. He warned her against taking candy from men and went so far as to talk about red-light districts. The patient was confused and did not understand what he meant. The analyst pointed out that becoming pregnant was related in the patient's mind with forbidden association with men and subsequent punishment.

During the following six interviews before her delivery, the patient's guilt and anxiety over her pregnancy were discussed. The guilt had two main sources: One was the unexpressed belief she had clung to all her life that she could never be like her mother and have children of her own. This function she could not allow to herself although she granted it to her younger sister, to whom she had always voluntarily taken second place—first by mothering and teaching her, and then by pretending to be stupid in front of her scholarly father. The second source of her guilt lay in her unconscious correlation of pregnancy with wrongdoing: to become a mother was to have committed some sin. Her deepest wish was indeed to have children, to be like the mother, as the unfolding unconscious material showed; but the fear of competition with her mother (and sister) and the early conviction that all sexuality was wicked, blocked her in the acceptance of her normal maternal function. It was this emotional confusion which brought her to the therapist.

In the interview immediately preceding the child's birth, the patient expressed her feeling that she must have some authoritative person help her defend herself against her wish to become a mother, by saying that she wanted a dictator to tell her what to do or not do, just as her father had when she went to the fire station. She yearned for independence, but when she tried to be independent she became frightened and saw the color yellow with red flecks in it, and became so overwhelmed with anxiety that she would retreat into passivity. She associated this color to a very early memory of seeing her father turn on the gas light when the family moved into a new house. The analyst pointed out that there might have been some relationship between the fear of the light and her father's later reproaches about red lights.

The patient gave birth to a daughter in a normal delivery. She was disappointed that she had had another daughter, since she had always felt little girls were "dirty," just as she herself was. Her parents came from another city to see her before the baby came but, when they visited her and the new baby in the hospital, she refused her father admittance because she "couldn't bear his solicitude," and saw only her mother.

A day or two after the delivery, the patient had a dream that her father was standing behind her with his hands over her mouth and that her mother was horrified at his "cruel treatment"; her father's fingers, however, were spread apart like a baby's in peekaboo. A conversation with her mother shortly before her delivery was largely responsible for this dream. In this conversation the patient had learned more about her father's peculiar behavior at the birth of the sister mentioned above. It seems he had not really been indifferent to his wife's suffering but had been very anxious to be with her; being a rigid person, however, and bound by the straitlaced conventions of his religion, he had been completely unable to explain this to his friend, excuse himself, and go to her.

In recounting the dream to the analyst later, the patient confessed that she had thought her mother was suffering from some misdeed that had angered her father. She now recalled that her father had taken the patient on his lap to comfort her, an act which had meant to her that she was "good" while her mother was "bad." The patient had always been told that any physical suffering was the result of badness; a stomach-ache meant she had eaten too much or the wrong food, a sore throat that she had gone without her rubbers. Her mother's suffering must also be the result of some sin.

Now that she knew her father had not been hostile to her mother in labor and realized that he was interested in and sympathetic with her own pregnancy, the patient felt guilty that she had denied what she knew to be true and dreamed, "Father will not let me do what I wish—deliver my baby." The father's open fingers, however, showed she realized that he was really permissive and was solicitous of her welfare.

Her depreciation of herself as a woman and a mother came out clearly in further unconscious material during the second interview after the baby's birth. The patient was then able to discuss her guilt at having orgasm, at menstruation, and at childbirth—all of which meant to her that she was dirty and debased. Everything associated with sex was regarded as degrading. She recalled an early incident in which her father had been very angry with her mother. Because the mother was then wearing a pretty new dress, the patient had thought he was accusing her mother of doing something wrong in trying to be attractive.

After her guilt over childbirth and her sexual life was somewhat relieved, there remained two chief problems. One was guilt because of her competitive feelings, especially toward her next younger sister. She frequently came to an interview in this period, saying that the analyst must think her a "hopeless case." She would then recount some social success she had recently experienced. For instance, a new member of her club had told her he thought her "quite a person" and met her modest, "No, I'm only the wife of a successful man," with "I think you very successful in your own right." In reaction to this compliment, she made a desperate effort to get a friend (who reminded her of her sister) elected to a position of prominence in the club. Her competitive attitudes toward her sister were mainly in the intellectual realm; she wished to impress men, to hold their interest, with her good mind, as she had longed yet feared to hold first place with her father because of her mental ability. Her early hostile competitiveness with her sister made her incapable of trying to have anything in her own right. Whatever she longed for she had to forego. This intense suppressed and overcompensated rivalry made her fear that even the analyst would be jealous of her success and would, in revenge, call her a "hopeless case."

The other problem was her need to sacrifice herself for others. She felt, for instance, that she should give up her own music and devote her time to training her older daughter to be a concert pianist. Dreams showed that she conceived of her relationship to her husband like that she had had with her father—merely as something to benefit another person. Whereas in her childhood this other person had been her sister, now her daughters must benefit. She did not expect to get anything from her husband for herself. Because of these feelings she was very angry with him and felt rejected by him.

Two dreams bring out clearly this attitude toward her husband, this need for martyrdom. "A man gave me two eggs. I was delighted and took them home to cook for supper. However, two guests came in and I had to give them the eggs, so I didn't have anything to eat myself." And the second dream, during a period of considerable sexual tension: "I was out on the street in my nightgown, without shoes on. I burst into a shoe store and asked the man for a pair of shoes for my baby."

Other dreams showed her conflict in regard to success. One is significant because it was repeated later on with an interesting change. "I was climbing a mountain of ice which was very slippery, trying to get to the top. As I rounded a curve I saw my mother and grandmother standing on top and I felt very guilty toward them that I had not succeeded in making it." The dream referred to her mother's ambitions for her. She felt guilt toward her mother because she had married and had children instead of being frigid and having a career.

It became increasingly clear that the patient was afraid to succeed socially and intellectually because she thought any success on her part would fascinate the husbands of her friends (sister- and mother-figures) and they would leave their wives for her. This repeats the childhood pattern: to have been more successful intellectually than her sister would have meant winning first place with her father. This was one of the most important causes for her regression to inactivity and depression uncovered in the treatment. The analyst suggested that she try to enjoy herself in social and intellectual situations, and was able to demonstrate to the patient the anachronism of her anxiety and guilt over any success for herself.

Following a summer vacation during which she and her family visited her parents, the patient returned to treatment. She reported that she had felt a great deal of hostility toward her husband and father. The anger at her father was because "he feels he understands life, but his ideals don't make sense to me." She had been unable to accept her father's and husband's affection; she had enjoyed her children, however, although she felt that she gave them little. She was sure the analyst was forming a poor opinion of her as she was talking. She had had a dream: "I was in a bank on a balcony overlooking the center of the bank, which was brightly lighted. Some people were at the cashier's window taking money out. Behind me in darkness it was like a church with stained-glass windows." The light reminded her of the gas-light scene. She thought her mother must have been pregnant at the time of this occurrence and that the dream must be related to a conflict between religion and sex.

In association to this dream the patient mentioned her father's indifference to money which had caused his family so much deprivation when she was a child. It was due to his religious discipline that he had always been reluctant to take compensation for anything he did. Further associations led the analyst to interpret putting money into a bank and getting it out as symbolic of the sexual act and the birth of a baby, both of which she felt were wrong and contrary to her religious upbringing. The patient then said she remembered hearing Stravinsky lecture on artistic creativeness as though it were a physical thing. He felt he had to dig for inspiration and when he got it he gave it to people and they loved him in return —so he got something back. The feeling that it was all right to get something back was what seemed reprehensible. The analyst said the patient was angry at her husband because he loved her for what she did, and that she felt it was wrong.

The patient continued to struggle with her feeling that it was wrong for her to do what she wished. This conflict was intensified on the one hand by the father's moralistic teaching, and on the other by the mother's disappointment that she did not pursue an intellectual career. It was further reinforced by her rivalry with her sister. Having anything for herself meant that she took from others; hence her constant need to placate others by giving. This pattern was brought out vividly in the patient's dreams, which the analyst consistently interpreted to show her how she had been limiting her life by trying to make up to her father, mother, and sisters for fantasied wrongs done to them in the past.

The following dream shows the patient's dawning realization of the restrictions she had put upon herself and her effort to grow up. "There was a ridge of snow and ice with a gap in the middle of it. I knew if I could climb up the ridge to the gap and go through it I would come to the following scene at the beach, a scene I actually saw when I was sixteen: a man struggling to put a bathing slipper on a young girl's foot, both of them red and embarrassed. When I actually saw this, I wondered how a girl could allow a young man to take such a liberty with her. In the dream I didn't know whether I'd make the grade, or whether I would slide back." She commented that this dream reminded her of the dream of the icy mountain, and recalled that on this same beach she had been kissed by a boy when she was an adolescent. Another memory was that a married man once made advances to her while she was in college.

The analyst suggested to the patient that she was afraid to be born (pass through the gap) and separate herself from her mother, because she was afraid that a father-figure (a married man) would prefer her to her mother.

The following hour was the last; the patient was now going to join her husband in a city some distance away. She came in looking very well and cheerful, and announced that she had dreamed she made a great hit with her brother-in-law by being very intelligent. The patient said she was tired of her destructive fantasies of breaking up the marriages of her friends and would like to turn her energies into constructive channels. She left in good spirits, and a few months later wrote the analyst to say that she had maintained her improvement, that what few depressions she had had were shorter and less intense, and that she was now able to enjoy her children and her husband much more than formerly.

Comments on Case I

This patient's neurosis was rooted in two conflicts: she was unable to accept maturity because of her dependent attitudes, and she could not allow herself to succeed in any social or intellectual enterprise because of her guilt feelings. Her maturation had been inhibited by certain early traumatic experiences which had made her believe that anything concerning sex was debasing. She felt that to her mother she had meant only deprivation and mental worry and disappointment; to make up to her for the wrongs she had done her (first in being born and then in growing up to do things her parents seemed to forbid) the patient felt she must cling to her mother. These infantile attitudes she had carried with her through life and had later transferred to her women friends and to her daughters. As a result, she came to feel that anything in the nature of personal pleasure or success was wrong—an attitude which was reinforced by her rivalry with the sister who had first place with the father. Her hostility was suppressed under the guise of conformity and good deeds, but it asserted itself in her depressive symptoms. The impending birth of a second child exacerbated her depression to such a degree that she sought help.

But for certain practical considerations, this case might have been taken for psychoanalysis. Indeed, much of the treatment was handled in the standard manner. Why, then, was this patient able to work through the type of material which usually occurs only in psychoanalysis proper, although she saw the therapist only once a week? Since good therapeutic results came with briefer treatment, the reasons for this therapeutic achievement must be examined.

This patient came in great distress and eagerness for help. She put her confidence in the therapist at once. She was both intelligent and intuitive; she produced unconscious material readily and she had both a flair for understanding interpretation and ability to use the insight gained. She was so grateful for help and (especially at the beginning of the treatment) so pressed by the exigency of her condition, that she worked through much of the material during the intervals, using each session as a lesson from which she took information to be assimilated and insight as a key to further understanding. She showed little resistance in the usual analytic fashion; the interval of a week seemed rather to help than to hinder her progress. In the best sense of the expression, she did her "homework" well.

That this patient did not develop a full-fledged transference neurosis may perhaps be explained, in part, by the fact that when she came to treatment she was on the eve of childbirth and was consequently concerned with practical matters of the immediate future; the infrequency of interview was partly responsible, and also the therapist's constant application of the patient's newly gained insight to new experience. Another factor that expedited treatment was the therapist's immediate recognition of the fact that, although this patient had what she most longed for—a husband and children—she lacked the permission (and therefore the freedom) to enjoy them. This she sought and found in the therapist and the stage was set, so to speak, for an expanded personality.

The patient's ego was good; in spite of her conflicts, she had married and had children. Thus the prognosis was far better than if the conflict had been severe enough to withhold her from marriage. Her life situation was actually what she unconsciously wanted, although it was very different from her conscious ambitions for a career and childlessness. She was abnormal only in her holding on to the childhood ambitions set up by her parents. This woman had a good capacity for warm human relationships; she was very much in love with her husband even though she was full of conscious hostility toward him. There was evidence that her husband was an adequate partner. She was consciously repudiating what she unconsciously desired.

Under these circumstances it was relatively easy to break down her neurotic pattern. The chief task of the analyst was to make the patient feel that her attitudes were out of date and that she was holding onto old patterns because she had never been able to free herself from the parental authority of her childhood. Acting as a new and permissive authority, the analyst helped her learn to trust the validity of her own wishes, to break away from the dictates of a conscience taken over from the parents, and to live her life as a mature person. In order to effect this character change, however, it was necessary first to activate her suppressed hostility and her guilt toward her parents and her sister, then to give her guidance and support in changing her attitudes, and finally to encourage her attempts at independent, mature behavior.

That the depression lifted is evidence that the guilt had, for the most part, been resolved. That she could enjoy her husband and children, and could engage in social activities with freedom and pleasure, would indicate that she had rid herself of adherence to anachronistic authority. As in all therapy, this constitutes the first step toward a greater freedom of the personality.

Only a follow-up much later on can determine the full results of the treatment. Perhaps the best proof of the therapeutic accomplishment in this case will be found in the patient's attitude toward her own daughters as they come into maturity.

Catherine L. Bacon, M.D.

———

The second case to be discussed required only fifteen interviews at intervals of a week to achieve the therapeutic goal. Here again, the psychotherapeutic problem was not the resolution of an acute conflict, but the relief of a character disturbance caused by a rigid, restrictive super-ego which led to a depressive and inhibited personality structure. This case, moreover, demonstrates the effect of cultural, as well as family, influences on the forming of personality patterns and the importance of arriving at an early evaluation of their significance. In this case, we were interested in discovering if a real change of personality could be achieved in an intensive treatment carried on in weekly intervals.

Case J

(Inhibited Type)

The patient, an attractive young woman of twenty-seven, presented symptoms of general nervousness and deep feelings of inferiority. Throughout the initial consultation, she was continually on the verge of tears and complained bitterly of how inferior and insecure she had always felt. Obsessed by the desire to have people like her, she feared nothing more than to arouse criticism. She had no self-confidence and had become very submissive in her behavior, constantly striving to "do something to please others." All her life, the patient had been tortured by an excessive feeling of guilt for which she could find no satisfactory explanation. Treatment was successfully terminated after fifteen weekly interviews extending over four months.

A striking feature of this case was the patient's inability to express any hostility. This repression had produced some obsessive and compulsive manifestations. She was constantly fearful lest an accident occur to her mother; she was superstitiously afraid that she might do something which would cause unhappiness to her friends and had sometimes thought that she might hurt them by merely looking at them. In regard to food she was very fussy and ate only that which she had cooked herself, rationalizing that her stepfather (who usually prepared the food) was not clean enough. She was an inveterate housecleaner and thought that no one could do it as well as she.

The following history was reconstructed from direct conversations with the patient, from memories, dreams, and associations. Here again, we are forced to give only a part of the vast amount of material produced.

The patient was a factory worker, an unsophisticated girl of Polish birth, the child of humble peasants. At the age of five she had come with her parents to America where her father secured work in a steel mill. There were two other children —an older brother and a younger sister. When the patient was about eight, the father was killed in an accident; the mother took the children back to Poland and left them in the care of the grandmother and an aunt while she returned to the United States to work for a living. After four years, when the patient was twelve, the mother (who had meanwhile remarried) brought the children back to America. The patient attended school through the ninth grade and then left to work in a factory. Now, eleven years later, she still had the same job.

The patient was extremely dependent on her mother and often felt that she could not live without her. The mother, a cold and domineering woman, had never shown any affection for the girl and posed as a martyr in order to enforce her will upon her daughter. When she was a child, the patient was frequently beaten by the mother. Her mother's method of "moral punishment," however, was far more impressive: the patient was told that if she did not obey her implicitly, her mother would die and then the patient would be responsible not only for her death but for harming her brother and sister as well. When the patient was about six years old, she occasionally wet the bed; for this, her mother punished her and once slapped her face so hard that she had a black eye. The patient was so ashamed about this that she did not tell her father, who frequently defended her against the mother. After the father's sudden death, the mother remarked triumphantly that now the child would have no one to fight her battles for her.

The children had been made aware of the fact that their mother considered them an oppressive burden. She often told them she would rather have died herself, since they caused her so much worry. When the children were taken back to Poland, they were again made to feel they were a burden. The patient retained no friendly memory of her life in Poland where she had been actively abused by an aunt who showed marked partiality toward her own children. When she came back to the United States, the patient was once more informed that she was unwelcome; the mother told her that she had remarried only for the sake of the children, that otherwise the immigration authorities would not have given her a permit for them to enter. The patient's mother consistently took the attitude that she was sacrificing her own life for her ungrateful and unworthy children.

It is no wonder that the patient developed feelings of excessive guilt and inferiority. She tried to avoid pangs of conscience by doing everything the mother demanded and became extremely submissive toward her. She had no conscious resentment or hostility against the mother; she would even try to find excuses for her behavior. In the same way, she gave no indication of jealousy of her brother and sister.

In spite of the mother's antipathy for men—she was derogatory of men in general and spoke of sex with scorn and disgust—the patient showed a normal interest in boys during her adolescence. At the age of twenty-two, she was married. Unhappily, her husband was passive, inefficient, and unwilling to build up a family of his own. He was overattached to his own mother and remained dependent on her, never assuming any responsibility toward his wife. In her marriage, however, the patient could act out clandestinely some of her hostility against her own mother and, at the same time, gratify her submissive masochistic needs, since her husband disliked her mother and was extremely critical of her. The patient did not find fault with her husband and was willing to earn a living for both of them.

The patient seemed to have had no sexual disturbance in the beginning of her married life, but soon her husband showed such indifference to her sexually that she consulted a physician. The physician advised divorce but this was against her religion and the patient continued to stay with her husband. The marriage deteriorated and the patient began more and more to take on her mother's attitude that sex was dirty and something to be avoided. The marriage finally broke down when the patient, at long last pregnant and consciously very anxious to have a child, was persuaded by her husband in alliance with her mother to have an abortion. Shortly after the abortion, the patient left her husband, returned to her mother and obtained a divorce. The abortion and the divorce became the source of intense guilt which the patient tried to attribute to the fact that she had acted against her religion and therefore made people think evil of her. Following the divorce, the patient's social contacts were largely centered about her night school (she was eager to improve her education), the art and music activities of a girls' club, and such church activities as singing in a choir.

Marked improvement was seen almost at once in the actual therapeutic procedure. Only during the first interview did the patient react toward the therapist (a man) in a tearful, infantile manner. After that, she was always composed, friendly, and very serious in her attitude toward the therapy. Throughout the treatment, the patient intellectualized very little. The weekly sessions were conducted on a high level of emotional participation, the intensity of treatment consistently greater than in a standard psychoanalysis of daily interviews. The patient was stimulated by the interviews and seemed spontaneously to "work through" her emotions during the week, showing new progress with each session.

It was evident that in the first interview the patient had identified the therapist with her sadistic mother and had therefore reverted to provocative, infantile behavior; but as soon as she was able to differentiate the reality of the treatment situation from her neurotic expectations, she calmed down and expressed surprise that the psychiatrist had not scolded her. It was in the second interview that this significant shift in the transference relationship occurred. She said she was much more comfortable and "felt like waking up." Now the first cautious interpretation of her behavior was given. The therapist pointed out that her submissive behavior toward her mother was not really justified; that by not taking any responsibility she could always blame her mother when she herself failed. To this the patient responded with some insight, saying, "Apparently I have never lived my own life!"

The patient now became conscious of the cruelties she had experienced and expressed a great deal of resentment against her mother, her aunt, and her husband. But her feelings still remained highly ambivalent and during the third interview she returned to the terrible sin she had committed in having had an abortion and in divorcing her husband. A week later the patient had already become aware of an increased self-confidence; she felt more equal to other people and was less disturbed in her mother's presence. "I used to be very nervous when my mother said anything; now it doesn't bother me at all!"

The patient's progress was reflected in a number of dreams she reported during the next weeks. "I was in a forest and soldiers were shooting. I came to a little house which had a shelf around it where dogs were seated. I didn't trust them, but I didn't want them to notice it, so I fed them. I said to another girl, 'I think if I feed them I'll gain their confidence and they won't bite me.' But the girl didn't believe me. She started to pet one of the dogs and he started barking and wanted to bite her." In association, the patient remarked that she was fond of dogs and not afraid of them, although once her sister had been bitten by one. In this dream the patient is expressing her first doubts as to whether it really pays to try to appease a hostile outside world.

In the next interview, the patient reported that she dreamed she was walking with her sister under a big umbrella, and a husky man, an opera singer, took her home through the rain. The singer was more interested in her than in her sister. The patient remarked to the therapist, "I hope it isn't a bad dream." The singer reminded her of Jan Kiepura and the psychiatrist. The dream is obviously a transference dream and shows that, since the patient now feels protected by the analyst as she had once been by her father (the Polish singer), she can therefore become less dependent on her mother.

Later the patient had the first of a series of shoe dreams: She was on a train with a group of girls with whom she worked; her shoes had somehow disappeared and everyone was helping her look for them. Secretly the patient picked up an umbrella and tried to take it away with her. Finally she found her shoes and put the umbrella into her purse. In this dream the patient is trying to become independent, to get on her own feet by finding her "shoes"; at the same time she tries to obtain possession of an umbrella which, in the earlier dream, expressed her desire for dependence on a man rather than on her mother.

The second shoe dream occurred several weeks later: "I was running from a lady who wanted to take my money. I was scared and ran away. Suddenly I noticed I didn't have my shoes on, but I didn't feel as badly without shoes as I did before. I got home safely. I thought it didn't make any difference whether I had my shoes on or not." In other words, the patient felt less threatened by her mother and less dependent on her.

In her last dream of the series, two weeks later, the patient was wearing a nice pair of shoes and felt very comfortable in them. "I never had any shoes that fit me so well."

This series of dreams is a clear reflection of her increasing sense of security derived from the treatment. She had been learning how to "stand on her own feet" again. As she regained confidence in herself, her excessive need for the approval of others decreased and she became less compulsive generally. The home situation now became less difficult for everyone.

This change in the patient's attitude, however, was no mere superficial manifestation of a positive transference relationship; it was the result of the gradual building up of an identification with the therapist. In the first phase, the early weeks of the treatment, the patient had slipped back frequently into her old pattern of self-accusation and self-humiliation. Then after about two months, the mid-point of the therapy, she displayed a kind of compulsive confusion for one interview; opposing tendencies were struggling with each other and she did not know which direction to take. "Maybe I am wrong, and maybe I am right at the same time." She wanted the therapist to tell her what her condition really was and tried to discourage him by emphasizing that nobody had ever been able to help her. She complained that she was wasting everybody's time and she felt as guilty about coming to the therapist as about everything else. The analyst interrupted her, however, and simply remarked that understanding her behavior was more important than complaining. The patient immediately felt better and told him that she had actually been much better and that her relationship to her mother had improved greatly. From this time until the end of the treatment, the patient became much more free and uninhibited in her attitudes. She felt more self-confident and no longer had the need to blame herself for everything. She realized that her marriage could never have worked out and no longer felt guilty about the divorce.

The patient discontinued the treatment on her own initiative, stating that she felt able to take care of herself. In the last interview, the patient said, "My mind is real clear now. I was blank before. I suppose I always was obedient and listened to my mother. Mother's will was so forceful, and I felt guilty whenever I tried to break away. I can think and answer better now, and I feel capable of going ahead."

The patient continued to live with her mother, however. This was not only an expression of unsolved dependence on her. It was also an acting-out of aggressive feelings against her mother as if she wanted to say, "You never gave me the care I wanted; now I'm going to stay, regardless of my own interests." As a matter of fact, the living arrangements in the patient's home were anything but convenient. The mother, the stepfather, the patient's sister and her child, and the patient herself, all lived in a small basement apartment, and the mother actually wanted the patient to live somewhere else.

About nine months after the therapy was terminated, the patient was seen in a follow-up interview. She had continued to feel well and was completely at ease during the hour. Although she was still living with her mother, she had frequent dates now and had "almost found somebody to go steady with." She took a more mature attitude than she had been able to before, declaring, "Of course I'm not always happy. Before, everything had to be the way I wanted it to be or I'd become moody. Now I realize one can't have everything. I have learned to be satisfied with what I have."

This interview concluded the contact with the patient. Later attempts to see her for other follow-up interviews were not successful. It is not possible, therefore, to say whether the patient's progress continued.

Comments on Case J

To understand the success of a psychotherapy in which the results are comparable to those achieved in a standard psychoanalysis and which, indeed, closely resembled the standard procedure in the handling of the individual interviews but which consisted of only fifteen interviews at weekly intervals, over a period of only four months, we must make a psychodynamic formulation of the situation which existed in the beginning of the treatment.

It is obvious that the patient was maintaining an infantile emotional dependence on her mother, that like the first patient of this chapter she had not been able to accept maturity. Her ego functions, however, did not seem deeply disturbed. She too had always maintained a good adjustment to reality; her history showed no severe breakdown. On the contrary, she managed a fair degree of adaptation to her environment in spite of a constant impact of traumatic events in her childhood. Here again, the patient—although frightened by her mother about sex—had married.

Her super-ego, however, had formed a pathological identification with the mother. Moreover, she had introjected her mother's sadistic attitude; that is to say, her hostility toward her mother, inhibited in its expression, had been turned back upon the patient as self-accusation and defeatism. As a result, both inferiority feelings and excessive dependence on the mother developed.

Her extreme guilt feelings might be said to stem from three sources: her identification with the nagging, reproachful mother who deliberately made the patient feel unworthy; her deeply repressed hostility against the mother; and possibly a strong oedipal attachment to her father in early childhood. The last source was not uncovered during the treatment but is surmised from the history.

The type of interpretation given this patient needs some amplification. Throughout the treatment the patient was encouraged to face her underlying hostility and resentment against the mother; this was explained to her as a justifiable and understandable reaction to her experiences. At the same time, her emotional dependence on the mother and her unconscious identification with her were pointed out to her as they became clear from dreams and fantasies as well as in her actions. All the unconscious material was related to the actual situation. In this way, the patient finally came to the realization that she did not have to respond to her mother as she had been, and she was able for the first time in her life to verbalize the great resentment she really felt toward her mother and to see that she could become independent of her. This made her ready to accept maturity.

More important than this intellectual insight was the fact that the therapist helped the patient to establish a positive relationship to him as a permissive father-figure and thus revived the childhood identification with her father. Through this identification the patient could reorganize her conscience; the punitive, rigid super-ego gave place to an authority which allowed her to seek pleasure for herself. This transference relationship to the analyst supported the patient in building up a feeling of security; it decreased her need for dependence and appeasement at any price; and it made her capable of facing her hostile feelings against her mother without anxiety. As a result, the patient in time became convinced that she could safely give up her mother and be an individual in her own right. Negative transference manifestations were not important in the therapy after the first interview. The transference neurosis remained at a workable intensity throughout.

In order to understand this patient's inhibited character, it was necessary *from the first* to accord the differences in cultural patterns their proper significance. Important years of her life were spent among Polish peasants. Even in the United States the home atmosphere was more Polish than American; she lived in a lower-class Polish neighborhood, had Polish friends, and always maintained close ties to the Polish Catholic church. She was self-conscious about her foreign birth, about her lack of education, and about her "foreign" way of speaking. She felt her command of English was poor and that she spoke with a marked accent. Actually, her vocabulary and manner could have been that of any American girl of her age and class, and her speech showed no noticeably foreign influence.

Although these complaints were used as rationalizations of her sense of inferiority, her foreign background had, in fact, contributed to her feelings of insecurity and inferiority. The powerful cultural factors in this case no doubt increased the difficulties of a personality already inhibited by a punitive, rejecting environment. Without the added burden of cultural differences, these personality difficulties would have been far less severe. We have evidence for this conclusion in that the patient could indulge with little or no difficulty in those social activities she allowed herself, and was successful in building up friendships within a circumscribed area. This adjustment, limited though it was, served as an indication of the patient's good ego capacity and justified the expectation that she could profit by a short, intensive treatment.

The therapist's initial decision (based on these considerations) that the patient's illness had not led to a severe disturbance of her ego functions, was confirmed by the course of the treatment. Basically she had remained a warm personality, many of whose interpersonal relationships were not severely disturbed. Apparently the treatment came at a favorable moment, at a time when her need for self-punishment had been fairly well satisfied and she was ready to accept the revised father relationship offered her by the analyst. During the treatment she showed ability to make new adaptations and a capacity for spontaneous growth. With this type of inhibited personality, it is on this last point that therapeutic success depends—the patient's adaptability and potential development. In this case a real personality change was accomplished; a patient having a deeper character disturbance would probably not have responded so well.

Discussion

The main task of the psychotherapy in both cases of this chapter was the same: to relieve guilt feelings and to help the patient gain self-confidence and reach maturity. The results in both cases were good. Although the course of the therapy in the two cases has been recounted, it might be interesting at this point to speculate on the effect the sex of the analyst had on the therapy.

The patients have similar character problems: exaggerated dependence on authority, deeply repressed hostility, fear and guilt regarding sexual matters. Their symptoms are practically identical: depression, inhibition, deep feelings of inferiority. In both cases there was a high degree of ambivalence toward the mother; both patients feared to disappoint the mother, both had been trying to live the life they felt the mother expected of them, and both felt they had failed. In the second case, the patient had overt evidence of her mother's attitude; she had experienced repeated rejection and abuse. Both patients had introjected a stern, forbidding authority; the first had taken this from both father and mother, the second from just the mother. There was reason in the latter case to believe that the father had been a warm person to whom the patient was deeply attached.

The first patient repeated with the woman therapist her old fears in respect to her mother, fears that the therapist would think her inferior, a "hopeless case," and the therapy consisted largely in the therapist's assuming a different attitude from that of the mother whom she felt she had disappointed. The second patient apparently expected the therapist (although he was a man) to scold her. This fear she evinced at once, but when she found he was a benign person, he became not the cruel authority represented by the mother but the good father of the past, a restoration of the warmhearted person who would "fight her battles." This was favorable to a good transference relationship; she accepted the new authority at once; she strove to understand the treatment and to profit by it. At the mid-point of the treatment when she started to regress to her old compulsive pattern, a kind admonition from the therapist seems to have been enough to bring her back to her efforts to reach maturity. Perhaps she could not have done this so readily with a woman.

The first patient did not reach this state of confidence so quickly. Had the therapist in the first case been a man, the therapeutic task in part would still have been the same—to relax the rigid super-ego—since this patient's father was ambitious like the mother, and stern to the point of being punitive. It would have differed in respect to her hostility toward the mother. With a woman therapist, this patient had to grapple with this hostility within the transference neurosis, whereas the second patient had to do this in her life situation. That the latter did not accomplish this completely is evidenced by the fact that nine months after termination of treatment she was still with the mother.

Perhaps because of the difference in the sex of the therapist, we find in the first case a more highly developed transference neurosis than in the second. It was easier to hold the second patient to reality because the therapist did not, could not, represent the sadistic mother; furthermore, there had been a good father in the past. Our conclusion is that a man therapist was the best choice in the second case; that in the first a man or a woman might have been equally successful but for one outstanding reason—the patient was pregnant and therefore more in need of a mother substitute than a father.

Dreams are used in both treatments; in presenting these cases, only a few could be included. Those quoted in the first case would indicate the use of deeper unconscious material, since the dreams in the second case deal chiefly (in symbolic form) with the progress of the treatment. In our research, we have often noted that the latter type of dream is more characteristic of our "brief psychotherapy," perhaps due to the fact that the therapist is making a more constant application of unconscious material to reality than is usual in the standard psychoanalysis.

Although both of these cases could be called modified psychoanalysis, the first "follows the rules" more closely than the second—in length of time, in the free use of unconscious material, and in the development of the transference neurosis. Neither therapist permitted the patient to become deeply dependent; both relied strongly on the corrective experience of the transference relationship to bring the patient into mature attitudes and behavior. In their therapeutic work, they were abetted by a fundamentally good ego in each case, without which a real character change could hardly be expected in a relatively short treatment.

Rudolf A. Fuerst, M.D

Chapter 13

ALLEVIATION OF RIGID STANDARDS

The following cases were chosen for presentation because of certain similarities in their dynamic structure which pointed the way to similar plans for treatment, and because in each case the environment could be effectively modified to meet the patient's needs.

From the evidence gleaned in the clinical histories it was obvious that all three patients had been able, until the onset of acute illness, to adjust themselves moderately well to the life situation in which they found themselves. In spite of the handicap of inner emotional conflict, they were able to carry on their work and social life without obvious display of neurotic symptoms. In other words, each patient possessed an ego of good strength in spite of certain restrictions in activity which had been imposed by the emotional problems.

Common also to the three were a severe and restrictive super-ego and (another similarity which became evident early in treatment) strong but deeply repressed dependent wishes. The main dynamics of the pathology in each case, therefore, was an unconscious conflict between the rigid conscience and the drives which were clamoring for expression. In each case, the symptoms developed when external circumstances became too stimulating to the drives and old methods of adjustment, developed at the behest of the censorious moral standards to keep the drives in check, were threatened.

In picking out a specific emotional conflict as the basis of the symptom formation in a particular case, the therapist does not mean to imply that this simplified emotional problem is the only one integrated into the personality structure. For purposes of treatment, however, attention is focused on the main

233

problem. This is justified by the experience that elimination of the disease-producing conflict clears the way for the solution of secondary problems—just as in surgery removal of a primary point of infection such as the tonsils may cure secondary arthritis, nephritis, etc.

In planning the treatment of these three cases, similar goals were formulated. The aim in each was, first, the alleviation of symptoms through the elimination of the pathological condition causing them, and, second, the achievement of sufficient dynamic change to increase the capacity for enjoyment and self-expression and to make possible the development of methods of adjustment more adequate than those previously in use. In all three cases, the therapeutic results were good.

Case K

(Phobia)

A senior in a coeducational college, an attractive, friendly twenty-one-year-old girl, requested treatment for a severe generalized anxiety and confusion which was most troublesome when she was away from home and particularly acute in the classroom and at dances. This anxiety had recently become so extreme that the patient insisted on staying at home and refused to let her mother leave her side. Excellent results were brought by a treatment which extended over a period of two months (interviews twice a week for the first month and once a week for the second), followed by two interviews a month apart to assure the therapist that the healing process continued.

Although the patient remembered that she had always been anxious and uncomfortable in social situations, these acute manifestations had developed suddenly about six months before, during a Christmas visit to the parents of a male friend. Her distress had increased so greatly that, upon her return from the visit, she ceased going to classes and regularly refused to attend dances or other parties. She had been thrown into acute panic upon several occasions—once in a large class with a male instructor, the other times at college parties.

Other symptoms of interest were anorexia, nausea with occasional vomiting, insomnia, and amenorrhea. She had been under endocrine treatment for amenorrhea for several months, but since there had been no improvement she had voluntarily stopped treatment. She had lost eleven pounds and was very slender.

During psychotherapy (with a woman analyst) the symptom picture of this case showed progressive improvement. The patient went back to her classes within the second week, and before treatment was concluded was able to take her final examinations, graduate, and enter into the gaieties of dances, parties, and other college activities—without symptom return and with the reestablishment of regular menses.

Sufficient historical material was freely given by the patient in the first interview to furnish a background from which to reconstruct the causes of the conflict responsible for the presenting symptoms. The patient was an only child. Her mother had been widowed when the patient was two and from the time of her husband's death had devoted most of her life to her child. The mother and daughter had lived with the maternal grandparents who were also very devoted to the patient. She spoke of her grandmother as being very dependent upon her mother, and of her grandfather as a gentle, lovable man who played a very unimportant role in the planning for the family—which was of definite matriarchal organization. She remembered having always been a very obedient child, although she had been told that, when very young, she had indulged in severe temper tantrums which had ceased suddenly at about four years.

At about ten, the patient was taught masturbation by an older girl in the neighborhood and had practiced it occasionally since then, but with a severe sense of guilt. She could remember no childhood curiosity about sex, but she was unusually ignorant of such matters and had felt embarrassed when she heard other children discussing them.

Being an intellectually precocious and musically talented girl, she was pushed in school and was expected to practice her music for long hours. She had planned to be a concert musician, but two years previous to her illness she had taken an aversion to her instrument and became anxious whenever she considered returning to her music. Socially, she had always had a circle of acquaintances, but during her school years her work schedule offered little time for them. Her main recreation as she was growing up was visiting adult friends of her mother, an occasional concert, and moving pictures.

When she went to college, her mother left the grandparents' home and established an apartment for the two of them near the college. Although the patient joined a sorority, she had little social life with the other girls for fear that her mother might be lonely during her absence. When boys visited her, she always included her mother and even took her on all dates other than college dances. Consciously she considered her mother as a "pal," but she admitted that because her mother was gay and good company she had often thought the boys liked her only because of her mother. One boy, however, who had been devoted to her for over a year, insisted upon omitting the mother from their dates. He proposed marriage to the patient and was accepted. Since she considered herself engaged, she had indulged in "necking" with him before the onset of her illness. Although she enjoyed it, she had felt guilty and was sure her mother would disapprove.

Her fiancé had invited her to his home for the Christmas holidays to meet his parents. During this visit, which was the first trip on which she had ever been away from her mother, she developed the severe symptom picture described. It started with insomnia the second night of her visit, after he had given her an engagement ring. She became fearful during the night that something dreadful might happen to her mother, and the next day became so ill that she insisted upon returning home.

It was evident from this history and from the symptom content that the girl had been precipitated, by the realization of the nearness of her approaching marriage, into a conflict between her dependent wish toward her mother and the more adult sexual wish toward her fiancé; this conflict was near the surface but not yet in consciousness. Fear of injury to her mother suggested also a stirring of unconscious hostility toward her mother who had always directed and shared her life, who stood in the way of her interest in sexuality and its coincident independent life, and who might also win away her fiancé as she had taken away the father, the grandfather, and (more recently) the other boys who had been attentive to the patient.

Guilt and anxiety thus played a role in producing the symptoms, the secondary gain of which was to solve the conflict temporarily by renouncing sexuality and an independent life. When she was so ill, she need not consider marriage or independent activity—as classes, dances, companionship and so forth. At the same time, she intensified her dependence upon her mother through her illness. Her mother dared not leave the patient, even in the home, for fear symptoms would develop in her absence.

In the first interview, the patient was given insight into her hostility toward her mother, with an explanation of how it grew from her mother's restriction of her independence and self-expression—a result of her mother's ambitions for her—and from the consequent restrictions of her social life. The therapist discussed with her the fact that all children develop such hostilities toward their parents, and showed the patient how, from fear of losing love, she had formed defenses against her own childhood hostility by exaggerated obedience, shyness, and avoidance of tabooed activity. An explanation was given to her of how the conflict had been intensified into severe symptom formation during her first trip away from home, because she was really deserting her mother in choosing to be with her fiancé and yet was enjoying herself. A hint was also offered her about guilt reactions to any enjoyment because of her training to sacrifice so much for achievement in work. This guilt in turn made her even more dependent upon her mother, the childhood disciplinarian whose presence could protect her from indulging her wishes for pleasure.

These interpretations were followed with a permissive suggestion that she might try to refrain from repressing angry feelings toward her mother when critical thoughts occurred, with an explanation of the naturalness of such feelings in spite of the traditional teaching that one should love one's parents under all circumstances. It was then suggested that some mild self-indulgence such as lunch with her sorority sisters or an after-class drink in the drugstore with them if she felt the inclination might aid in her recovery, and that she go to classes or begin to study again only when she felt comfortable and wished to. But, in order to protect her from losing prohibitions too rapidly, she was urged not to indulge herself beyond her feeling of comfort.

In this first interview, the sexual component in her conflict relative to pleasurable indulgences was not touched upon. Since this element seemed to be much more deeply repressed than her conflict between her dependent and independent wishes, and since it was emotionally charged, it could be handled only after some freedom from the mother had been achieved and the dependent transference to the more permissive therapist had gained strength.

In the second interview, three days later, the patient's manner was less tense and she reported that she had begun to feel that she would recover. She had not been back to classes but had spent her days at the sorority house studying. In the afternoons, she had worried lest her mother be lonely and had returned home early for dinner. She had not seen her fiancé although he had telephoned daily.

Tears came when the patient reviewed in detail memories of deprivation as a child, when she had longed to play with other children and had been made to practice or to visit adults with her mother. Occasional excursions with her grandfather, to the circus and to the zoo in particular, were marred by her mother's criticisms of the grandfather who kept her out too long. On these trips she was happy and felt her grandfather was like Santa Claus, but her pleasure was always tempered by fear of eventual criticism. Sympathy for her deprived childhood was offered by the therapist, and again the hostile feeling of any child toward a parent in such a situation was discussed with her. In order to soften the guilt resulting from the anger which was obviously reaching consciousness, she was helped to recognize the fact that parents, meaning well, often deprive children unwisely in an attempt to do the best they can for their training. Her response expressed relief. "I feel better to think that mother wasn't really mean, and maybe wanted me to have the best of things."

At this point the therapist asked permission to talk with the mother in order to explain the patient's need for freedom and to warn her that her daughter might occasionally be irritable at home during the treatment period. The patient was assured that there would be no discussion of confidential information.

In the resultant interview, the mother proved quite willing to cooperate, both because she was truly distressed by her daughter's symptoms and because she suffered some personal discomfort from the patient's intensified dependence upon her. Not only was the mother able to be tolerant of the girl's whims but, following the therapist's suggestion, she also began to develop a richer social life for herself and to renew old friendships. At the same time, she did not withdraw her "mothering" completely and the patient's dependent satisfactions were not cut off abruptly as she experimented with greater freedom in satisfying her own wishes. That this gradual change of attitude on the part of the mother had a profound influence on the patient's progress could be seen with increasing clarity as the therapy proceeded.

In the third interview, the patient brought the information that she had been sleeping well, had gone to classes, and, although there were sudden moments of anxiety, had not had to leave the classroom. She had lunched daily with friends; and the previous day she had taken a walk along the lake with her fiancé which both had enjoyed, but after about half an hour she had begun to worry about leaving her mother alone and had gone home. A new symptom, however, had developed which was frankly hostile to her mother. She had impulsive wishes to hit her mother when away from her, and when she was with her she heard what her mother said but could not see her clearly. Although these symptoms had not really frightened her, they were startling and convinced her of the intensity of hostility toward her mother.

In this interview, insight was offered in two realms. The transference relationship was discussed in detail and it was suggested that in indulging herself now she was doing it partly to please the therapist, who was momentarily a parent-figure, just as she had always inhibited herself previously to please her mother. And she was shown the split which had occurred in the parent-image—the therapist as the good parent and her own mother as the bad one who could be hated. At this point, an explanation was given of her conscious and unconscious need for dependence, and of her use at the moment of the therapist as the person upon whom she depended. Again she was encouraged to enlarge her social experiences by the use of opportunities as they presented themselves. In giving advice of this kind it is, of course, essential for the therapist to be quite sure not only of the needs of the patient, but of both the external situation and the patient's capacity to act independently without an increase of anxiety. It would be highly traumatic, naturally, to a patient if in trying to be friendly he were met with rejection.

The second point in this interview was her attitude toward sexuality. This subject was introduced easily by the discussion of possible reasons for the precipitation of the anxiety symptoms at a time when she was with her fiancé and away from her mother and girl friends. She was encouraged to talk freely of her fiancé and of her concept of marriage. She revealed fear of sexual intercourse and a puritanical attitude as well, saying that she had thought of it as an evil to be endured because of the "base nature of man." For a person of her generation, her general sexual information was very vague. As is often true of persons brought up by persons with strong sexual taboos, she did not remember ever having been curious about birth, sex differences, and so forth, nor did she remember masturbating as a child. She admitted having indulged in masturbation as an adolescent after she had been taught by an older girl, but she had done this only rarely and with tremendous guilt and fear.

Sex information was therefore given to this patient as part of the treatment procedure, just as one often teaches a child in the course of psychotherapy. As with the child, answering the sex questions of an adult whose information is confused or incorrect has a two-fold therapeutic result. It tends to relieve unconscious guilt connected with sexual curiosity and (through the transference) it tends to bring sexual wishes to consciousness, since the good parent in the form of the therapist does not condemn interest in sex.

At the beginning of the fourth interview, the patient was again tense and cried while she told that her fiancé was begging her for dates and was urging her to go to a dance the following week. She had been preoccupied since the last interview with sexual thoughts, and had felt that marriage would be impossible since the idea of sexual relations with him revolted her. She told a fragment of a dream she had had the previous night: She was running from a large man along a dark street; then she found herself in a small basement room and just as the man was going to grab her she saw that he had no arms. She awoke screaming and trembling.

She offered two enlightening associations to this dream. One was that her fiancé had a slight limp as a result of childhood poliomyelitis, and the second was a memory of seeing a man expose himself in an alley when she was a small child. Her recollection was of seeing an enormous penis and of running home in terror, but of being afraid to tell her mother of the experience.

The patient then confessed that she had recently doubted her love for her fiancé and thought that perhaps she was sorry for him, although his paralysis had not been severe enough to handicap him in athletics or other activities. She wondered if she did not cling to him for fear that other men would not love her if they knew her well. The therapist interpreted only the safety which she felt with the man in the dream when there were no arms, which was similar to her previous feeling of safety with her fiancé when she had thought of him as also injured. It was suggested that her fear arose only after he gave her the ring which might assure marriage and make her face relations with a real man. Her reaction to this was a smiling admission that her fiancé was certainly much more dominating than she had first thought him.

The next three interviews covered details of her doubts about her fiancé, her decision that she really did not love him, her plans to move to the sorority house while her mother visited friends in another city, and questions concerning possibilities of seeing other men. She also reported active classwork and weekly parties.

In the following interview she reported another dream fragment: She was in the woods and started to take hold of a tree trunk when she noticed that she was holding a penis which was attached to herself. In telling the dream she laughed and said it reminded her of the time when as a little girl she tried to urinate standing up and the urine went over the toilet cover. She had no memory of seeing a boy urinate, but admitted that she must have. The therapist told her of penis-envy in little girls and the hostility which sometimes developed toward boys as a result. She admitted then the despair she had always felt in her musical achievement because she believed that men would always be more successful.

Little fresh insight came with further interviews. There was repetition and elaboration of the material of the previous hours, and much of the time was consumed by reports of her activities and requests for detailed suggestions about how to meet certain social situations, such as dates with men other than her fiancé or the correct behavior as bridesmaid at a wedding in which she decided to take part although she had previously refused for fear her old symptoms would reappear. Her menses had been reestablished, and except for some insecurity socially her symptoms had ceased. Plans for the summer were also worked out with her and her mother so that she could spend half the time with friends and half in a resort with her mother.

Seven months after the termination of treatment, the patient was seen again in a friendly visit, and she appeared as a charming, self-reliant young woman. She had returned to her music; was engaged to be married but to another man, this time with inner conviction of success; and was working temporarily in an office while making plans for her marriage. She had encouraged her mother to return to the grandparents and was living in an apartment with a college chum who was also working. She stated that she saw her mother about once a week and enjoyed her as a companion. She could now feel amused at both her previous dependence on her mother and her hostility toward her.

Three years after the last treatment interview, her marriage of two years' duration was still obviously happy and there had been no symptom return.

Comments on Case K

Several factors operated to bring about a therapeutic change in this patient. Of greatest importance was the opportunity for a dependent relationship to a mother-figure (the therapist) who was neither demanding of love nor ambitious for success, and who was permissive of the patient's sexual interests and of her wish for pleasure with friends of her own age. Insight concerning her sexual and independent wishes made the relationship with the therapist clearer and more acceptable. But insight alone was not the curative factor; it was rather the new relationship, a framework in which she felt free to experiment emotionally and socially.

The absence of transference repetition in this case was accomplished by the mother's changed attitude toward the girl. Because of this and because she was still living with her mother, the patient was able to re-live the disturbing feelings with the original object rather than to transfer them to the therapist. In this way, the patient experienced a corrected mother-daughter relationship, not only within the therapy but in her life situation as well. This accelerated the therapy and made it possible in a short treatment to reach a deeper conflict, her fear of men.

This conflict, her fear of men and her castrative wishes against them, was brought out as the repression of her sexual wishes was relaxed. Insight into the meaning of the two dreams which showed a deepseated masculine identification made it possible for her to identify herself still further with the permissive therapist and to accept as normal the passive feminine wishes which had been thwarted by her mother's (and thus her own) earlier attitude of contempt and aversion.

Case L

(Peptic Ulcer and Examination Anxiety)

A junior medical student, a young man of thirty-one, was referred because of examination anxiety. In the last examination period, although he had studied well and conscientiously, his mind had become "blank" and he had been unable to think of anything to write; as a result he had failed two tests and did not even hand in papers for the others. He had always been afraid of examinations of any kind and had never done well on them but, because of excellent classwork, had received good grades in his courses. In addition, the patient was under the medical care of an internist for a duodenal ulcer of about five years' duration. He had had gastric difficulty from infancy and had been a "feeding problem" as a baby. In spite of his ulcer, he smoked almost continuously. Good results were brought by treatment consisting of 37 interviews over a period of fifteen months.

The patient was a very slender man of medium height, with a friendly but not overly aggressive manner. He was the second of three children, with a sister four years older and a brother eight years younger. His mother, a very ambitious woman, had been disappointed that her first child was a girl and when the patient was born she had turned her major interest and ambition toward him. He had been greatly indulged. The household had centered around him and even his older sister had been forced to give in to him and to defer to his wishes—at first because he was the baby and later because he was the boy. At the same time, however, much had been expected of him. He had been taught parlor tricks at an early age and had been called upon to recite poems and play the piano before he was four years old. His mother had called him "my big man" constantly, and had later held him up to the younger brother as an example of perfect behavior.

At the early age of six, he had been given tasks to perform in the family business. He was often assured that he would own and run this business when he came of age. The mother had constantly depreciated the father to him, exhorting him to be better and more reliable than his father. He remembered that he had always felt the responsibility for the family's future support an oppressive burden, and had feared he could not live up to his mother's expectations. Although the family had been well-to-do in comparison with the standard of the small town in which they lived, he had from an early age been expected to work after school rather than play with other children.

As one might expect, the father played an insignificant role in the family. He was easy-going, passive, and completely dominated by the mother. With the help of a good manager, he ran the business which she, an only child, had inherited. He never took part in decisions concerning the children or in their discipline. By the time the patient reached adolescence he, rather than his father, was the master of the house. The mother turned to her son for advice, expecting him to punish his younger brother when he misbehaved and in other ways to play the father role. The brother had always outwardly adored him, imitating him, and even now still asked his advice, as did the older sister. In college the patient had been academically successful, conscientious in his work, but not popular. After graduation he became the manager of the family business and his father retired.

He worked very hard and reorganized the business so that it became a much more successful enterprise. During this time he had many periods of digestive difficulty, and a physical examination by a specialist revealed a duodenal ulcer. He was put under ulcer management and urged to take a long rest. During convalescence, he became interested in medicine. This interest was further stimulated by a wealthy girl with whom he fell in love. She was two years older than he and ambitious like his mother. She helped him make plans whereby he could leave the business and go to medical school.

His mother, greatly disappointed in him, put the younger brother into his position in the business and withdrew all support from the patient. He persisted in his plans, however, married and entered medical school, using his wife's money for his training. According to both the patient and his wife, their marital adjustment was good, their sexual relations completely satisfactory for both.

Characteristically it was the wife, the more aggressive of the two, who urged the patient to seek treatment and made the first visit to the therapist (a woman) to prepare the way. She was very distressed over his condition and begged to help if there were anything she might do. She was an attractive, intelligent, and energetic person. Later in the treatment she proved that she could cooperate in a plan to help her husband when the opportunity was offered her.

For the first six months of the therapy, interviews were held once a week, except for a two-week interruption at the spring recess. Following the three months' summer vacation, the interviews were resumed and held at irregular intervals—never more frequently than twice a month and then only on the initiative of the patient. During this period it was suggested that regular appointments would not be necessary but that, from time to time, he might wish to discuss certain situations or reactions as they occurred, in which event he should feel free to call for an appointment.

In the first interview, the patient reviewed various examinations he had taken and told of the fear of failure which blocked his thought processes. No interpretation of the possible causes was offered by the therapist at this time, but assurance of symptom relief through treatment was given. He was told something of the connection between a person's symptoms and his general pattern of behavior and life experiences.

To the second interview the patient brought details of his life history as outlined above. He laid much stress upon his mother's ambition for his success, stating that she was like the mothers who dream of their sons as President. When asked if he too were not ambitious for his own success, he said he was a "double person," that he wanted "inordinate" success but would like it to come without any effort on his own part. With some embarrassment, he said, "I wish I had a wealthy relative who would leave me a million dollars." He accepted the therapist's interpretation that his tremendous ambition probably stemmed from a wish to please his mother who expected so much of him, but that his fear of failure and also his reluctance to exert himself might be due in part to his mother's pushing him when he was still too young to accomplish what she expected.

The next three interviews were somewhat repetitive, but new information led to a discussion of the humiliation he felt because of accepting financial support from his wife during his medical training. His method of assuaging the guilt was to work very hard and to refuse relaxation through recreation or extra rest periods. But he admitted that the harder he worked, the greater was the severity of his ulcer pains. When this distress was very great, he had to take time off for the frequent milk and powders of the ulcer treatment. When the patient was able to recognize, through the therapist's discussion, the repetitive cycle of his behavior—dependence (in the present situation, upon his wife's support), guilt and shame, compensation through overwork, illness following overwork, dependent indulgence to cure the illness, guilt again because of indulgence, and so on—it was possible to describe the psychodynamic factors in ulcer production to the patient.[1]

He was made aware of the intensity of his unconscious dependent wishes, but at the same time the therapist discussed with him the strong defenses he had built up to protect himself from the indulgence of these wishes. He was shown that, first, the wishes persisted because of childhood deprivation; second, his mother's disapproval of childish desires developed an aura of humiliation about all dependent wishes; and, third,

---

[1] F. Alexander, *et al.*, "The Influence of Psychological Factors Upon Gastro-Intestinal Disturbances: A Symposium," *The Psychoanalytic Quarterly*, Vol. III, p. 501, 1934.

his own masculine pride caused him to be ashamed of them. The desires were consequently denied indulgence and a compensatory ambitious exterior dominated his personality until imbalance broke it down and symptoms resulted.

To avoid, as much as possible, injury to his pride and to his conscience in facing the admission of this dependent part of his personality, he was given help in recognizing that all people, even adult men, retain from childhood some wishes to be cared for, and it was suggested that his present wishes might be stronger than those of some other persons because he had never been adequately satisfied as a child but had been forced into mature, responsible behavior before his capacity for it was developed.

Following this interpretation, the therapist saw the patient daily for three interviews. The purpose of the temporary increase in frequency was two-fold. In the first place, to a patient with such strong defenses against unconscious wishes, recognition of these wishes inevitably creates a feeling of inferiority (narcissistic injury) and the patient needs added support during a period of adjustment to the ego-alien material. Secondly, by seeing the patient more frequently, the therapist assures him that the wishes are acceptable to the therapist and that a repetition in the treatment situation of the parents' attitude will not occur. In this way, his shame is partly assuaged and the therapist temporarily plays the role of a less critical authority.

In the first of these three interviews, the patient related the following dream: He was on a beach with a lot of people; someone was drowning and the patient was expected to save the man. He was frightened that he couldn't swim that far, then someone pushed him from behind and he fell into the water and started to swim toward the drowning man. He kept feeling that he was going under. He thought, "They will have to save me." Then he was sitting on the beach being fed ice cream by some woman. He woke up thinking anxiously, "I have to get back and save the man."

Associations to the dream were: *Eating ice cream* reminded him of stealing ice cream from the refrigerator when he was a boy. He used to feel very guilty but could not resist. Once his sister told on him and his mother spanked him. Regarding *swimming,* he said he was an excellent swimmer, but his wife was a better diver. *Saving life* made him think of saving life as a doctor. He was always afraid that he might make some mistake; maybe the responsibility was too great. He might fail, as he did in examinations. He wished he were not so ambitious. With emotion he said, "If mother had left me alone, I would have been happier."

The therapist discussed the dream material only in terms of the meaning of that part made obvious by the associations. The conflict between the dependent wish to be cared for and fed, and the need to be responsible and successful was pointed out to the patient and correlated with the discussion of the previous day. He was shown also that this conflict interfered both with adequate pleasure in passive indulgences and with adequate exertion of his energies in adult, masculine, responsible activity. It was suggested that the conflict could be lessened by certain changes in his attitudes and habits: he should accept some of his passive feelings as normal, and he should allow himself some experience in dependent satisfactions of a socially acceptable nature. He was assured that it would be quite normal, for example, to let his wife or his laboratory assistants do odd jobs which he had previously insisted upon doing himself.

Dependence on the therapist was encouraged as a temporary means of trying out his capacity to accept passive pleasures. He was assured that the therapist would be glad to work out details and give advice if needed. This instituted a period in which the patient became rather lazy and demanding; he was satisfied with about half a day's work and rationalized that his ulcer would make it impossible for him ever to be a great success.

At this point, the wife's cooperation was sought; she was encouraged to give him sympathy and extra tenderness, to make no demands upon him but to show interest and appreciation of his work whenever he discussed it with her. As he became more interested in work again, in about two weeks, the help of the internist supervising his ulcer management was also enlisted. He arranged that in his hospital work the patient be allowed to examine and plan the treatment for some ulcer patients. The cooperation of both wife and physician was discussed with the patient so that he was aware of the therapist's recommendation; and resistance which might have grown out of a wounded pride was lowered by assuring him that both persons had been asked to do these things only if they wished to, and were requested not to go beyond their own pleasure in carrying out the recommendations. An interpretation of the use of his illness as a secondary gain for passivity and dependence was discussed with him as a morbid, rather than a healthy, way of securing satisfaction, whereas allowing his wife, his physician, and others to help him so that he could gain greater pleasure in adult activities was a more mature method.

For some time he had difficulty in accepting his wife's more maternal attitude and turned to the therapist for advice, with questions such as, "Won't it make me soft if I allow her to write my letters for me?" or "She got tickets for the theater for this Saturday; I ought to study; won't it be a bad policy to start going to the theater weekends?" He was reassured and recreation as a normal human need was discussed with him.

The situation of the transference was laid before him as he kept asking for reassurance, comparing his need for acceptance by the therapist to the need of any child for acceptance by his mother. Since his mother had disapproved of childish pleasures and had demanded adult behavior of him at an early age, it was hard for him to believe that the therapist would not take the same attitude. He was encouraged to allow himself greater leeway in personal pleasures, both active and passive, and it was explained that as he continued to enjoy and express himself more fully he would find that no harm would come to him, but rather a greater feeling of satisfaction and self-sufficiency.

At spring recess of that year, for the first time that he could remember, the patient was able to allow himself a complete ten-day vacation. He and his wife spent the time in

Florida "just loafing." He came back eager to work and settled into a life of work and pleasure with only a few twinges of conscience. A new symptom, however, reared its head as he became more active and successful in his work. This was disclosed in a dream fragment which occurred a week after the patient returned from Florida: He and his favorite professor were examining a woman patient. She was very uncooperative and kept telling them how to conduct the examination. She was critical of the professor and finally said, "You get out of here and let Doctor A. (our patient) take care of me." The professor looked at her with disgust but smiled at our patient and said, "Go ahead with the old witch." Our patient felt very uncomfortable, continued the examination but could find nothing wrong with the woman, and went out to the professor saying, "I can't do it, I don't know how." He awoke with the same feeling of despair he used to have in examinations.

The few associations to this dream were revealing. He respected the professor extremely, was convinced he himself could never be as good, but often fantasied discovering some new treatment which would make him even more famous than the professor. Another thought which was provoked by the dream was that lately, since he was doing so well in his classes, he had a guilty feeling in relation to the other students. He often wondered if they were jealous of him. In association to the woman in the dream, he laughingly said, "I used to think women were all uncooperative and bossy. I said I'd specialize in a man's kind of illness. Maybe that is because my mother was so bossy."

As interpretation of the dream, the therapist suggested that perhaps the dream indicated that successful competition with a father-figure (the professor) in relation to a woman made him feel so guilty that he had to fail in order to assuage his guilt. The failure in the dream was compared to his failure when taking examinations, and a hypothesis was offered that this guilt for his success in a competitive situation might be a second cause of the examination anxiety. He was reminded by the therapist that in childhood he succeeded to his father's place with his mother, and it was suggested that this may have made him feel guilty since he was fond of his father. The patient accepted this interpretation, but said that the professor was much more successful than his father. He added that he did not believe he was so successful that he really made the other students jealous of him; he guessed that it may have been mostly imagination.

Toward the end of the school year, the patient made up the examinations he had failed, and passed his junior finals. Although he was irritable and demanding at home during the examination period and admitted some anxiety before starting the examination, he had no fear after he began writing.

The summer vacation was varied; he and his wife took a trip for a month, he spent a month at home helping his brother with some difficulties in which the family business had become involved, and the final month he and his wife spent at the summer home of his wife's parents. There he spent part of his time enjoying himself and part studying for his medical board examinations. On his return in the fall his appearance was that of a normal healthy man; he stated that he was now off ulcer management and needed only to be a bit careful in his diet, that he had decreased his smoking from two packages of cigarettes a day to about half a package.

During the following year, the patient was seen only when he wished to discuss specific situations, such as the choice of interneships, extra work offered to him in the department of medicine, and advisability of vacations. At these times he was advised when necessary. There were frequent rediscussions of the conflict situations interpreted early in the treatment, but no deeper material was delved into. His dependence became increasingly less and his fear of competition and failure ceased. Since he accepted an internship in a hospital at some distance, he was not seen again after graduation. Two years later word came from him that he had established himself in general practice in a middle-sized town, and that he was doing well and was enjoying life. He then had a three-months-old son. He had expected to be jealous of the child, knowing of his old passive wishes, and was pleased that he was not. He was determined that his son should have a happy, irresponsible childhood.

Comments on Case L

As with Case K, an important factor in the symptom relief here was the patient's experience of a relationship (to the therapist) different from the one he had known with his mother. In this case, permission to accept and indulge in dependent pleasures allowed him to enjoy satisfactions which were denied by the mother. The cooperation of the wife increased the facilities for "acting out" at home, for being passive, and offered an opportunity for an evaluation in a real life situation of the dangers versus the pleasures of a less overcompensatory masculine attitude.

As a result of an acceptance and assimilation of his dependent wishes, the need to repress them by means of an exaggerated ambitiousness made it possible for the guilt concerning his competitive masculine wishes to come near consciousness, as the dream with the internist indicates. Through insight into the cause of the guilt he was then able to overcome his fear of success in competition, and to attempt a normal masculine professional life.

Interpretation of the causes of his neurotic attitudes as they operated in his early life aided his recognition of the differences between the treatment relationship and real life on the one hand and his childhood experiences on the other. Such insight through interpretation is valuable mainly in that it serves to emphasize the difference in the two situations and thus frees the patient to release repressed feelings and to relive them in the framework of the transference relationship. From this point, he then becomes able to try a new version in his everyday life.

In this case, it was significant that the therapist was a woman; the sequence of emergence of the two main conflicts was probably determined by this fact. Had the therapist been a man it is very likely that the fear and guilt in relation to masculine competitiveness would have been stirred up first.

The resolution of the conflict in relation to the dependent wishes toward a woman, made possible by a woman therapist in this case, decreased the intensity of the masculine over-competitiveness and thus decreased the guilt associated with it.

Case M

(Vaginismus)

A 35-year-old woman came for treatment because of vaginismus, tearing pain during intercourse, and fatigue from overwork. A physician had tried to dilate her vagina with instruments but without success. Even after the dilation caused by childbirth, ten years earlier, the symptom had persisted. (The child, incidentally, was delivered stillborn.) Good results were achieved by a treatment consisting of seven interviews at weekly intervals.

An attractive woman who talked freely and frankly, the patient was the second of three sisters brought up by very religious, puritanical, but devoted parents. Until she went to college, her social experiences had been restricted to the closely knit family life and to church activities. Dancing, card playing, smoking, and drinking were all taboo, and sex life of any kind was never mentioned. She could remember no sexual curiosity or activity as a child. Upon the onset of menstruation her mother had told her that the menses would occur regularly and explained how to care for herself at the period, but offered no explanation of the meaning of the function.

The patient was the favorite daughter of her father who called her his "little boy," insisted that she dress in over-alls, and taught her carpentry, his avocation. She in turn adored her father, and told him when she was still a child that she would never marry but would stay at home with him. She had no conscious hostility toward any member of the family and professed love for everyone in the statement, "One can find something to love in all."

She had left home for the first time at twenty, to go to a denominational college in which the social activities were similar to those of her home. She had become engaged to a "student volunteer," but had broken the engagement because her parents did not want her to go so far away as his missionary activities would necessitate. Later she married a man whom she had met at a church party and who had an upbringing similar to her own. He was in business rather than in religious activities and her parents approved of him.

She claimed that she had entered marriage completely unprepared for sexual experience. She had envisioned marriage as an affectionate idyll, which God would eventually bless with children. On her wedding night she had been horrified by her husband's advances and had said to him, "If my mother and father had known what kind of a man you are, they wouldn't have let me marry." She eventually submitted to intercourse, but only after her husband had wooed her tenderly for several weeks and had explained to her the relation of sexual intercourse to child bearing. The relationship was always painful to her, however, and often vaginismus was too severe for coitus. She had never experienced orgasm although her husband explained to her that women did. She insisted that, in spite of these unpleasant experiences, she still adored her husband and was devoted to him. When she became pregnant two years after her marriage she believed that she was completely happy and was inconsolable for a while after the stillbirth of her child. Some postpartum difficulty had necessitated a hysterectomy, so that it was impossible for her to have more children.

Her husband had never been very successful financially. At the time of treatment he was cooperating with the patient's father in a business project but was making no more than expenses. The patient had been supporting them both for two years on a meager salary for clerical work. She had to work long hours, often in the evenings, and did her housework after business hours.

In the first interview she frankly admitted that she still felt, emotionally, that "sex was bad" although intellectually she had accepted it as something which should be pleasant. Consciously, she wished to enjoy it and to satisfy her husband. In discussing her puritanical upbringing with the therapist (a woman), she insisted that she had loosened her attitude some-what in recent years; she danced and played cards occasionally, although she still disapproved of drinking and smoking.

This change which she had undergone without feeling guilty was used as a point from which to discuss the difference in attitudes toward morality between generations, and it was suggested that as a very small child she might have been punished for some innocent sex play and, although the memory be lost, the moral taboo might still unconsciously influence her behavior. The vaginismus, then, might have developed as an unconscious protection against her normal sexual desires. The development of such a need for protection as a result of a childhood fear of punishment or loss of love was discussed with her. It was also pointed out that her method of protection, the avoidance of temptation by some evasive device, might cause her to wish to run away from treatment if discussions stirred up fear or guilt. Laughing self-consciously, the patient answered, "You think I may be afraid to come next time and maybe will pretend I am cured?" In the second interview, she explained rather sheepishly that she had become distressed by her wish to "dig into the dirt" and thought fleetingly that really she was too busy to keep weekly appointments. Remembering the warning that she might wish to run away, she deliberately made herself think about all those "dirty things." Facing these issues in the interval between appointments made her feel less ashamed of sex thoughts and more eager to learn the truth about such things. She then discussed frankly the attitudes of various groups of people toward sexual activity. She compared her parents' puritanical attitude with that disclosed in novels she had read, and admitted guilty feelings over sexual sensations she had experienced when reading love passages in books. She expressed interest in the anatomy and physiology of sex, and the therapist lent her a book on sex information.

In the third interview, she admitted the development of an absorbing interest in sex information and said laughingly, "I'm making up for my ignorance as a child, when I should have been taught." This was used as an opening to discuss the hostility which children often develop toward their parents as a result of repression and deprivation. The patient, at this time, was unable to accept hostility toward anyone, much less toward her parents, but said that her mother was "too good" to her, always doing things for her and giving her advice. When questioned, she admitted that often she wished her mother would stop doing so much for her. She would sometimes prefer to stay at home cosily with her husband when her mother, to relieve the patient of work, insisted upon their coming to dinner at the parents' home.

It was suggested tentatively that such a reaction was natural, but that because she loved her mother it was difficult to allow herself to feel irritated or to be more independent. It was explained how often the most devoted mothers are selfish too in smothering their children who need independence. She was told also that it would be excellent for her health, as well as for the success of her marriage, if she could admit normal hostility and assert a little of her independence. She was assured that, as a rule, mothers can adjust themselves to a gradually less close relationship to their children and still be content.

In the next interview, the fourth, the patient brought two pieces of news which she offered as if she were presenting a gift to the therapist. First, she had had intercourse twice without pain and with some pleasurable sensations, although as yet without orgasm; second, she had spent Sunday with her husband on a picnic instead of attending the usual family dinner. The patient was complimented and smilingly told, "You said that as if you knew I would be pleased." The patient laughed with some embarrassment but then admitted frankly that during the week she had often wondered if the therapist would approve of this or that thought or action, but she had also felt relieved that an adult she respected could approve of what she now accepted as normal feelings.

The nature of her relationship to the therapist was discussed with her; she now complied with what she thought the therapist expected of her just as she had been obedient in childhood to her mother. She was assured that this attitude in a treatment situation was normal and indeed useful as a frame in which

she could experiment safely with the expression of feelings
and thoughts, the prohibition of which had led to her symptoms.
The temporary nature of this dependence was emphasized, and
a hint offered of future independence with the assurance of
a richer life which would not be constricted by unnecessary
repressions.

The patient admitted jealousy of her sisters, both of whom
had been allowed more independence than she. She had now
begun to suspect that she had been the favorite child only
because of her consistent obedience and conformity. This
thought stimulated antagonistic feelings against her mother
who had put so many restrictions upon her. Some insight was
offered at this point into the fact that since she had obviously
been the father's favorite from the beginning, her guilt in
taking him away from the mother might have made her
propitiate her mother by being overobedient. Her obedience
had become a defense against her feelings of guilt. In general
terms, the growth of a little girl and the importance of the
oedipal phase in her development were discussed with her.
With surprising intuition, she said, "Perhaps that is why I
never could believe that my father really did have intercourse
with mother. Such a belief would have been too tempting to
me in that stage." She might have added, "No wonder I had
to build up idyllic notions of marriage." Following this acceptance of her early repressions, her other two defenses, sexual
prohibition and masculine identification, were hinted at as
other methods of protection.

The patient then suggested that perhaps she played a masculine role even now with her husband. She earned a large share
of the living expenses and she also helped with his work by
giving advice, checking accounts for him, and so forth. The
therapist pointed out the element of masculine protest in her
symptom, and showed her that vaginismus constituted a deeply
hostile attack against her husband since it thwarted his sexual
satisfaction. In respect to her playing the role of the man in
the family, it was suggested that she might enjoy being less
active, letting her husband do his own work except when he
definitely asked for help. In the time thus freed, she could

indulge herself in pleasures long denied. She confessed that she longed to read novels, but did not because she always felt as if she were wasting time. She laughingly admitted that it would be hard to allow herself such pleasures, but said that she would try. She added that her husband often scolded her because she refused to be "cherished as a wife should be."

In the fifth interview she was again jubilant over her success and discussed a philosophy of life she was developing, the gist of which was the pursuit of personal happiness accompanied by avoidance of hurting other people. Instead of making duty the core of her life, she was giving some place to pleasure, even though she continued to protect herself by a good control of her hostility. Although their sexual relations continued to be about the same, she was optimistic about the future, and told of her husband's having asked to read the book lent her by the therapist. He had decided that if he were now a more adequate lover, all would be well. She conveyed his request for an interview with the therapist to talk over some of the suggestions in the book.

An appointment was therefore arranged with the husband who appeared to be a friendly but definitely inhibited person. The therapist encouraged the husband to accept his wife as a less repressed individual now, and to feel free to experiment in their sexual relations. He was also given much credit for his tolerant attitude toward his wife's treatment. He left stating that he was relieved by the change in their mutual relationships and would try to equal his wife's gain.

The rest of the treatment time consisted of two more interviews with the patient in which the previous discussions were reviewed and elaborated. In the first, the therapist told the patient of the conversation with her husband. She accepted this very well but was relieved that there had been no discussion of the more intimate information. With embarrassment, she confessed that she had worried some that her husband and the therapist would be interested in each other and that she would be less important. When the therapist pointed out that the triangle situation was similar to that of child-mother-father, she accepted it easily and was interested in the ease with which a patient repeats childhood attitudes in the transference relationship.

In the last interview she was encouraged to attempt a period on her own, but was assured that she could return any time she wished. The similarity of this separation to weaning was talked over with her and was related to the earlier discussion of the transference relationship.

She returned only once, after six weeks, to report that she had experienced orgasm and that the pain and vaginismus seemed cured. She told of much contentment in her social life, most of which was now away from her parents' home. She also said that she was much less fatigued; she was helping less with her husband's work and so had more time for sleep and rest as well as recreation.

Comments on Case M

The therapeutic change in this case was accomplished (as in the other two cases) mainly through the experience of a relationship with a mother-figure who was different in attitudes and behavior from her mother. The difference lay in the therapist's acceptance of sexual experience and sexual satisfaction as desirable instead of "dirty," in her willingness to discuss and explain sexual matters rather than be secretive and disgusted. Interpretation of the factors in her rearing which were responsible for the repression and guilt and exaggerated obedience made the difference in the therapist's attitude stand out more clearly. With this insight, a continuation of transference repetition became untenable and the patient therefore reacted to the actual situation in a realistic way.

This patient, like the first, had a strong masculine drive, due to her early identification with her father. She was able to relax this masculine attitude partly because of her insight into how this identification came about and partly because of the therapist's permission to enjoy feminine satisfaction, but it came about chiefly as an automatic continuum. When she was able to accept sexuality as a woman, her need to deny her femininity through masculine strivings became no longer necessary. The presenting symptom, vaginismus, was relieved because there was no longer a neurotic purpose for it to serve.

Discussion

In the opening paragraphs of this chapter, it was mentioned that these three cases had in common a good ego, a restrictive super-ego, and strong, deeply repressed dependent wishes; in each was found the same basic conflict between inner repressed drives and the rigid standards of conduct imposed by the super-ego.

In Cases K and M, sex wishes and feelings as well as hostile aggressive attitudes were denied by the super-ego; in Case L hostility (especially that produced by rivalry) and dependent wishes were taboo. When external circumstances reinforced these repressed drives, the increased pressure broke down the defenses and acute symptoms developed. In the first instance, Case K, pressure for marriage threatened the sex repression; in the last one, Case M, marriage itself was the disturbing experience; while in Case L the attitude toward masculine success—first in business, later in medical school—plus the pressure of increasing responsibilities stirred up unconscious hostile rivalry as well as passive dependent longings.

The therapeutic task in these cases was three-fold. It was necessary, first of all, to soften the severity of the standards and to achieve sufficient flexibility in the ethical rulings to allow the personality to meet more adequately and without guilt the demands of both his own drives and society. The second task was to broaden the ego so that it would allow such socially acceptable emotional indulgences as legitimate dependence, sexual experience, and a reasonable amount of aggressive competitiveness without causing such internal conflicts as guilt feelings or injury to pride. The third task, tentatively formulated at first but actually carried out during treatment, was the manipulation of the patient's environment in order to increase the possibilities for healthy satisfaction in his life and at the same time to decrease, temporarily, the external pressure conducive to symptom formation.

In the conduct of the treatment of these cases, two tenets common to the usual psychoanalytic treatment were kept in mind. Insight into the causative factors of the patient's emotional repressions was used as an agent for the release of the emotion, defenses against which were responsible for the production of symptoms; and (still more important) an opportunity was given the patient to re-live, through new and obviously different objects, the old feelings which had caused distress in childhood. These emotions emerge from the neurotic repression to find attachment first to the therapist (within the transference relationship) and later to persons in his daily life. It is this new personality constellation which aids in changing symptomatic behavior to healthy behavior.

In these cases, interpretation of personality conditions was based in part upon information derived from the history of the patients, from their behavior, and from dreams when they were presented, and in part upon scientific knowledge of the causative factors of certain syndromes. In most instances, information from all these sources was so synchronized that it could be used together. For example, in Case L, the dream of eating ice cream on the beach after his failure at a heroic adventure exposed in both content and associations the same psychic conflict which we know from earlier research to be characteristic of the neurotic pattern of ulcer patients—the conflict between deep dependent desires and conscious masculine strivings. Such a personality difficulty could be discussed with the patient when related to the historical information.

The same kind of correlation could be made in both of the other cases in which knowledge gleaned from earlier investigations made it possible to recognize the repressed sexual conflict at the base of the phobic symptoms in Case K and of the vaginismus in Case M. This knowledge of the structure of the cases made it possible to formulate the psychodynamics of the individual case quickly and to shorten the therapeutic period by eliminating the months of free association which would be necessary if the dynamic pattern had to be reconstructed from the words of the patient alone. This knowledge is the therapist's "reference book," and as such is highly important in determining his whole plan of treatment.

Interpretation of his conflict to the patient was timed according to his capacity to endure the resultant emotional release. In these three cases, a comparatively strong ego made them capable fairly early in treatment of accepting insight into ego-alien trends. An introductory interpretation of a main facet of the conflict was therefore offered, in all three, within the first few interviews. In Case K, the hostility toward her mother was discussed and elaborated by the second interview; in Case L, the conflict between passive and active wishes was interpreted by the fourth and fifth session; and in Case M, the patient's guilt and fear in relation to sex were interpreted in the very first visit.

In giving interpretations, the spacing of the interviews was always considered. In Case K, where "acting out" was a personality tendency, the patient was seen twice a week during the period of most intensive treatment, frequently enough to protect her from acting out too impulsively and yet infrequently enough to give her time to use the new emotional freedom for expression in her world outside the treatment period. The transference repetition was thus kept at a minimum, and was dependent in nature. There was a minimum of ambivalence within the transference relationship, since the hostile angle of her repressed emotion was directed toward the original object (the mother) rather than toward the therapist.

In Case L, spacing of interviews was also adjusted to the patient's capacity to stand insight without new symptom production. When the traumatic interpretation of his deep infantile passivity was offered, this patient was seen daily to support him through the trying period; and when his strength to accept this element of his personality was marshaled, he was seen weekly so that the emotion could be used in establishing a richer relationship to his wife, rather than in the development of too great dependence upon the therapist. As has been indicated earlier, by so controlling the intensity of the transference relationship in ulcer patients, the tendency to project hostility to the therapist, a complication occasionally encountered in some of the psychoanalytic cases, can be avoided.

In Case M, where one of the patient's methods of solving her difficulties was, with hostile detachment, to avoid meeting the situation, the interval between appointments was kept at a week. The interpretation of this defense of evasion, which might have operated as a wish to interrupt treatment or as criticism of the therapist for permissiveness, was given to the patient at the same time that her sexual conflict was discussed. In this way she was protected against reestablishing her neurosis, not by the support of more frequent visits as in the other two cases, but by the forewarning that she might feel hostile in the interim and not wish to return. This "interpretation in advance" served to help her through her resistance as shown by the report of her thoughts during the week.

As with interpretation in standard psychoanalysis, the method of giving insight in these cases was to correlate current attitudes, symptoms, and transference behavior with infantile experiences and conflicts; to point out the various ego defenses which had developed to protect the individual from suffering in his childhood and which remained as part of his personality although no longer pertinent to his present adult life.

Dreams, when offered as in Cases K and L, were used as collaborative information in an interpretation, and only that part dealing with the conflict in the focus of treatment was discussed. Such use of dream material kept the patient oriented always toward reality and avoided severe regressive behavior which could prolong treatment unnecessarily. This principle is valid for every treatment based on psychoanalytic theory.

In all three cases, an element in the method of offering interpretative insight should be pointed out: the phrasing of the information in a tentative and suggestive rather than in a factual manner. For instance, the interpretation was preceded with "Maybe," "Perhaps," or "It could have been that." This may seem an unimportant preoccupation with an insignificant detail since, to many analysts, this procedure is the rule in presenting any interpretation. But particularly with such cases as these—in which interpretations were offered early and were based upon a minimum of information given in the conversation of the patient and a maximum of scientific knowledge concerning the dynamics of the specific disease—such tentativeness avoided a tremendous amount of resistance to the interpretation, a resistance growing partly out of wounded pride and partly out of a shocked conscience reaction. The tentativeness of the interpretation lowered the resistance because it allowed the patient more easily to accept what his own strength could bear and to discard the rest for the time being, rather than force him to defend himself against the whole.

The relationship of these patients to the therapist played an important role in the treatment process. The fact that the therapist was a different kind of person from the parent, and particularly that she assumed a different attitude, made it possible for each patient to test the validity of the demands of his conscience against the more permissive attitude of the therapist and to experiment tentatively with changed attitudes in his life activities. In Cases K and M, the permissiveness was in the realms of hostile feeling and sexual wishes; in Case L, it was related to the satisfaction of dependent and passive pleasures. Permissiveness was not expressed by the therapist merely by an uncritical attitude as is characteristic of the standard psychoanalytic technique; the uncritical attitude was fortified by discussions of the causes for such a censorious conscience and of general attitudes toward these human trends, and by tentative suggestions that the patients might experiment —but carefully—with richer life experiences. With patients of strong ego capacity such as these three possessed, the transference relationship becomes a frame in which they can allow repressed impulses to come to expression, not in a primitive, unrestrained manner but rather in socially acceptable ways.

Weaning from dependence on the therapist thus became a minor problem. Each patient was able to continue on his own as soon as his newer reactions in life became sufficiently strong to bring him happiness and pleasure to such a degree that he could allow himself to dispense with the security and acceptance supplied by the treatment situation.

As suggested above, the actual life experiences during the treatment period were also utilized therapeutically in all of these three cases. Thus the patient had already learned by the end of the treatment more adequately adjusted methods of behavior, and had been able to develop these new reactions in a period when he could still evaluate them objectively in discussions with the therapist. At the same time, since new experiences are educative in themselves, the changes in life situation achieved during treatment became therapeutic for the patients In order to use to the utmost these everyday events, the therapist intervened in various ways. Where advisable, environmental situations were manipulated in order to change a repetitively traumatic environment to one more conducive to healthy life satisfactions. In Case K, an interview with the patient's mother achieved a lessening of restrictive pressure and finally a willingness on the part of the mother for her daughter to have an independent life. In Case L, cooperation of both the wife and the patient's internist made possible the satisfying experience of a healthier dependence upon his wife and a work experience under the tutelage of a respected superior in a field which allowed him to transform wishes to be cared for into caring for and feeding others. In Case M, education of the patient's husband in the art of the marital role made the sexual experiences of the patient healthier and more satisfactory and thus aided in eliminating the sexual block.

The therapist encouraged each patient also to expose himself to richer living by suggestions of various activities which were safe to initiate at the particular stage in the treatment. Such advice is theoretically avoided in a standard psychoanalysis, although many analysts do not hesitate to give such aid when it seems necessary. If the advice, however, is given as a tentative suggestion which can be taken or left at the patient's discretion, it usually does not cause resistance but gives a support which is valuable in strengthening the patient's ability to travel the road to health.

The therapy in each case was terminated when it became obvious to the therapist that the energy released by the solution of the central conflict was sufficient to make the patient able to carry on more efficiently than before—but only after the patient had demonstrated this by actual improvement in adjustment. That progress would continue seemed a safe assumption in these cases since the potentiality was great, both within the favorable environmental circumstances of each patient and within the patient's ego itself.

Margaret Wilson Gerard, M.D.

Chapter 14

CORRECTIVE EMOTIONAL EXPERIENCE
THROUGH RAPPORT

In this chapter two cases will be discussed in which therapeutic results were achieved through careful manipulation of the therapeutic relationship and without the production of an intense transference neurosis.

Therapists have long been fascinated with the *similarities* between transference feelings and previous neurotic conflicts, but the *differences* between the new feelings and the old have sometimes been overlooked and the importance of these differences many times underestimated. As is well known, the new edition of a neurosis is never an exact duplicate of the old conflict. It is by virtue of this very dissimilarity that therapeutic results can be achieved.

In the first interview with each of these patients, the dissimilarity between the attitude of authoritative persons in the earlier life of the patient and the emotional attitude of the therapist stimulated in the patient a warm feeling of trust and confidence in the therapeutic relationship. Such feelings of rapport have always been a part of any effective doctor-patient relationship. It was through the utilization of this congeniality that therapeutic results were here produced.

The first patient (Case N) felt that the initial comment of the therapist revealed understanding of her problem. This immediate sympathy was in marked contrast to her husband's hostility, which had so bruised the patient's feelings that she had retreated to the dream-like state of the chronic alcoholic. The sense of being understood by the therapist restored to her a feeling of adequacy and a desire to live again in the real world of her home and children.

With the second patient (Case O), the sense of alliance with the therapist came about when she saw that her husband could not distract the therapist's attention from the patient to himself, and when the therapist refused to place the patient on a lower plane than her daughter. The feeling that someone would act wholeheartedly in her interest was a new experience for this patient, since all of her previous relationships had been intensely ambivalent in character. Seeming never to have had the security of genuine love, the patient had not dared to rebel openly against any of these ambivalent relationships, but her feelings of frustrated rage found expression by means of multiple hysterical and vegetative symptoms.

Case N

(Alcoholism)

The patient, a woman of fifty-six, consulted the therapist on the advice of her oldest daughter. She came because of chronic alcoholism which had become increasingly severe over a period of ten years. She was seen for eight interviews covering a period of six weeks, with satisfactory results.

The patient, a quiet cultured woman with a timid manner, came eagerly for psychotherapy. She felt very much ashamed of her drinking and guilty about the effect her behavior was having on her six daughters. In describing her drinking, she seemed neither to exaggerate her consumption of alcohol nor to underestimate it in an attempt to deceive the therapist (a woman). It was particularly striking that she made none of the protestations so characteristic of the alcoholic that she had taken her "last drink." She said she would like to stop drinking but did not know whether she would be able to. She had no idea why she had such a constant urge to keep herself in a dazed or comatose state. The desperate need of the patient for some person to understand and help her was tragically evident.

The patient said that in the first 45 years of her life she had never sought alcohol of her own accord. Only when her husband had insisted on her taking a cocktail with him before dinner, or when the social situation had demanded it, had she taken a drink—and then never more than two. About ten years ago, however, she had started drinking at home, usually within the confines of her own room. For the past three or four years she had kept herself in a comatose or semi-comatose state most of the time, utterly unable to care for her children or household.

After the patient had described the onset and progress of her drinking, the therapist suggested that some person close to her must have hurt or failed her in some way to make her need the comfort of alcohol. This remark won the full confidence of the patient. She at once disclosed—for the first time to anyone—the distress and bewildered resentment she had known when, at the birth of each child, her husband had blamed her for not bearing him a son. Instead of loving consolation for her own disappointment, she had been subjected to his bitter rage and vituperation.

About the time of the birth of the last daughter, the husband had insisted on building a large suburban residence. This decision resulted not only from the increase in the size of his family but from the increase in the size of his fortune, due to the stock market boom. The patient had hoped to win back her husband's love and admiration by planning the arrangement, furnishing and management of this new home, but even in this —ordinarily considered the realm of women—he scorned her suggestions and taste. Every particular of the construction was of his planning, and all the details of its management were dictated by him. This had made the patient feel a complete failure as a wife; not only had she failed to give her husband a son but now she was deemed incapable of planning and running her own home.

A complete history of this woman was never elicited, but these few facts were gradually revealed during the course of the eight interviews. The patient had lived all her life in a large middle-western town where her family belonged to the wealthy, secure aristocracy of the community. After a finishing-school education, travel, and debut, she was married. Her husband, an ambitious dynamic man, fifteen years her senior, was already successful in business at the time of their marriage and in the following years became very wealthy. The patient, who had always been genuinely devoted to her husband and whose happiness lay in satisfying his demands, received in return the knowledge that she was the beloved wife of a man (seemingly strong) who was a leader in their community. She never questioned his intellectual opinions and beliefs; like a good Victorian wife, she accepted him as lord and master and carried out his orders—in the house, with the children, in their social life, and in her political convictions.

One wish of her husband, however, she could not gratify— his narcissistic desire to have a son. She was not robust physically and would not have had such a large family voluntarily; but in an attempt to satisfy her husband's obsessive insistence on a son, she had had six children. When the first three children disappointed him by being girls, he blamed his wife but still found pleasure in the fact that they were beautiful children. Moreover, he found some consolation in his belief that, just as he had never failed to produce and achieve anything he desired in business, he could not fail to produce a son. When he was told that the fourth and fifth children were also girls, he cursed and berated his wife and would not visit her in the hospital. To the birth of his sixth daughter, he reacted with extreme rage; to spite and punish his wife (whom he held responsible for this unkind trick of fate) he disappeared from home for three weeks. And then the onset of the climacteric closed the door forever on the possibility of the patient's giving him the son he so pathologically desired.

A few years after the establishment of their elaborate suburban home, the stock market crashed and her husband's business enterprises were hurt severely by "that man in the White House." This was more than his inflated self-esteem could bear; he gradually sank into a severe depression colored by paranoid delusions. Four years before the wife entered treatment, her husband had been placed in a sanitarium near their home. She saw him daily but he was not allowed to leave the sanitarium.

It was evident that in the last fifteen years of her life the patient had been made to feel that she was a complete failure as a woman. Unconsciously she accepted the blame for not creating a son, but at the same time she resented the injustice of her husband's indictment. In addition, his compulsive dictatorial demands had become more and more inordinate as he became more threatened by the actual economic situation. While he was still at home she had at least the illusion of his emotional support, but with his depression and subsequent hospitalization she felt totally alone.

The actual situation which she had to master alone was considerable, consisting of a large house for which it was becoming impossible to find servants, six daughters who should (according to her tradition) be given debuts, education, and socially acceptable husbands. Toward her first two daughters she seemed to feel some real maternal affection; toward the four youngest she showed only a sense of duty. She had turned over to governesses the complete responsibility for the last two. She had never been a strongly maternal woman; her whole emotional life was centered in her husband and, until he failed her completely, she never even felt the need of an intimate woman friend or confidante. Her realization that she was completely alone made her turn more and more to alcohol in an effort to find comfort and strength.

Drinking had been encouraged by her husband. Both to please him and to buoy herself in social situations in which she felt shy and unsure of herself, she would take a drink— but never more than a socially acceptable amount. After her husband had so brutally turned on her about her children, she began gradually to take more and more alcohol. It made her feel less insecure. It was, furthermore, a gesture of defiance and revenge against her husband since her silly behavior after two or three cocktails enraged and humiliated him. With her husband's complete collapse she also collapsed, regressing to a confused infantile Nirvana-like existence. This was her condition when her daughter brought her to the therapist.

The therapist made it clear that she felt the patient had been cruelly treated by her husband at times when she needed understanding, not only because of physical weakness but because of her own disappointment at not giving her husband a son. The patient accepted the therapist's attitude that a sense of grievance and anger in such a situation was normal and need not be a source of guilt; she accepted this just as unquestioningly as she had taken first the opinions of her parents (perhaps her father) and later those of her husband. Her faith in the therapist was like that of a trustful child.

Therapeutic results were apparent almost at once. In the second interview, the patient said she had not taken a drink since the first consultation and did not feel any need for alcohol. She was, even then, attempting to find adequate servants for her household and displaying surprising energy. During each of the following interviews, the patient revealed not only more resentment against her husband but also that she was making a belated adjustment to her daughters in her everyday existence. Finally, in the eighth interview, she told of her one act of successful defiance to her husband's overweening authority. This was in regard to the home her husband had built and furnished without consulting her wishes. She had set her heart on one beautiful piece of furniture, an antique, and (backed by her husband's secretary) had remained adamant to his objections. This antique became a symbol to her of the narcissistic core of her personality. She would not relinquish her right to that core, since her husband had broken her unconscious bargain with him to love him in return for being loved by him.

After this significant confession, the patient herself suggested discontinuing the interviews. She had done no drinking in the last six weeks, she was making daily visits to her husband in the hospital (and, where before she had resented this duty, she now faced it with equanimity), she was planning a debut for one daughter, and she was encouraging another daughter to marry a suitable young man. The therapist acceded to her desire to interrupt treatment, feeling that the patient's confidence in the therapist would enable her to come for further help should she need it.

The discontinuation of the treatment was undoubtedly an unconscious defiance of the therapist, just as the purchase of the antique had been a conscious defiance of the husband. But to the therapist this defiance seemed a healthy sign of growth in a woman who had shown so little ability to assert herself and such an inordinate capacity to submit to the authority of anyone whose love she needed and to whom in turn she gave her love and confidence. For the therapist to insist that the patient continue treatment would have indicated a lack of faith in her and a ruthless disregard for her independent strivings. Her reaction to such treatment at the hands of her husband had been a regressive flight to alcohol. It seemed probable that the slightest pressure on the patient toward remaining in treatment, or the vaguest intimation of lack of confidence in her capacity to act maturely, would have started a similar regressive flight.

In terminating the treatment, the patient was acting out in reverse the trauma of being rejected by her husband. She was now rejecting the therapist with whom she had had a dependent relationship similar to that she had had with her husband. She had reversed the roles: what she had endured passively, she now experienced actively. An emotional equilibrium was reestablished.

About six months later, the therapist heard that the patient was ill. She had done no drinking in the interim and had been well except for some vague gastrointestinal symptoms suggestive of gall-bladder disease. Finally she was hospitalized. An exploratory laparotomy revealed carcinoma of the gastrointestinal tract, and within a few weeks the patient died. After the patient's death, the daughter who had suggested that her mother consult the therapist wrote a letter thanking the therapist for making it possible for her mother, before she died, to reinstate herself in the eyes of her children and friends. Her mother's ability to stop drinking and lead a normal life before her death was a tremendous comfort to the daughters.

Comments on Case N

It is impossible to evaluate the therapeutic results obtained in the eight interviews, since actual physical disease ended the patient's life within a few months. There is a possibility that all the dependent care which was necessary during her severe illness was in itself an adequate substitute for drinking. The trauma to her 'feminine narcissism had been partially healed by the psychotherapy. It is pertinent, however, to attempt an analysis of the symptom and the dynamics of the therapy.

The drinking itself had a double meaning. It was a method by which she could re-live highly pleasurable experiences with her husband in their ceremony of a cocktail before dinner, when both husband and wife felt relaxed and somewhat erotically stimulated. This positive symbolic aspect of her drinking the patient made clear in the course of her treatment. On the other hand, drinking was a method of expressing her anger and resentment against her husband. The punishment for such an expression of hostility was also implicit in the drinking, since she was ashamed of the consequences of intoxication.

This patient seemed only partially to have reached a mature feminine character. She exemplifies the second type of feminine character delineated by Deutsch.[1] She had identified herself with her husband and his interests. Certainly on her fell the "larger share of the work of adjustment." She left the initiative to the man, and, out of her own need to be loved, renounced her originality, expressing her own self only through identification with her husband. By this identification she had tied her husband securely to her until, driven by his narcissistic need for a son, he turned on her. When her entire adjustment to her overvalued husband crashed, the patient regressed to an oral infantile form of gratification. Since the patient gave the most meager information concerning her early life, there is no data of psychogenic factors responsible for this regression.

Another psychological reason for her drinking was the patient's anxiety and insecurity aroused by the progressive disintegration of her husband's personality. Unconscious guilt

---

[1] Helene Deutsch, *The Psychology of Women*, Grune & Stratton, 1944.

over hostile feelings against him for his brutality intensified this anxiety greatly. From this conflictful situation the patient sought freedom in an alcoholic state.

The aim of the psychotherapy was to allow the expression with the therapist of the traumatic experience which the patient had suffered in her relationship to her husband. In this repetition, the therapist's attitude was the opposite of the one shown by the husband and therefore acted as a corrective emotional experience for the patient. The danger that intense regressive forces would be stimulated by dependence on the therapist was a clear indication against any extended type of therapy. Even in brief treatment the therapist was careful never to stir up the unconscious dependent longings of the patient. The manifest therapist-patient relationship throughout was that of two friendly equals, although unconsciously the patient was seeking guidance and love from the therapist.

The initial positive feelings stimulated in the first interview when the therapist sensed the patient's deep hurt, gave the patient sufficient confidence to give up the support gained from drinking. In the next seven interviews the patient made neither demands for advice, nor protests of dissatisfaction because no advice was given. In the initial interview the therapist did not urge the patient to return at a specified time but instead asked the patient if and when she would like to come again. Throughout the six weeks' period, the patient was allowed to control the frequency of interview. In terminating the treatment the patient took the initiative.

The choice by the daughter of a woman therapist of about the same age as the patient undoubtedly played an important part in the initial positive reaction of the patient and in her ability to accept the therapist's attitude. She was permitted by a mother-figure to abreact her real feelings and still be accepted by that mother. Since the patient had never had an intimate woman friend, we assume that she had an unconscious fear of women. This fear would have been increased by her conflict over having only female children. No data is available concerning the genesis of such a fear in the patient's relation to her own mother.

By bringing her mother to the therapist, the daughter was acting in a sense as a mother to her own mother. This in itself must have alleviated some of the patient's conflict and guilt toward her daughters. With the added permissiveness of the therapist, the patient was able to have with her daughters the same relationship the analyst had with her; she could allow herself to accept them as companions and to enjoy them.

Because of her husband's resentment toward her and her daughters, her normal maternal feelings had been rendered intensely conflictful and had been repressed. Her feminine narcissism had been deeply injured not only in her wifely feelings but also in her maternal feelings. With the healing of the narcissistic wound, these maternal feelings again sought normal expression in eager plans for her home and children. Even a kind of maternal affection toward her husband became possible. In the treatment the patient could abreact traumatic feelings without guilt. Because her guilt was relieved by the therapy, and not engendered by it through competition with the therapist, no new conflict developed.

How much progress this patient would have made is, of course, a matter of conjecture: Would the healing process have continued its work? Would she have remained fixed at her present state of health? Or, with new conflicts, would she have again regressed to an alcoholic Nirvana? It could be surmised that she would have sought increasingly the pleasure of companionship with her children and that, as a grandmother, she could have reached a thorough satisfaction of her deeply repressed maternal longings.

Case O

(Chronic Anxiety State)

The second patient to be discussed, a fifty-year-old married woman, was referred for psychotherapy by an internist. She herself had never thought of consulting a psychiatrist and firmly believed that her physical ailments, of which she had a long and varied history, were purely organic in nature. For some

twenty years, chronic gastrointestinal distress and a multitude
of hysterical symptoms had kept her under the constant care
of a physician. Then, a few months before she came to the
therapist, she developed a new symptom—a pain in her right
arm and shoulder so severe that she could not move the arm.
This partial paralysis was diagnosed as due to arthritis of a
cervical vertebrae; she was hospitalized and her spine was put
in traction. No relief was obtained and she felt bitter toward
the orthopedic surgeon and the internist who had advised such
drastic treatment. It was this latter physician who now sent
her to the psychiatrist. Treatment over the period of a year
(58 interviews in all) brought satisfactory therapeutic results.

The patient came to the first interview accompanied by her
husband who at once attempted to intrude himself into the foreground of the situation, assuming that he would be present at
the interview and act as liaison officer for his wife. The
therapist (a woman) resolutely ignored his efforts to divert
her attention to himself and saw the patient alone. In the course
of the hour the patient revealed that they had one child, a girl
whom they had adopted in infancy. This daughter was now
twenty-two years old and had been under the care of a psychoanalyst in a neighboring city for nearly two years. It was while
she and her husband were visiting the daughter that the pain
and paralysis in her arm had suddenly begun. Finding an un-
finished letter in her daughter's room, she had read it and been
horrified at the adolescent, exaggerated account of a drinking
party at which her daughter said she had gotten "tight." The
patient became greatly excited, weeping and "imagining the
worst" about her daughter. She awoke in great pain the next
morning and found that she could not move her arm above
the elbow.

In view of the long-standing chronic character of her complaints, therapy seemed futile. The therapist frankly did not
want to attempt a psychoanalytic treatment which would certainly be tedious and the outcome of which was extremely
doubtful. During the first interview the therapist, therefore,
said no more than that another diagnostic consultation was
desirable.

At the conclusion of the interview the patient and therapist rejoined the husband. He immediately began to ask many questions about what had happened and to bargain with the therapist about the fee. The psychiatrist mentioned a sum which was suitable for his income and standard of living. To this he objected strenuously and said, "That is what I pay for my daughter. We are under great expense and I can't afford that much for my wife." The therapist refused to reduce the fee and remained firm in the face of argument. The patient watched the therapist intently. When the therapist refused to give in to the husband's neurotic attempt to depreciate his wife by paying less for her treatment than the daughter's and was not sidetracked into becoming more interested in the husband than in the patient, the patient began to smile. She now showed genuine eagerness to return and left happily. This was an indication to the therapist that the patient would give her confidence to the therapist and that something could be accomplished in treatment.

The husband accompanied the patient on the second visit also. Again he expressed his wish to be present at the interview; again he countered the therapist's refusal with a demand to know what took place; again he insisted that the fee be reduced. Defeated a second time, he did not return.

In the course of treatment the following pertinent anamnestic material was obtained, although the patient never gave a complete history. From the beginning—when the patient revealed that her daughter was adopted—the therapist refrained from asking many questions, such as why she had no children of her own, and from probing into her sexual life generally.

The patient was the only daughter in a family of six children. She had three older brothers and two younger. The patient spoke of her mother and brothers in the most glowing terms; indeed, the entire picture given by the patient of her early life was obviously idealized. The family had always been dominated by the mother—a beautiful and intelligent, but apparently also a demanding, woman. The mother had always shown a strong preference for the patient's youngest brother. She suffered from a chronic illness and the patient nursed her devotedly during many long sieges. Her father seemed to have played little part in either her past or present life; toward him she felt only a perfunctory sense of duty.

In her early twenties, the patient had been married to a man almost as old as her parents. In many ways he resembled her mother; he was sweet and apparently very considerate but, unconsciously, extremely demanding. He had been very successful in business and soon retired, ostensibly because of an obscure chronic malady. The patient nursed her husband through repeated illnesses and followed him in and out of one hospital after another.

At one time the patient was in constant attendance on both her husband and her mother. It was during this period that she developed the spastic colitis and gastric distress from which she was still suffering at the time psychotherapy began. For these functional disturbances she had for many years been under the care of a very handsome physician who inspired strong, erotically tinged feelings in his patients. The weekly or biweekly visits to his office had afforded the patient great emotional satisfaction, although she complained that he always gave her too little time.

After a few years of marriage the patient and her husband adopted the little girl. Without ever assuming any responsibility for the care of the child, however, the patient handed her over to a nurse to whom the daughter became greatly attached. The patient's rationalization for neglecting the child was that she had to care for her husband and her mother. Actually she and her husband would travel or stay away from home for months at a time. Then when they returned home, after having left the child alone with the nurse (a compulsive woman but devoted to the child), the patient would resent the strong bond between the two. That the husband also depended greatly on this nurse created still further resentment in the patient. The nurse lived with the family for years and ruled it in much the same way the patient's mother had dominated her own family.

In spite of all these tensions and conflicts, the patient achieved a not-too-unsatisfactory equilibrium until she was 48

—two years before entering treatment—when several changes occurred. She reached the menopause; her husband became totally impotent; and the handsome physician whom she consulted for her many physical ailments moved out of town. Added to these difficulties was the fact that her daughter developed a severe neurosis; now even her ambitions for her daughter were frustrated. Because of some early evidence of musical talent in the child, the entire family had believed that she could become a great concert pianist. When it was finally all too apparent that she would never realize this ambition, the daughter developed a severe anxiety state which made it necessary to put her under the care of a psychiatrist in another city. It was when the patient and her husband visited the daughter and she read the letter, that the new symptom developed—the pain and paralysis in her right arm.

Of the 58 interviews comprising this treatment, 42 took place during the first half-year. For nearly four months the patient used the interviews chiefly for hypochondriacal complaints about her many symptoms: gastrointestinal distress, paresthesia in various parts of the body, transient headaches and flushing, sensitivity to heat and cold, insomnia, and the partially paralyzed arm.

As she brought up one symptom after the other, the therapist patiently reiterated that the patient must be suffering some discontent or conflict within her family, even though she consciously believed that she was completely satisfied with her husband and daughter. The fact that the onset of pain in the right arm was coincident with reading the daughter's letter was stressed. The abnormality of her life—devoted to nursing first her mother and then her husband—was related to the multiple functional illnesses from which she had suffered so many years. The concept of expressing emotions in body language was explained. It was pointed out again and again how she used physical symptoms as a way of expressing rebellion against being the one who always gave help and never received it.

At first the patient protested violently that she never wanted or asked for anything; she was always the generous giver. She admitted she had often felt others accepted attentions and service much too easily from her. This secondary gain, her feeling of being generous and good, she was loath to relinquish. As time went on, however, she expressed her unconscious rebellion against her self-imposed martyrdom bit by bit. She began to complain openly that her husband was spoiling their daughter, and that the nurse was more devoted to both the husband and the daughter than she was to her. It was clear that, in the patient's feelings, the daughter was like a sibling rival for dependent gratification. (The envy of her daughter, in relation both to the nurse and to the husband, seemed to be a repetition of a childhood envy of the youngest brother, her mother's favorite. This infantile envy of the brother in relation to the mother was never interpreted to the patient.)

The patient's relation to the therapist was mildly positive throughout. The rapport began from the moment the therapist refused to give in to the husband by reducing the fee and it became firm when, through friends, the patient gleaned a little personal information about the therapist's life. The fact that the therapist had suffered a disappointment about her own child increased the patient's bond with her and made her feel that the therapist was, in a sense, her equal. As a result she did not experience the feelings of inequality characteristic of the usual patient-doctor relationship.

For mutual convenience of patient and therapist, the interviews were held in the office in the psychiatrist's home. The patient was always loath to end any interview. In order to terminate the consultation the psychiatrist often took the patient home in her automobile, a natural and friendly act since the patient had no car and the analyst was going to her downtown office. In this social aftermath of the interview proper, the patient gave the analyst advice and critical comments about her clothes, her house, and her maid. She frequently brought some small gift, such as a special kind of candy or food. Once, when the therapist commented in the following hour that there might possibly be a symbolic meaning in this giving, the patient became very defensive and was deeply hurt. It seemed to the therapist that the slight positive aspects of the transference relationship would have been destroyed if any of the guilty restitutive or negative side had been made explicit; the relationship was too tenuous to bear discussion.

Soon definite improvement could be seen. By the end of the first half-year, the gastrointestinal symptoms were occurring infrequently and were less severe. Only rarely did the patient mention hypochondriacal feelings of hot or cold tingling. Her resentment against her husband and the nurse for their greater devotion to the daughter had been abreacted. She stopped hovering over her husband, began to go out socially and even defied the nurse and her husband by asking friends to her home. She had gained some insight into her jealousy of the daughter, both as a sibling rival and as a rival for her husband's attention. With the working through of these feelings, the pain and paralysis in the arm disappeared.

From the first interview it was apparent that one of the most powerful unconscious motives for being in treatment was rivalry with the daughter. Throughout the first half-year this unconscious narcissistic wish to have as much as the daughter was a powerful incentive for her to continue treatment.

After this conflict had been fairly well resolved, the therapy became centered around the symptoms obviously arising out of sexual tension. These were feelings of pressure in the bladder, rectum, and vagina. Of her own volition the patient consulted a gynecologist, a man who aroused erotic feelings in her. This physician substituted in part for the handsome internist who had deserted her. There is no doubt that the gynecological examinations and conversations with the gynecologist were sexually gratifying to her.

Treatment was terminated at the patient's own suggestion. During the last eight or ten interviews she had struggled unconsciously with the temptation to seek out some sexually gratifying partner. She would talk around such a possible solution for her tension and then immediately deny any feeling of sexual deprivation or frustration resulting from her husband's impotence. Unconsciously she was frightened by her sexual feelings. It was obviously to avoid further discussion of this that she decided to stop the treatment. Her training, background, and the reality situation itself made the likelihood of any extra-marital outlet not only remote but highly disturbing. It seemed wisest that the therapist not probe more deeply and the therapy was concluded by mutual consent.

The therapy in this case might be said to fall into two parts. The first and more intensive brought a resolution of the patient's conflict with her daughter and with it considerable relief from her long-standing gastrointestinal and hypochondriacal symptoms. This was accomplished through her relationship to the therapist who accepted her as an individual and therefore just as worthy of consideration as her daughter, restored her self-esteem, and gave her permission to enjoy herself without constant self-sacrifice. It was the patient's awareness of the therapist's confidence in her that constituted the corrective emotional experience without which these changes would not have come about. In the second part, when the patient's sexual tension dominated the therapy, the permissiveness of the therapist, by which the patient had gained so much, became somewhat threatening, and termination of treatment seemed advisable in order to hold the patient's good, though limited, adjustment.

In the two years after treatment was terminated, the patient called the therapist on three occasions to give a report and ask in a friendly fashion about the psychiatrist and her family. Twice the therapist telephoned the patient as a friendly gesture, and once, at the patient's invitation, dined with the patient and her husband.

During these two years the patient's husband was ill a great deal of the time, confined to bed at home or in the hospital. The patient, conscious of some irritation at the restrictions this imposed on her, endeavored to go out in as normal a fashion as possible during the day with women friends. In the evenings, however, she felt awkward at being a "lone woman" and so stayed home with her husband who kept her busy doing innumerable services for him. The husband was trying to get the daughter to return to the home, but the patient said frankly that it was better for all of them to have her live elsewhere. The daughter had written an extravagantly fanciful letter to her parents about being in love with a young man whom she described in great detail; this story she later confessed was pure fantasy. The mother took the letter with a fair degree of calm but was concerned by the implications of such a fantasy.

During this period, the patient had only occasional gastro-intestinal symptoms. She had discontinued her practice of running to doctors and consulted one only every few months. The only symptom which still bothered her was her insomnia. This she attributed to the fact that her husband "disturbed" her. It seems certain that continuous, unrelieved sexual tension was mainly responsible for the insomnia.

Comments on Case O

Here we have a patient, unconsciously a dependent, narcissistic individual, who was always thwarted in the satisfaction she sought. She was jealous of her mother's affection for a younger brother and so had a strong ambivalent attachment to her. By her marriage to a man the age of her mother, her dependent needs were displaced to the husband. His severe illnesses, however, reversed the relationship; he became dependent on her and demanded constant care from her. She repressed her rebelliousness at these demands and developed an over-helpful martyr-like attitude. Her rebelliousness and her need for attention asserted themselves in multiple gastrointestinal symptoms. These symptoms gave her a reason for consulting a physician from whom she for many years received dependent and erotic gratification, but he finally moved to another city. Her relationship to her daughter was ambivalent also; when her narcissistic ambitions which were to be realized through the adopted daughter's achievements as a concert pianist were foiled by the daughter's failure and illness, she had feelings of both resentment and pleasure. She was relieved when the daughter was away from home and began unconsciously to hope that the nurse and her husband would now shower on her the love which had been given to the daughter. In this she was disappointed again.

At this time she suffered more frustration; her sexual problem had been greatly accentuated as a result of her husband's impotence and of the probable increase in her own sexual energy because of the climacteric. When the daughter's letter made her suspect the girl of sexual promiscuity, her rage was aroused that her daughter had the sexual gratification which she was denied. This rage was expressed by the paralyzed arm.

For the treatment of this patient a limited goal was planned from the initial interview. The age of the patient, her social and marital situation, and her restricted ego span as indicated by her past history, made it seem probable that even the most intensive therapy could achieve no more than could a relatively brief treatment. In a long-term therapy there was danger of unearthing new, perhaps insoluble, conflicts which would leave the patient in a worse and not a better state of emotional health.

The patient's many ailments throughout her marriage and her failure to have a child indicated that there had been something radically wrong and unsatisfying with the patient's marital life for many years. Yet even in the face of so much dissatisfaction, the patient had been unable to make any serious attempt to change the situation. It had never even occurred to her consciously that she was unhappy. She claimed that hers was one of the so-called perfect marriages. At her age, tied to a demanding husband, surrounded by a close and gossipy social group, divorce or an extra-marital solution was impossible.

No inquiry was ever made concerning the reason for adopting a child. The seeming lack of curiosity on the therapist's part concerning important psychosexual problems in the patient's life was merely a wariness lest problems be stirred up in a patient who the therapist felt was, to a great extent, untreatable. After the first interview the therapist, therefore, deliberately avoided the problems of her psychosexual life.

There was, however, some therapeutic gain. The patient improved considerably in her psychosomatic symptoms; she was relieved of the hysterical paralysis and, for the most part, of her gastrointestinal distress. This is evidence of her having found some emotional satisfaction, of having gained a modicum of insight. Following treatment, she was able to accept her life with less strain and allow herself more social pleasure—all without the necessity of enduring constant physical ailments.

In this case, the therapist kept the transference relationship at a low pitch throughout by deliberately allowing the patient to feel that her sexual frustration was due only to her husband's impotence, even though it seemed probable that this stemmed from a severe internal conflict which must have existed from earliest childhood.

Discussion

From a rigid theoretical viewpoint, the two cases just discussed might have been judged almost inaccessible to any form of psychotherapy—even a long-term psychoanalytic treatment. Both patients were in their fifties, both had lost the possibility of any marital sexual life. In the first patient, severe drinking developed late in life in response to an extremely traumatic situation in her marriage. Previously this patient seems to have been a rather immature and inhibited woman but essentially healthy, with no psychosomatic or neurotic symptoms. The second patient had a long history of many functional disturbances in the gastrointestinal tract and of multiple hysterical symptoms. Engrafted on the chronic illness was an acute conversion symptom of recent origin. From her illness and neurotic behavior this patient had secured so much secondary gain that she had little incentive to give up her symptoms.

Indications for treatment in both cases were slender. The therapist's decision to attempt therapy was, in each case, based on the feeling that the patient had confidence in the therapist's ability to relieve the immediate distress. In response to the therapist's remark that the patient had been hurt by someone near to her, the first patient, a shy, moderately inhibited person, took the therapist into her confidence. She felt that the therapist understood the narcissistic injury which had led to her drinking. The goal of this therapy was to heal the injury and restore the patient's self-esteem. How was this accomplished?

The positive feelings toward the therapist were utilized in encouraging the patient to abreact her hostile feelings against her husband. With growing recognition on the patient's part that her anger against her husband was justifiable, she felt more able to accept the therapist's confidence in her ability to act maturely. The therapist avoided any mothering, dictating, or advisory attitudes; she did not at any time reassure the patient about the drinking or warn her of its possible recurrence, as this would have been interpreted by the patient as an expression of doubt concerning her newly regained mature behavior. After the patient announced in the second interview that she felt no further desire for alcohol, drinking was not mentioned again. As another token of her confidence in the patient's capacity to act and decide for herself, the therapist allowed the patient to determine the frequency of the interviews. This attitude toward the patient was the exact opposite of the husband's depreciatory condemning treatment. As a result of the difference in the attitudes of the therapist and the husband, a psychological healing took place in the patient's ego. This increased the ego's capacity and enabled the patient to handle her own situation; to stop the drinking which she had used as a revenge against her husband for his lack of confidence and affection.

Neither this patient's unconsciously strong dependent needs —these must have been strong since she had developed drinking as her regressive solution—nor her sexual feelings were stimulated in the therapy. To have pushed analysis further in this case would have meant either a long therapy or the patient's anxious withdrawal from treatment before any change in attitude could have taken place.

In the first interview with the second patient, the therapist saw no indication for undertaking treatment until after the session when the therapist realized that her refusal to reduce the fee gave the patient a feeling that at last she had found someone who would not depreciate her. With this moment, the patient gave the therapist as much confidence as she was capable of, and the therapy could be said to have begun. But the prognosis was poor; the chronic character of her symptoms, the long-standing secondary gain from her hypochondria, all seemed to indicate the futility of any type of therapy. Resolution of the acute conversion symptom, the paralyzed arm (which was clearly related to her conflict with the daughter), could have been defined as one goal of therapy, yet it seemed doubtful whether this symptom could be cured without running the risk of becoming hopelessly involved in the chronic and other severe neurotic difficulties this patient presented. The narcissistic competition with her daughter seemed to be a motive which could be used safely and constructively in the treatment.

Because of her rivalry with her daughter, the patient would have enjoyed four or five interviews a week. Such intensive treatment would have satisfied her unconscious dependent and strong latent homosexual longings, and would also have served as a revenge against her husband since he would have had to pay more for her treatment. Two facts made the therapist decide at once against the standard form of psychoanalysis: the difficulty of weaning such a deeply dependent patient from treatment and the great improbability of the patient's making a better sexual adjustment in view of her age, background, and social status.

An initial positive transference relationship was established when the patient felt that the therapist was aligned with her and would not let the husband interfere. This positive transference, plus the narcissistic rivalry with the daughter, gave sufficient impetus to the patient to continue treatment and eventually to gain some insight into her conflicts. Since the positive feelings were not intense, the treatment was not complicated by the frustrated rage which would have arisen had the patient become emotionally more involved with the therapist. Such negative feelings as existed were expressed in the socially acceptable ways of giving advice or mildly criticizing the therapist's clothes, house, and maid and these did not need to be analyzed.

In both cases, the patient was enabled to meet her present situation with greater satisfaction and without the necessity of maintaining the neurotic behavior which had become chronic —in the first instance over a period of ten years, in the second over a period of more than twenty.

The therapeutic results in these two cases may be called "transference cures" in the sense of the definition given earlier in the book. The positive aspects of the transference relationship were not interpreted but were used throughout as a motive for treatment.

Although the results with these two patients are not great, they are commensurate with the situation in each case: the age of the patient, the family circumstances, and the social possibilities. These cases may be used as examples of the value of setting a limited goal for treatment rather than being dissatisfied that more drastic changes could not be effected. They show, furthermore, how much can be accomplished in a transference relationship which is kept within the limits of a good rapport.

Helen Vincent McLean, M.D.

Chapter 15

VARIATIONS IN GOAL AND TECHNIQUE

If the great variety of clinical material that every therapist meets is to be handled expeditiously and efficiently, a flexible approach to the problems presented is imperative. The determining factors in the choice of goal, general approach, and subsidiary techniques—such as the clinical problem, the practical realities of the patient's situation, etc.—are discussed elsewhere in the book. The cases to be presented in this chapter illustrate the fact that although depth of therapy varies only in the matter of degree, the diversity existing in personality and reality factors makes necessary great differences in approach and technique.

In the following cases, two outstanding factors determine both the main strategy and the tactics of each phase of therapy: the functional efficiency of the patient's ego, and the particular knowledge and experience of the therapist. An early evaluation of the ego strength is invaluable in the treatment of all infrequently seen cases and becomes of paramount importance when an uncovering type of approach is used. The therapist's training and experience determine not only his skill at using (and thus his predilection for) certain techniques, but also his knowledge of the psychodynamics in those problems which have been ascertained by years of intensive research.

It will be noted that the degree to which the therapist deals with conscious and unconscious material varies widely in the five cases to be discussed. In the first three, a great deal of unconscious material (as revealed by transference reactions and dreams) was analyzed frankly and in detail. In the last two, the therapist was consciously careful to deal with only the more immediate problems, and in analyzing them to evaluate carefully how much could be done without mobilizing deeper conflicts.

The first three cases are similar in that all are analyses of fundamental conflicts. They differ, however, in the depth to which their unconscious conflicts are treated, so that even in these three cases the analyst's approach varied, from case to case, in the selection of material. Case P is restricted to the analysis of a traumatic nucleus discovered early in treatment; Case Q is concerned mainly with a central conflict already determined and understood from previous research in the treatment of similar cases; while Case R is a thoroughgoing analysis, comparable to the standard psychoanalysis, leading to extensive personality change.

In these cases, positive and negative transference reactions, as well as the dreams, were observed and utilized exactly as in a standard psychoanalysis. No effort was made to avoid the initial development of a transference neurosis—although it was, of course, so controlled that it did not become an impediment to therapeutic progress. Intellectual discussions were avoided as diligently as in a regular psychoanalysis, the therapist waiting for feelings and associations and dreams. This was true whether the patient sat up or lay down; in fact, only one patient ever chose to lie down and then only for two or three interviews.

When patients come for only one hour a week and sit vis-à-vis the therapist, it is believed to be of greatest importance to wait for emotions, since the patient may otherwise try to convert the interview into a social hour. At times, in such a situation, the therapist may become uncomfortable and feel called upon to say something; this, however, will only slow down the development of the transference relationship. When the therapist avoids intellectualizations and quietly waits for the patient's true emotions to manifest themselves, even though he must wait through periods of silence, transference feelings often develop even more rapidly and with more reality than when the patient is reclining.

In contrast to the first three cases, Cases S and T illustrate the frequent need to define *how little* the therapist should do at times to ensure the best health of the patient and those associated with him. This means a careful defining of one's goals and may entail any degree of handling unconscious material— to the extent of not touching it at all, as is shown especially clearly in Case T. These last two cases also involved very conscious attention to keeping transference reactions at a minimum, just sufficient to ensure a good "working relationship."

———

The first case to be discussed illustrates that it is sometimes possible, following an early, careful exploration, to isolate a nuclear situation in a patient's life which has immediate bearing on the present acute illness. By concentrating one's attention on this conflict, ignoring all lesser disturbances, the way may be opened for a resumption of growth in a relatively short time. The following case involved first careful exploration and then definite direction of the treatment as soon as the traumatic nucleus was suspected. In this instance, the encapsulated traumatic nucleus lent itself to ready revival in the relationship to the therapist.

Case P

(Acute Depression)

A highly intelligent young man of nineteen, who was to be inducted into the Army in three months' time, came for treatment because he was so depressed that he was unable to concentrate on his classes at a technical school; this depression was aggravated by anxiety lest he fail and have to face his father's disappointment. The patient could come for no more than twenty minutes at a time, once or twice a week, but was seen for a total of 35 interviews in the short period before his induction. He was found to be dependable with regard to his appointments and unusually sincere in his desire for help so that, in spite of the brevity of both individual interviews and the treatment as a whole, excellent therapeutic results were achieved.

In giving his history, the patient had great difficulty in reporting the fact that his mother had been accidentally burned to death when he was three. He said he could remember nothing about her and had assumed that his stepmother (whom his father married a year later) was his own mother until she suddenly told him the truth when he was eight. He reported that at the time he had made no comment but had felt stunned. Asked how he got along with women, the patient looked at the therapist (a woman) through narrowed eyes and said, "You seem to be receding further and further into the distance." To the comment that possibly he had some anxiety in relation to women, he answered irritably, "Maybe so."

Although he at first stated he had never felt anything but love for his father—"I love him too much"—it immediately became clear that the patient had very mixed feelings toward him. Now a skilled laborer, the father had for years owned and operated a string of gambling houses. Even though the patient was ashamed of his father's past occupation, it was only in gambling that he felt he could be as successful as his father. Conscious of a great need to look up to his father, he told boys from good families that his father was an "electrical engineer" and boasted to the gamblers' sons that his father was the best gambler of any of them. He had always wished that his father were either an engineer or an Army man, and now his father wanted *him* to be both. The therapist suggested that possibly there had been a feeling of being hurt and humiliated in those earlier years and that now, in a sense, he wanted to disappoint his father by being just a gambler. The patient said he was quite conscious of this and that he had the feeling that he could not be better than his father.

Early in the treatment all the fears connected with the fact that his stepmother had been unusually seductive with this boy came to the fore with much resistance. This resistance gradually became more obvious as his tension and resentment toward the therapist increased. His possible fears of the seductiveness of the treatment relationship were interpreted, but before his erotic transference feelings became conscious the patient angrily left treatment for a week. While struggling with sexual feelings and conflicts, he asked to lie on the couch so as not to see the therapist, but after a few interviews the patient of his own volition sat up again.

His class work began to improve, but still the patient felt depressed. What was the use? He said that everyone seemed "cold" to him. There were long philosophical recitals of his feeling that all his life he had been "looking for something in reality that is familiar, that I knew a long time ago. I don't know what it can be. It is something steadying. Some day I feel I'll find it." The therapist suggested that he might possibly have known steadying influences before his own mother died. The patient said he remembered nothing, then added that he knew hers was a fine family since he had come to know some of them in recent years. But when the analyst ventured the opinion that his first great inhibition in integrating reality might, perhaps, have come with his mother's being burned to death, the patient dropped the subject at once, saying stubbornly that he did not even know her maiden name.

The feeling of unreality about women, the longings for "something familiar that was steadying," and the defensiveness about recalling the mother's death led the therapist at this point to focus on that incident as being possibly of primary importance to the patient. All subsequent analysis was pushed in that direction.

By the beginning of the third month of treatment—when the patient was doing good work in his classes and was getting along better with his father—the therapist thought he seemed ready to grapple with his underlying conflict. In reply to a question as to whether he had ever asked his father about his own mother, the patient said, "No," adding, "But did I tell you I went to the hospital and got my birth certificate three weeks ago?" When asked why he had done this, he replied, "To find out my mother's last name." The therapist asked what it was. "Can you believe it?" he said, "I can't recall it now,"—then added with depreciation, "I think it sounded sort of middle class." The next hour he said he had not looked up the name, but had tested his father by telling him he had dreamed that he (the patient) had set fire to his mother; this had elicited only a "Hmmm" from the father.

The therapist's comment was, "You must have repressed angry feelings towards your mother. I wonder if, since you

were only three years old, you took her death as a desertion?"
The patient became irritable and replied obliquely, "I must
have been a stinker, for no relative would take me." He was
told that he probably hadn't been a stinker but that one feels
so when he is not sure of being loved and is angry. Asked if
he could look up his mother's name, the patient silenced the
therapist with an angry, "I don't want to." He hesitated, then—
"I have it on me. I don't want to look, because before when
I looked at it, I was uneasy for hours afterwards."

After a pause, the patient continued, "In the Army I will
improve my gambling." When the therapist asked if he were
trying to punish someone he answered, "My parents." He then
took out his wallet, looking for the birth certificate. He handed
the contents to the therapist—driver's license, ration book, false
birth certificate with the stepmother's name on it, bills, etc. At
last he came to the certificate bearing his own mother's name,
but did not hand it over. He commented, "The name is G—,"
and replaced the paper in his wallet.

"You hand over everything but the certificate bearing your
mother's name," said the therapist. "That you keep for yourself. I feel you have been repressing not only your angry feelings for her, but also, perhaps, the fact that you and she loved
each other." His eyes on the distance, the patient said, "I was
thinking of writing my aunt for a picture of Mother." Suddenly tears welled up and the patient threw himself sobbing on
the couch. After ten minutes he grew calm and said, with
great feeling, "Silly, but I feel as if my own mother were all
around me here. It's something so familiar."

The emotional change in the patient was dramatic, he was
ecstatically moved. Turning his attention to the therapist, he
ordered her, "Tell me all about *your* standards. I will accept
them. Tell me what is right about sex, possessions, religion.
Talk to me as you would to an adolescent." He had never
asked any opinion or advice before. When the therapist answered some questions, the patient rushed on to others, as if
he were less interested in the answers than in the experience of
talking. At the end of the interview, he said, "I know who
I've been talking to—my mother! And I feel wonderful!"

From this point on, until he left for ASTP a few weeks later, the patient felt no more depression and worked in his courses with enthusiasm. He was more considerate of his parents but recognized their inconsistencies and conflicts.

The patient continued in the ASTP for ten months, rising to be student commander of his group of 400. When the ASTP was abandoned, he wrote the therapist realistically about it. He has since returned twice to see the therapist socially, when he has had leaves, and appeared healthy and happy. At present, two years after he left treatment, the patient is a commissioned officer in the Army and writes that he has never been so satisfied with his relationships with people as now.

Comments on Case P

What happened in this boy's treatment?

To reconstruct his early trauma, we find a boy losing his mother at three. The treatment brought the tremendous longing for the mother into consciousness, which (with the tears) was the beginning of acceptance of her death as a reality, a renunciation. For him emotionally, she died at this moment, and the weeping was the resolution of his conflict. Now, at last, he could begin the identification with father-figures, his officers. His wish to fail in his courses seemed to be an acute mobilization of his long bitterness, of hating everyone, of refusing to accept anyone in his mother's place. This bitterness may have been mobilized before induction because soon he must leave home, a home about which he had great ambivalence, both anger and longing. It was as if he said, "I refuse to identify myself with my father or to do anything for anyone except Mother."

Several questions arise as we review this treatment. Since the patient had to leave for the Army shortly after this abreaction, was the death of the mother thoroughly digested? This boy had suffered many rejections: his mother had died when he was small, his relatives had refused to take him, his father had remarried, and his stepmother, whom he at first regarded as his own mother, had told him abruptly that he did not belong to her. The therapist neither rejected nor deserted him; he left her with a new confidence in people. Will this confidence sustain itself through the rigors and deprivation of Army life? Much depends on his experience in the Army. Up to the present, all seems to be well.

Is this patient on the road to recapturing loyalty to his father? or is it just to the Army? Since the mother died when the patient was three years old, he never had a chance to work through the oedipal battle and establish a real identification with his father. This patient certainly established a good relationship as a man with the therapist; but she did not send him away—it was the Army who took him away—so one wonders whether he has really emancipated himself from her and can become a man with *any* woman. His future heterosexual relationships will answer this question.

Another question may well be raised. Can this nineteen-year-old man, through this short abreactive experience and its interpretation—and possibly through a continuation of the transference relationship—do that which otherwise he could not have done? Can he go on through a fairly normal growth, be successful, have more security and gratifications? Can he do all this without a further, and intensive, therapeutic procedure? Such breaking of a fixation often happens in our civilian patients and frequently leads to a good therapeutic success. What this young man meets in the Army may be too traumatic to allow for the same growth he might have had in civilian life.

This case shows the need in any type of psychotherapy to search as rapidly as possible for clues pointing to a significant, possibly traumatic, nuclear life experience. The pressure of his prospective induction probably helped the therapy in speeding up the mobilization of the encapsulated trauma, the separation from the mother, as related to the imminent separation. Progress can be attributed also to the fact that this relatively isolated situation was the particular source of the acute and immediate difficulty which brought the patient to treatment, and to the fact that the therapist was a woman so that the trauma could be reenacted within the transference relationship without difficulty.

To find such a center of conflict is especially important in brief treatment and demands careful exploration of the entire problem at the outset, with attention gradually becoming focused on what may be the most significant factors in the immediate illness. The rationale of such a treatment—restricting one's attention to an encapsulated trauma—is that after resolution of that nucleus of trouble, growth formerly impeded by it may now go on, gratifications be forthcoming and confidence increase. This does not mean a working-through *in the treatment* of all conflicts, but one of such significance as to make for real change. The great importance and broad implications of this chain of events have been emphasized in an earlier chapter. In view of the results obtained in similar cases, the prognosis for continued growth in this particular case seems good.

———

The next case shows how a therapist can, *from the first interview,* consciously direct the treatment through the resolution of a deep and widespread personality problem with psychosomatic expression, if he understands the fundamental dynamics of the disorder. In this instance, the knowledge gained through painstaking research by psychoanalysis in intensive analyses allowed the therapist to effect a resolution of the neurosis within a fairly brief period.

Case Q

(Bronchial Asthma)

A recent graduate of a medical school, twenty-four years old, single, came for treatment because he felt unable to practice on account of severe asthma attacks. He had a history of asthma since the age of fourteen when he had gone on a diet and had reduced his weight from over 200 to 155 pounds. Four years before coming for psychotherapy, tests had found him allergic to beef, pork, and chicken. He was seen approximately once a week over a period of nine months with good therapeutic results.

The therapist (a woman) was able, because of her previous knowledge of the fundamental dynamic structure of the asthmatic disorder, to direct treatment at once to the central problem—deep dependence on a mother figure plus the fear of becoming estranged from her by somehow offending her.[1]

The patient's mother had died when he was three. Of this event he recalled only her leaving for the hospital on a stretcher, and crying as they took her away. The next six years the patient spent with an aunt and uncle, then returning to his own home when his father remarried. The patient was at first hostile to the stepmother, but soon became fond of her. The patient expressed great disgust at the beginning of the treatment at his aunt's "infantile greediness and obesity"; he remembered, however, that as a child he had longed to be fat like her. This attitude toward his aunt's stoutness may be taken as indicating a relationship which later became plain—that his own obesity had served as a defense against the conflict arising out of his erotic attraction to the stepmother.

Almost immediately the patient developed a strong dependent attitude toward the therapist and wished her, like other women, to assume full responsibility for his behavior, erotic or otherwise. Although this dependence was pointed out to him, the patient made no resistance. He was elated over his treatment interviews and refused to listen to any warning that resistance might come later. He was certain nothing could interfere with his friendliness toward the therapist.

The first time the patient came to an interview suffering from an attack of asthma, he attributed it to having had to

[1] T. M. French, F. Alexander, et al., "Psychogenic Factors in Bronchial Asthma," *Psychosomatic Medicine Monographs*. 1941.

hurry in the morning. In discussing it, he recalled his resentment at his aunt's attempts to keep him infantile, his anxiety when his uncle chided him for being snuggled too closely by his aunt, and his uneasiness with girls from the time he was six. He added that he was now conscious of the fact that he felt insecure when he was alone. The therapist had encouraged him to take a job to cover his expenses, and he said that the asthma attacks were severe whenever he was left alone there at night. It was suggested to the patient that his asthma might come whenever his dependence was threatened. The therapist indicated that since his attacks began at fourteen, she wondered whether the asthma had some relationship to impulses in him that might threaten a pleasant relationship with a mother-person. Immediately to this the patient associated that his step-mother had been very young, voluptuous, and openly seductive with him. In the five years from the time he went to live with her until he was fourteen, the patient was often consciously aroused sexually. Then, wanting to become more attractive physically, he had reduced. Although from that time on he had attacks of asthma, he was no longer conscious of sexual feelings toward his stepmother.

Hostile dependence toward the therapist, however, was soon mobilized. When she refused to offer to intercede for him with his draft board, the patient's asthma became worse. When she continued to refuse despite his constant hints in this direction, he developed an intense rage and said that even though the draft board ridiculed her for placing his asthma on an emotional basis, she should be willing to risk her reputation as a physician to save his life. The therapist's acceptance of his rage as belonging to his conflict, coupled with this frustration of his dependence on her, constituted the first and most basic step in the resolution of his conflict and the relief of his asthma.

After this, the patient felt more independent. He began dating girls and even had the courage to ask for another date when refused the first time. After dating one attractive girl for some time, however, he became concerned over the fact that she still entertained some affection for a former beau, and so he broke off with her. His insistence that the therapist give her opinion about this provoked from her the comment that perhaps what he really wished was to find out something about the therapist's personal life and attitudes. The patient was surprised but admitted the charge.

For several interviews thereafter, he expressed anger over the "faithlessness of married women." Finally the therapist suggested that he was more in conflict about those who were faithful to their husbands. His rejoinder that he could not have any conflict about the therapist as she was "too old" for him, was met with the comment that possibly he feared he was "too young." The patient was breathing heavily and expressed amazement that he could think of nothing to say. Only rarely, he said, did he feel so uneasy in talking to "men or women." Asked, "Why bring men into it?" he retorted resentfully, "Why not?" At this point, when he was breathing with difficulty and seemed on the verge of an attack, the therapist observed quietly that possibly his concern had something to do with her husband. The patient appeared startled, but relaxed almost immediately, his noisy breathing subsided, and he admitted he had been wondering about him.

Just after this, the therapist went on her vacation. An interview shortly after her return may be regarded as the second decisive step in the treatment.

When the patient came to the office, he was in the midst of a severe asthma attack which had not responded to ephedrin, and was obviously suffering great distress. He said that he had had several attacks during the week, but always at night. This attack he again explained on the basis of having had to hurry. After a few minutes, he said he could remember nothing they had discussed before her vacation. It occurred to the therapist that he was probably angry with her for going away with her husband, so she mentioned that when he had found his girl was still somewhat attached to a former suitor, he had dropped her immediately. The patient understood the allusion. "Oh, yes," he said, "and this probably brings up your husband whom we were discussing as a rival before you left." Suddenly the asthma stopped completely. The patient began to laugh and said he could hardly believe it, that not even adrenalin had ever ended an attack so suddenly. He was at last convinced that he had been inhibiting feelings toward the therapist and he now confessed erotic impulses to her.

In the following interviews, the patient expressed resentment and humiliation as if he had been a rejected suitor, and he depreciated the therapist. Within a few weeks, the asthma had subsided entirely and the patient, for the first time, began to want to share things with women on an equal plane. Having found that rejecting the analyst and depreciating her as a woman was accepted calmly, the patient said he no longer felt anxiety about telling a girl he did not love her, he no longer feared that such a rejection would precipitate a rage in the girl that he would not be able to endure. He now felt a great sense of freedom and could act with both friendliness and masculine aggressiveness.

As a result of this improvement, not only in removal of the symptom but in a general change of attitude, the therapy was terminated in the ninth month.

The patient has now been an officer in the medical corps for three years and is feeling very well. He has had only one slight attack of asthma, a few months after he entered the service when he was in a difficult situation. When heard from last, he was engaged to be married.

Comments on Case Q

This case illustrates the need for a therapy relatively less intensive than the preceding case, but one which accomplished an *actual analysis* of the conflict because the therapist already knew the dynamic structure of the asthmatic syndrome and knew that the chief mechanism in its resolution is confession. As a result, the interpretations were designed to facilitate the patient's confession of disturbing impulses and were directed toward relieving the disturbance arising from the frustrated dependence and the anxiety engendered by his sexual wishes toward the therapist which threatened his dependent relationship to her.

It is believed that a real ego change was achieved in this case. The therapy was directed in such a way as to avoid intellectual discussion and to encourage a re-living, in relationship to the therapist, of the patient's dependence with all its threats of frustration and of anxiety aroused by intruding erotic impulses.

It must be reemphasized that, since the therapist had the advantage of knowing the fundamental dynamic constellation in asthma cases as worked out in earlier research, she could work more rapidly and with more assurance than would have been possible without this knowledge. As soon as a significant issue arose, the therapist felt free to encourage its analysis immediately. Especially in cases such as this, where interviews are infrequent, must the therapist be careful not to fall into the error of discussing the dynamics with the patient intellectually, but to use his knowledge to promote the treatment by mobilizing those feelings in the transference relationship which are necessary for a resolution of the conflict.

———

The following case demonstrates that a thorough analysis, leading to extensive personality change, can be carried on in weekly interviews. That little more conscious direction was required of the therapist in this treatment than in a standard psychoanalysis of such a problem, was again due to some knowledge of the dynamics involved, although in this case they were neither so well known to the therapist beforehand nor so dramatically portrayed as in the asthma case just reported.

This case also shows that an adolescent girl who has a relatively good ego can be analyzed without taking her away from her environment or attempting to treat simultaneously the most significant adult in her life. Such a patient might have been seen far more often were the therapist uneasy about controlling the situation, although this patient was not much inclined to act out her impulses. It will be noticed that this therapy is conducted much as in cases where the patient is seen very frequently.

Case R

(Neurotic Conflict in an Adolescent Girl)

A fifteen-year-old girl was brought to treatment by her mother because of a complicated picture of general anxiety, depression, and habitual vomiting. She was seen for a total of 65 weekly interviews over a period of seventeen months, with excellent results.

At the initial interview the mother, well-dressed, intellectual, and an obviously successful business woman, said that ever since her daughter had started to school at the age of six, she had exhibited a constant nervousness and pallor, with vomiting each school morning. During examination periods this vomiting became so severe that frequently she either missed the examination or had to go to bed for weeks afterward. Connected with this was acute anxiety lest she not be among the top three in her class. The mother was also concerned because the girl refused to go anywhere unless accompanied by either her mother or her one friend, a girl who dominated the patient easily. As for friendships with boys, the idea filled the patient with panic.

Of herself, the mother said she and the patient's father—a brilliant, attractive man—had been married after a courtship of eight years, that she had continued to work and they had lived with her parents. A year later the patient was born. Leaving the baby in the care of the maternal grandmother, she returned to work. The father proved unsuccessful in business, irresponsible, and secretive about accumulating debts—which his wife had to meet. This situation created much strife between them; she repeatedly threatened to divorce him and he, in the presence of the child, said he would commit suicide if she did. Finally, when the patient was five, they separated and were divorced a year later. When the patient was twelve, her mother remarried and brought her new husband home to live with her parents. The patient was said to have been "delighted" about this marriage and also about the birth of a sister a year and a half later. As both the mother and stepfather worked, the standard of living was excellent. The children were left in the grandmother's care.

The mother said the patient had always been a feeding problem, vomiting often in infancy. During the first five years of her life she had had many serious illnesses, so that an unusual amount of nursing care fell to the grandmother who became overprotective; even now the grandmother displayed great concern over the patient's vomiting and constantly urged the girl to eat more. The patient was said to have been a well-behaved and reasonable child who was not demanding and for whom punishment was unnecessary.

The mother added that before the divorce the patient had been "passionately attached" to her father and was with him constantly, as he spent most of his time at home. When the grandmother (who disliked him) depreciated him to the child, the patient staunchly defended him. For the first year or two after the divorce, the patient continued to see him with fair regularity; then she seemed to change toward him, fearing that he would try to take her away. She was said not to have thought of him for many years. This version of the patient's difficulties was later found to contain many distortions of the facts.

Since this psychotherapy covered seventeen months and was by nature an intensive character analysis, the amount of material accumulated is too great to permit a full report of the treatment progress. We shall attempt only a brief résumé of the more salient features.

During the first months of treatment the patient was extremely tense, cried frequently, and talked in such a low voice that at times the therapist (a woman) had great difficulty in hearing her. Even from the very beginning, however, she reacted to the treatment situation much as would an adult with a good ego. She took the initiative at each interview and spontaneously reported dreams when she found they were acceptable. Almost no advice was given her at any time; intellectual discussions were avoided; interpretations (confined to the present realities) were grasped with intelligence and relative quickness.

During the early sessions, the patient's main preoccupations were with her scholastic standing and the rivalry at her school for grades. She said she had vomited every morning from the time she started to school and, before that, sometimes when she wanted to make her grandmother give in to her. In these first few interviews, she expressed resentment at her father for leaving her mother, and concern because her mother had to work so hard. The patient recalled her father's great kindness to her as a child, and her affection for him in those first years, followed by bitterness when he left. He had told her he would come for her some day. Once, when she was seven (barely more than a year after the divorce), she awoke from a nap, saw him in the yard and ran screaming for her grandmother. She recalled a haunting fear of meeting him on the street, but made no connection between this and her present fear of going out alone.

Soon the patient began very cautiously to reveal—with many tears—that the reason she was depressed was that her mother was "disgusted" with her. Since early childhood, she had resented her mother's violent temper. At the same time she had felt guilty because it had been repeatedly pointed out to her (by both mother and grandmother) that it was for the patient's sake that the mother worked so hard and was never in the home. Usually some such comment as, "If you are ever half as good as your mother . . ." had been added. The therapist agreed that it must have been difficult for her not to be allowed to be angry when the adults could and did lose their temper, and then discussed ambivalence in general with her.

The patient mentioned that when she was four her grandmother had once been delighted when the child had cried for hours because the grandmother went away. The therapist took this opportunity to talk of the need some adults have to keep people dependent on them. This led at once to accounts of similar episodes with her own mother. The patient now became much more free in expressing disappointment and annoyance with her mother and grandmother. She began to observe and recount incidents between her little half-sister and the grandmother which she felt were similar to her own early experiences. This kept the discussion in the interviews quite concrete.

As time went on the nervous weeping ceased and it became evident that this girl had a truly warm nature and an unusually interesting mind. The patient was now feeling more confident and self-reliant, and several interviews were concerned with tales of her mother's frustration of her tentative gestures toward independent action, toward freedom, followed by an angry refusal to accept the patient's attempts at appeasement. Other sessions brought accounts of the mother's having held over her daughter for years the threat of sending her away to boarding school and college—a prospect which had terrified the timid girl. She had implored her mother to allow her to remain at home and attend the university in the city, but the mother had been adamant.

The patient made steady progress in the therapy. Just about five months after she began treatment she stopped vomiting, took her examinations with ease, and decided not to work any longer for more than average grades. She had become much more self-confident and felt less guilty toward her mother. She had acquired many girl friends, but was as frightened as ever with boys. The patient now decided that she would actually like to go to a university half-way across the state, but her mother did an about-face and declared that she could not afford it, that the patient must go to the one in the city!

It was significant of the girl's personality that even though she made a strong identification with the permissive therapist, she rarely acted out her feelings. For instance, when the mother now said, "You'll have to go to the university here in the city," the patient's comment to the therapist was realistic: "It's clear what she's up to—but I'll let her stew over it. I don't go to the college for over a year yet anyway. No use arguing that out now. Maybe she'll eventually get used to my not being her baby any longer."

Moreover, in her new detachment she could now recognize that her mother had never freed herself of her dependence on the grandmother, and that it was her mother's own guilt and resentment toward the grandmother that led to the frequent conflicts between them. Instead of feeling as irritated with her mother as she had been, she could now feel somewhat sorry for her.

It became evident that the patient and her mother had always competed for the attention of the father-figure. Her earliest memories were of being taken by her own father to watch him play ball in the neighborhood lot. (She had now recalled much more about her own father; for weeks the interviews were filled with depression, as her resentment at his desertion and her guilt at turning against him came out.) Since her mother's second marriage, the patient had often gone to games with her stepfather. Her mother had no interest in sports and it was evident that the patient, who knew the name of every player in the big leagues whatever the game, went with her stepfather much as any young lady might. Not athletic herself, she played the role of the very feminine, charmed supporter.

At this stage of the treatment, the patient was becoming uneasy with her stepfather—especially when he kissed her, as he did every day. She noted with satisfaction, however, that he never kissed his own little girl. She recalled that she had had a great crush on her stepfather when he was courting her mother; that she had been sick with bitterness the day she helped her mother buy her wedding dress; and that when her mother became pregnant she had been furious. At this point the therapist commented that it was natural for girls to have such crushes; they wanted all evidences of love and attention.

The patient was still not quite conscious of her sexual feelings for her stepfather when the analyst left for a two weeks' vacation. During this time, the mother told the patient that her stepfather loved her more than he did his own child. This constituted permission for the girl to love her stepfather. When the analyst returned, the patient came in beautifully dressed. She said that she had felt tearful and depressed. She was oversolicitous of her mother, but she had planned every detail of her dress and behavior to please the stepfather.

In the period of the therapy that followed (after approximately a year of treatment), the patient, although she did not act out her hostility against her mother in an obvious manner, subtly calculated every move to monopolize her stepfather. For weeks she was sure she could love no one else. Then she alternated between love and rage at him, with dreams of turning from her stepfather to a younger man. During this phase the mother returned to her original decision that her daughter should go to a college away from home. This the patient saw only as a device to keep the stepfather to herself.

After an interpretation by the therapist that the patient might possibly be re-living with her stepfather the early deep affection and love she had known for her own father, the patient reported a dream of being a grown-up woman, very much in love with a Navy aviator. She then revealed for the first time that she had kept up a desultory contact with her father and that he was now a Navy aviator. The next week she reported that her feelings for her stepfather were subsiding and that she now recalled many incidents she had forgotten— of begging her mother not to divorce her father and of threatening to join her father whenever she became angry with her mother.

The patient had now become a much more mature personality, charming and self-assured. She reported that she no longer minded going out alone on the street; she no longer feared meeting her father or hearing about him. She also began to be popular with boys. Soon she reported a "wonderful" dream in which she had married a young man of her own age. "I was so in love. We said goodbye to my mother and stepfather at the dock and sailed for Europe. On the boat my husband and I saw a movie of ourselves happily waving farewell to my parents."

The patient said she was happy and at ease in most situations, got along better at home with her mother and grandmother, and that all her symptoms had disappeared. However, she was a little fearful about leaving treatment yet. On being questioned whether she thought the therapist would be annoyed if she tried to get along without help now, the patient looked relieved and said she would try it on her own until after the Christmas holidays. After the holiday season, she reported that she had had a fine time and was willing to break off the treatment.

Later this girl went to the downstate university where, although she had an unusually good mind, she received only slightly above average grades and was very popular with both boys and girls. The most recent check-up shows that now, six years since she left treatment, the patient at twenty-two has remained well and is happily married.

Comments on Case R

Thus we see that an extensive personality change can, indeed, be carried out in weekly interviews covering only seventeen months. This treatment was far more intensive than either of the preceding cases and can be compared to a standard psychoanalysis in the general approach and handling, although the transference neurosis was carefully controlled by relating all interpretations to present realities. The individual symptoms were not analyzed in the interviews, but the therapist, knowing their dynamics from previous experience, could use this information in interpreting the present-day reactions as portrayed in the dreams. When the patient gave up her rivalry and hostility toward her mother, the symptoms disappeared.

The stereotyped pattern of vomiting before school can be easily understood. In her early years vomiting had proved an effective means of gaining her ends. The fact that the divorce coincided with the patient's first school experiences could well account for her taking refuge in this formerly efficient weapon of resistance. It was useful in obtaining the attention and concern of her mother and grandmother, and became a powerful weapon against her mother in her ambition for her daughter to be an intellectual success. The patient's anxiety lest she not lead her class was reinforced by the displacement to her schoolwork of her neurotic need to be the first, the most loved at home. The concomitant of this anxiety was depression when she felt that she did not come first—whether in her parents' affections or in her studies.

The patient's warmth of feeling indicates that this patient could not have been an emotionally deprived child. Her grandmother had given her devoted care as a baby, her father had evidently enjoyed her companionship, and the mother herself, although deeply ambivalent and her rival for the father's and the grandmother's attention, had not been overtly rejecting.

An explanation of the girl's attitude toward her mother must then be sought in the events which followed her earliest childhood: the parents' quarrels, the father's threat of suicide, the separation and divorce (by which the father was sent away), the subsequent remarriage, and the birth of the half-sister. Although the child's relationship to her own father had been favorable to normal oedipal development, it had been cut off before the conflict could be resolved and (because of the painful loss of her father) she had had to repress the whole situation. The oedipal feelings were readily reactivated, however, with the mother's second marriage when the girl again became a rival to her mother. It was as if she said to her mother, "You took my father away from me; now I'll take my stepfather away from you."

Particularly interesting is the effect of the therapy on the environment. No attempt was made to see the significant adults in the patient's life and through them to ameliorate the environment; rather by working a change in the patient's attitude, a slight but definite change was produced in those around her. The grandmother, especially now that she had the baby half-sister to absorb her, learned to react toward the patient as to any self-reliant individual, giving up her nagging and her oversolicitousness. The mother came to accept her, in time, as a person with a mind and will of her own and could enjoy her companionship in little things.

The patient's progress was partly due to the fact that, since her first dependent relationship had been to the grandmother, she could face competition with her mother in the treatment without too much pain. But primarily success was due to the fact that the patient was emotionally ready for the corrective experience offered by the therapy.

The patient's apparent dependence on her mother and grand-mother was due more to frustrated independence than to un-satisfied dependent wishes. She was therefore prepared emo-tionally for the more permissive authority which she found in the therapist.

It is imperative, especially in cases such as this when the patient is seen only once a week, that the therapist know exactly how much lenience can be offered, and in just what spheres indulgence can be safely granted. Moreover, the therapist must make sure that each new bit of insight is thoroughly assimilated and the new attitude carefully experimented with, for with adolescents unassimilated insight leads easily to "acting out"— the patient may accept the therapist's interpretation as permis-sion to give in to his impulses rather than an incentive to grow up to them.

It is this thorough digestion which makes this case longer than most cases treated by flexible psychotherapy; indeed, this case covered a longer period than any other case reported in this book. Since the adolescent is still in the process of char-acter formation, much time may be required for each change of attitude to "catch hold," to be tested again and again until it has become an integral part of the more mature personality. It is because of this that therapy with adolescents must neces-sarily proceed at a slower pace than with adults.

———

In the treatment of these three cases, transference reactions and dreams were used by the therapist very much as in an analysis. The therapist varied the approach, however, accord-ing to the depth of the patient's difficulties and focused atten-tion directly on that unconscious material which was needed to help the patient mobilize and resolve his central conflict. The next cases illustrate further our flexibility in approach. In the handling of these two cases, the therapist made little or no use of unconscious material and strove deliberately to keep the transference reactions at a minimum.

Case S

(Pathological Family Constellation)

The first of these two cases demonstrates a therapeutic approach to a problem in which the therapist is aware of the total pathology in a family situation. Ann, the sixteen-year-old girl, was never seen. Her mother came to the therapist (a woman) quite depressed and bewildered because Ann was on the verge of failing everything in her senior year at high school. The girl was subject to intense rages toward her father and an older sister, and especially toward her mother. During the past year she had become increasingly fearful of remaining in the house alone, or even going to another floor in the home unaccompanied. Both the parents and her teachers believed Ann to be seriously in need of psychiatric help, but she absolutely refused to see a therapist.

The mother came to the therapist to ask what could be done —"because should Ann fail in her high school work, she will not get away to college, and I shall go mad if she is around home another year." At the end of the first interview, the therapist told the mother that since Ann would not come for help, there was a possibility of easing the situation through enlisting the mother's insight and feelings in trying to understand what procedure to follow. To this statement of plan, the mother agreed. The therapist saw the mother once a week for about six months, with satisfactory results.

Ann was vicious in her verbal attacks on her mother but, at that time, the mother was completely unaware of her own hostility toward the girl. She had some awareness, however, of her own need for help and talked freely of her past, of her attachment to her father and of her distress over her parents' quarrels. She spoke of her own adolescence as harried by guilt because she enjoyed the "pleasures of life" and found satisfaction in companionship with boys. She had been a conscientious, driving student and could not bear the thought of a scholastic failure. She could not accept the thought of Ann's choosing any but an outstanding eastern college. The mother could speak easily of her antagonism toward her own younger sister, an adventurous, creative, colorful, and fiery woman. When it was suggested, she could readily accept the fact that she identified Ann with this sister and also that she was possibly envious of this sister who had seemed to be their mother's favorite.

At once the therapist noticed that Ann seemed to be able to blackmail the mother into helping her with her studies, through constantly threatening to fail. She carried the blackmail further by forcing her mother to write unjustifiable excuses to the school for cutting classes. With this information, the therapist decided that although Ann, by this time, certainly had well-established neurotic patterns, there was a possibility of interrupting this vicious circle of ambivalence and blackmail through solving just enough of the mother's conflicts to improve her relationship with the daughter so that the girl could pass her courses and get away to college. The therapist decided not to go deeply into the mother's own conflicts.

Ann's mother was so terrified of her daughter's rages that she never flared back. She wrote the deceptive excuses for the school because she feared Ann's rage when thwarted. This was pointed out to the mother by the therapist. It was not revealed directly to the mother, however, that an important factor in her own reaction was her deep need to lead the girl to her self-destruction. Instead, this attitude of the mother's was analyzed indirectly by helping the mother to become more conscious of her hostility toward this difficult girl. As she grew to see more clearly her identification of Ann with her sister, her jealousy of her sister, and her attendant guilt, the hostility to Ann became more conscious.

Another profound factor in the mother's hostility and mistrust toward Ann was her identification of Ann with herself— that self that had achieved gratification out of the closeness to her own father during parental quarrels. It became clear that although Ann's parents did not quarrel and, on the whole, had a rather good relationship, the mother resented the fact that her husband seemed more sympathetic to Ann than to the older daughter. The therapist consciously avoided stirring up an oedipal problem in this woman, often omitting anything but the most superficial discussion of dreams bearing on this problem. More emphasis was placed on the immediate reality—Ann and her attachment to her father, and the mother's reaction to his undue sympathy toward Ann.

The therapist felt that the treatment should first be focused on the significance of Ann's blackmailing her mother into writing fraudulent excuses to the school. As this situation was analyzed, the whole relationship changed. At the beginning, the mother was very pleasant and sweet to the therapist, and it was early called to her attention that this reaction could hardly be entirely true. When the therapist suggested that Ann must have anxiety about her ability to corrupt her mother, the mother was amazed. The therapist indicated that, angry as Ann might be at her mother for not writing an excuse, still her anxiety would lessen when she felt strength and incorruptibility in her mother. The therapist went into the matter no deeper than to indicate that this impulse possibly sprang from the mother's resentments toward Ann. The mother was depressed and then recognized her hostility toward the therapist for pointing out her corruptibility.

Although the mother had not yet worked out her own conflict, she now wanted to be approved by her therapist and so took a firm stand with Ann, telling her there were to be no more fraudulent excuses. Ann accepted this blandly, but soon put her mother to the test. The mother stood firm in the face of Ann's rage, and for a week afterward Ann was charming toward everyone in the family.

The mother, however, had deeper needs to injure this girl because of her hostilities. Soon Ann made another demand of her mother—who gave in this time, with many rationalizations to herself. At once Ann became violent at home again and the mother came to the therapist with great guilt and fear. In this interview, the therapist was silent for the greater part of the hour and the mother, finding her rationalizations elicited no reaction, became defensive and for the first time quite angry at the physician. With all her rationalizations, she was trying to corrupt the therapist as she and Ann corrupted each other.

The therapist suspected that a similar relationship must have been present between Ann's mother and her own mother, and now seemed the time to break into the vicious neurotic pattern. The therapist listened to and observed all the hostility with no reassurance. Finally she was challenged with, "You do not feel my reasons for writing the excuse hold water." To this the therapist agreed; they did not. For some time the mother was angry with the therapist, who accepted it calmly. From that point on, there was no further problem about the excuses.

The next situation to be analyzed was the mother's fear that the girl would fail and her morbid wish to help the girl at any hour of the night Ann decided to study her lessons. It became clear that the mother's anxiety arose from her deeper wish that Ann fail, and this sprang from at least one highly significant source. She had envied and hated her own sister for her casual approach to schoolwork; she hated it in Ann; and yet she unwittingly fostered it as a means of getting, unconsciously, some of the gratification she had achieved as a consequence of her sister's behavior. This envy had, in her girlhood, been mixed with gloating whenever her sister failed, because then their mother (although she actually preferred the sister) had upbraided her for not being more like her studious older sister.

As all this became clearer to her, and when she recognized as well that Ann taunted her with possible failure as a means of punishing her for what Ann no doubt unconsciously recognized her mother felt toward her, Ann's mother was able to leave the girl more and more to work out her own problems. Ann was resentful at first, but soon did her own studying and talked no more of failure.

There were many side issues, such as insistence on breakfast in bed and demands for slavish care of her clothes, which were used by Ann to punish her mother. To be sure, the mother was also using these as a means of keeping the girl dependent and thus was thwarting Ann's own growth. These issues were again solved through the analysis of the transference relationship, the mother in dreams and in behavior indicating her wish that the therapist do much more for her. If the therapist were silent or noncommittal when asked for advice, the mother might pass it off in a friendly manner for one interview. In time, however, her anger flared toward the analyst and automatically, without much discussion, she became less slavish to Ann.

Ann was passing her courses, she no longer minded being alone in the house, and she went about her life much more independently. Her mother permitted her, without any anxiety, to choose her own college. The quarrels largely subsided.

It now became clear from her dreams, however, that the mother's own conflicts about sexuality were being mobilized, and here again the frustration was closely related to her attitudes concerning Ann and boys, and her envy of Ann's growth and gratification in this area. Ann would be leaving home for college in two months, and the therapist felt that it would be far better for both the mother and Ann if the girl went away with her conflicts about men, which by no means prevented her from dating. To have gone into this problem with the mother would never have been sufficient, it is believed, to resolve Ann's deeper conflicts about men; moreover, Ann could herself seek help in a few years if it became necessary. As for the mother, any mobilization of her sexual conflict seemed definitely contraindicated at her age. The therapist, therefore, left such dreams alone and gradually decreased the interviews, giving the mother considerable approval now for the excellent attitude she had taken all along in assuming the burden of treatment when Ann refused to seek help.

After Ann left for college, her mother came for the final interview. She reported the following dream: "I dreamed Ann was in a prison and everyone was mean to her. I told Ann I would do all I could to help her get far away from the prison, since those people would always be mean to her. I finally succeeded in helping her, and she went far away and was very happy." The mother herself saw the entire significance of the dream and said she guessed it would have been an endless job to resolve all her hostility toward Ann. She is a well-informed woman and, although guilty toward Ann, achieves conscious comfort from the knowledge that some day Ann can get psychiatric help when she needs it.

The girl is making an excellent adjustment in college, scholastically and socially, although she may need help later in working out her sexual problems and also in handling her own children. The mother is very happy and busy with community activities, an area in which she has much to contribute.

Comments on Case S

What was accomplished in this family situation? Ann had been failing in her schoolwork, was blackmailing her mother into writing fraudulent excuses and helping her with her studies, was displaying violent temper at home and developing increasing fears of being left alone anywhere in the house. The mother's own ambivalence toward Ann was fundamental in the neurotic reactions displayed by the girl.

Treatment, directed toward resolving some of the more immediate causes of the mother's hostility toward Ann, led to a real ego change in the mother. With the realization of her contribution to Ann's difficulties, the mother not only was able to give up her hostility but at the same time she was freed to exercise the restraint that Ann had demonstrated she needed. She then became a truly responsible parent. Ann reacted to this change automatically by passing her courses, lessening her rage and anxiety at home, and assuming personal responsibilities she had never before accepted. The automatic effect on the child of the treatment of a significant parent is well known to all therapists dealing with children.

The following case illustrates, even more clearly than the one just reported, the need to evaluate the clinical picture early and, if need be, to limit therapy drastically with regard to analysis of underlying conflicts.

Case T

(Potential Psychosis)

The patient was a young man of nineteen, a brilliant student in engineering at a nearby university. After much hesitation and long talks with gifted friends of his who had been helped by analysis, he finally came for treatment with a great longing for help and, by that time, almost *too little* resistance to therapy. He was seen over a period of a year with interviews first every week and then at intervals of every two or three weeks. The results, although limited in scope, were highly satisfactory.

The patient's major complaint was that, although he knew he was capable of brilliant creative work in his field of mathematics and architecture, he would for weeks at a time become so anxious and depressed that he would stay away from school. He also recognized that he had much anxiety in regard to any close association with girls. Having read and talked much about psychoanalysis before he came to treatment, the patient in the first interview literally "poured out" his life story, making many complicated and *correct* interpretations of the dynamics of his underlying conflicts, especially those dealing with oedipal material. The therapist (a woman) was relatively noncommittal.

In the second interview, the patient revealed that in the first session he had withheld a dream which he now wished to relate. This proved to be an oedipal dream, the elements of which were complexly disguised. In reality, he already knew of his strong love for his mother and resentment toward his father. The fact that he had withheld the dream before, a dream much disguised, should have served as more of a warning to the therapist than it did. The patient was allowed to bring associations to the disguised elements, and did so with eagerness.

No marked anxiety was evident during this interview, but a few days later the patient called the therapist for an appointment, obviously very much disturbed. In this interview, it was learned that the patient had stopped both his schoolwork and his job—by which he earned money to pay for the treatment. He had stayed away from school and work because he felt his men teachers and his employer were hostile to him, and he remained in his room because he felt they would follow him on the street "to see what I was up to." Obviously, a paranoid reaction had followed the mobilization and deeper analysis of his oedipal conflict.

The therapist knew from his history that his mother had always protected him from his authoritative, harsh father, and it was felt that this had only served to intensify his attachment to her and deepen the conflict. At once the therapist told the patient, therefore, that she knew he was upset and guilty and fearful of these men, but that since he had ended his job what were his plans for paying for his treatment? The patient appeared startled and then visibly relaxed as he seemed to be thinking. The therapist felt that, at this point, the patient would only become worse if she protected him from his employer and charged no fee—this was exactly what his mother had always done. It seemed he not only had become guilty from the analysis of the dream, but also had the unconscious intention of pushing the therapist into taking part in his deeper impulses.

After some thought, the patient ventured, "You could not see me for a while and excuse the fee?" The therapist assured him the issue was *not* the fee but what it meant, and she briefly pointed out to him that he seemed to have some wish to push her into exactly the same position his mother had held, in indulging him and protecting him against the father. The therapist said no more, and at the end of the hour the patient said he felt far less anxiety and would return to school and work.

The next hour he returned, calm and pleased with himself for having resumed work but also resenting the fact that the therapist had withheld help. He was able, however, to see that intellectually her point was well taken.

From that time on, the patient brought in very few dreams, but talked mostly about his studies, in which he was astonishingly brilliant. Personal contact with some of his professors before this had revealed to the therapist the amazing gifts of this boy. The therapist decided to encourage him and to show her appreciation for all his creativeness, in no way to mobilize any erotic attachment to her, to decrease his interviews gradually, and to attempt to stabilize this nineteen-year-old at a creative level. It was thought possible that some years later, with the added self-esteem which productivity would bring, the patient's ego might be better able to stand analysis.

During the rest of the year of treatment, the patient became increasingly sure of himself and pleased by the realization that he possessed true genius. That the therapist knew she was inferior to him intellectually could be conveyed to him easily by the nature of her questions and by her evident respect. His own mother was a woman of only average intelligence and vision, whose capacity to appreciate his intellectual gifts was extremely limited. The therapist could at least follow his ideas closely enough to give him real gratification from seeing that her admiration was not superficial flattery but true appreciation. He proceeded to win her approval and admiration on an intellectual level, and repressed—or possibly sublimated, in part—his erotic feelings.

His earlier relationship to his gifted father changed to mutual admiration and a productive exchange of ideas. The patient became deeply absorbed in his studies and research, received many awards for his achievements and rarely mentioned any interest in girls.

After a year, treatment was terminated except for a rare communication as to his progress. A year later he entered one of the armed services, and now (three years after the therapy was terminated) he is functioning well in a highly specialized technical group in that branch of the service. Occasional letters have expressed his intense gratitude for what he is able to accomplish.

Comments on Case T

What the eventual effectiveness of this young man's intellectual sublimations will be, remains a question. Certainly at the time he was first seen, before he had achieved the unusually high professional status that is now his, to have pursued an analysis of his pregenital and oedipal conflicts might well have precipitated a psychosis. Had he been several years older, the therapist would have been more confident of a safe outcome in a psychoanalysis.

This young man is fortunate in having within him the elements of genius. His tremendous intellectual gifts make it possible for him easily to outrank most of the men with whom he deals so that for the present, at least, he has no great threat from men. It is to be hoped that he will continue to function chiefly in the intellectual realm, where he will surely gain unusual recognition. At some later time, perhaps, he may again succumb to emotional pressure and need help. At that time his security and self-regard though achievement, added to his increased age, should be sufficient to carry him through analysis if it becomes necessary. At present, in an entirely unexhibitionistic manner, he recognizes his rare gifts and wins the praise of men and women.

This case demonstrates the need to deal immediately and specifically with the clinical picture as presented and to avoid any routine or usual mode of procedure. It emphasizes the necessity of stabilizing a patient, if possible, at a level at which his gifts and emotional defenses can be productive. Those therapists who treat adolescents or late adolescents often must formulate such a plan. A *complete* intellectual and emotional life cannot be achieved for everyone. If the therapist has such an aim, in many instances he may destroy the patient's opportunities for achievement in *any* area. This fact applies to any form of treatment; it is not peculiar to the briefer psychotherapy. In this particular case, it might have been catastrophic to have seen the patient in daily interviews and to have analyzed unconscious material. (In fact, much *conscious* material was also deliberately passed over by the therapist.)

In summarizing the structure of this case, the therapist is greatly limited by the fact that, from almost the very beginning, no attempt was made to understand the experiences contributing to this young man's emotional conflicts. It is believed, however, that the boy's earliest relationship to his mother was probably unsound and involved with considerable ambivalence on her part. The mother failed him not just because of her limited intellectual abilities and incapacity to appreciate him on that level, but probably also because of a resentment which he displaced to her lack of intellectual appreciation. Through the treatment relationship, the patient experienced a warmth and lack of ambivalence from the therapist which he had not had in relation to his mother.

It is felt that the oedipal conflict was a later disturbance, stemming from the deeper earlier ambivalent relationship with his mother. The therapist doubts if the dependent yearning characteristic of the dreams told in the beginning of the treatment was wholly regressive. Such speculations, however, must rest until treatment is resumed at a later date.

Adelaide McFadyen Johnson, M.D.

Chapter 16

THE USE OF NARCOSYNTHESIS IN WAR NEUROSIS

As a final example of flexibility in psychotherapy, we present a case of war neurosis in which narcosynthesis *in one week* brought relief from depression and anxiety of a year's standing. This case illustrates not only that an acute neurosis may become chronic if not treated quickly, but that relief can be secured even after a long period of disturbance if the psychodynamics of the case are understood. It also illustrates a new, very brief form of psychotherapy which may be found applicable to a wide variety of cases.

Flexible methods of procedure are especially applicable in military psychiatry, since treatment is in many cases extremely brief. Discovering the dynamic basis of the neurotic reactions as quickly as possible is a vital necessity. The standard psychoanalytic technique is too time-consuming, so new methods have been devised. One method which provides quick access to pertinent material is the use of sodium pentothal. This drug acts as a sedative, decreasing the intensity of the emotion, overcoming the resistances of the super-ego to the exposure of unacceptable trends, and permitting the ego to face them without neurotic flight. There are several methods of therapy with the same drug: narcoanalysis (a procedure for obtaining information), narcohypnosis (a chemical hypnosis during which the patient is persuaded to give up his symptoms), and narcosynthesis.

The name "narcosynthesis" implies that under narcosis the ego tends to synthesize previously isolated material; since it is rarely able to do this completely, subsequent synthesis in a conscious state is usually necessary. This method of treatment, first developed in a base hospital in North Africa, has been

proved successful in severe cases of war neurosis seen immediately after the breakdown. Its use has been extended to hospitals behind the front lines and is now employed in convalescent
hospitals in this country.

In the case to be recounted, the following steps in treatment
will be noted: (1) abreaction; (2) support of the ego through
identification with the therapist; (3) desensitization from
memories of anxiety-producing situations through repeated recounting of traumatic experiences and through reality testing;
(4) neutralization of the severe super-ego reaction of guilt to
actual or imagined failure; (5) insight into personality trends;
and (6) return to mature attitudes and adult activities. These
are not separate procedures, employed in chronological order
as in a surgical operation. Careful timing is essential and
several steps may be combined in a single interview.

Case U

(War Neurosis)

A 25-year-old captain in the Air Forces was sent to a convalescent hospital because of objective symptoms of depression.
Treatment was successfully terminated in a week.

A flight leader in a pursuit squadron, the patient had fought
successfully until about his twenty-fifth mission, a year before,
when a friend flying on his wing went up in flames. Although
the patient had felt bad and was depressed, he continued fighting and successfully completed his tour of duty, a total of sixty
missions. Refusing an opportunity to remain as commanding
officer of a squadron, he then returned to the United States
where he was reassigned to a job he liked very much and
wanted to keep. His depression continued, however, accompanied by severe startle reactions; when anyone came into his
room, making a sudden noise or turning on the light, he would
jump out of bed with great anxiety. In addition, he suffered
from insomnia and from dreams which repeated some of the
severe traumatic incidents of his combat experiences. Nevertheless, he maintained fairly good control of himself and con-

tinued to fly. He tried hard to forget his experiences but found it impossible, and drinking only increased his anxiety. Finally, his condition was thought so serious that he was referred for treatment.

At the initial interview the patient presented an expressionless face; his muscles were quite rigid, indicating a great deal of tension; his speech was retarded and he did not volunteer much information. The physician learned that he was single, a university graduate who had studied hard, had made excellent grades and had been given a fellowship in animal genetics which he had given up when he entered the Air Forces. There was no history of any previous depression, and there was no incident in his life that showed he could not adjust himself to his normal experiences and environment.

That afternoon he was given 0.25 grams of sodium pentothal, intravenously. He was told that he was up in the air on a strafing mission and that the man on his wing was aflame. Then the therapist commanded, "Go ahead and talk."

Immediately the patient went into an emotional state, shouting to his friend whose name was Slim. "Pull up and bail out!—Why doesn't he pull up, why doesn't he bail out? I hope he doesn't think it's my fault. He's such a nice boy. Such a swell fellow. I hope I'm not responsible for his death. We were together all the time. He lived in the same tent with me and would share anything that he had. When we were on low rations he would give as much as he could to everyone else."

Accompanying all this were tears and sobbing and repetitions of, "I hope he doesn't think it's my fault. He wasn't a good flyer. Oh, if I had only picked out another spot, a safer target; but that is where they told me to go, right over those trucks. If I had gone some other place he wouldn't have got it. Why did he do it? He should have stayed in formation. He didn't stay where he was supposed to. He came up and took the lead position with me. Maybe I should have given a talk before we went, about staying in formation. Why didn't I do that?"

Then he spoke of the letter he and his comrades had written home to Slim's family and how he couldn't bear to read it.

"I can't get him out of my mind. I couldn't see his family because I didn't want to stir them up." In this fashion he went over and over the traumatic situation, crying and sobbing. (This is the phase of *abreaction*.)

As this reaction subsided, the patient was allowed to close his eyes and sleep for a few moments. Then the analyst awakened him and handed him a lighted cigarette. He looked at his watch and said, "I must have been asleep. I had a dream about Slim." His comment on the fact that his pillow was wet with tears was, "Gosh, I perspired a lot." The physician said, "No, you were only asleep for a few minutes, but you talked to me about Slim and you told me all about it. Let's talk about him some more."

Then, in a conscious state, he went over the situation just as he had when he was asleep, but one further bit of information was elicited: Slim had not been appointed a regular flight leader because he was a "mechanical" flyer; the patient had been given the job instead. Next the patient talked about another boy who had crashed in a low-level flight, maintaining radio silence according to instructions although he was in need of help. Then the patient told of feeling bad about killing Germans. The therapist ended the interview by telling him that he had assumed a responsibility for the death of Slim that did not seem to be based on fact. (*Identification with the therapist* and *desensitization* has begun.)

The next morning the patient entered the interviewing room and stated, "I feel like a load has been lifted from my mind, like a great relief. I slept well last night and didn't even dream; I woke up once but I went right back to sleep. This morning I feel good." There was a silence, then he said, "I guess I blamed myself unnecessarily." The therapist said, "Yes, you did. Now let's try to figure out why you blamed yourself. Tell me something about your background."

The patient then said that he had lived on a large farm. His father was very successful as a farmer and had made enough money to send his children to college. The first child of this family had been born dead; then came the patient, followed by two sisters at two-year intervals and a brother nine years younger than the patient. The mother was mild-man-nered and religious. The children had gone to Sunday School and church although they were not forced to do so. The father was kind and gentle, but strict in his attitude. He had rarely spanked the patient but he expected him to live up to his re-sponsibilities. If the patient failed to do so, his father would look pained and disappointed and say, "This was your job," and then do it himself. The patient said that this was worse than a spanking. He had always been on very good terms with his father and would rather work with him than with anyone else.

He then began to talk about his commanding officer who, he said, was an exceptionally strong leader; a person who went on the most dangerous missions himself, a man who was fair and expected everyone to do his job. The analyst commented, "Your C.O. was very much like your father." The patient replied, "You know, I often thought he was like my father, doing things he didn't have to, and always doing everything he could to help us but expecting the best from us. Of course not in the same way, because he was a fighter."

The physician said, "Now let us summarize the things for which you blame yourself. Slim's death. But you were ordered to hit the target even though it was dangerous; you could do nothing else and you could not be responsible for his death. Then you blame yourself for not giving explicit formation in-struction, but you were all experienced flyers and had been trained in formations for six months and every man knew his position. You blame yourself for killing Germans, but you know that was to save the lives of our own troops. You blame your-self for the boy who crashed on the low mission, but it was agreed beforehand that radio silence was to be maintained. So you have a lot of disapproving attitudes toward things which are not really your fault. You behave as if you were still reacting to disapproving attitudes that your father might have had toward you. You act as if your father's image were looking at you with a disappointed expression." Here we see the beginning of the *neutralization of a severe super-ego.*)

"Well," said the patient, "I have always taken responsibilities and duties seriously. I have never been able to feel that I did give my best unless I worked terribly hard." "And now," the therapist went on, "your behavior, which is depressed and completely unhappy, is just as if you were determined to keep on punishing yourself and never let yourself have any fun or pleasure." The patient replied, "That's it. I can't enjoy things. I wonder why I take his death so seriously?" The physician echoed, "Yes, I wonder why?" and terminated the interview.

The next day the patient entered the interview smiling and stated frankly, "I must say I haven't felt so good for a long time. I slept well and didn't dream." He felt as if he could carry on and asked to go back to duty. He now realized that he took his responsibility too seriously, but he had always felt that he "didn't want to let anyone down."

Then he told about a younger pilot, 21 years old, whom he had taught to fly formation. The younger pilot looked up to him as to an older man or father. The therapist suggested, "Something like your own younger brother," and he answered, "Yes, he used to think I was a great guy. I taught him how to shoot, how to hold a gun, and how to play all sorts of games. . . . Our C.O. always spoke quite frankly about his opinion of the conduct and performance of the boys; he either disapproved or complimented. If a fellow did his work properly and if he asked for a day off, he always got every consideration."

It was explained to the patient that because of guilty feelings he was punishing himself for Slim's crash a year before. The physician added that this feeling had persisted without any cause in reality; that, therefore, this sense of guilt and the punishment which he had been giving himself must be due to some inner feelings; that it was not possible to master such feelings until they were unearthed and brought to light.

The therapist continued, "Now you have told me nothing but good things about Slim. You told me how attached you were to him and what a fine fellow he was. But I think your guilty feelings about him are due to some negative attitudes toward Slim that you have not yet discussed. Perhaps these feelings were unconscious and are a source of your sense of guilt." (Here begins the *loosening of unconscious hostility*.)

The patient then said, "Of course no one is perfect, but Slim was the easiest person to get along with. He drank a lot and had to be taken care of. Once when we were in the desert we got drunk and Slim tore up the tent in the middle of a sandstorm. There was a family quarrel with the four tentmates."

The therapist then drew his attention to the fact that Slim was not made flight leader—had Slim been envious of the patient? The patient then reconstructed the flight; Slim was flying on the left wing of the patient who was the leader. Slim flew on the left slightly behind, but he veered to the right and forward in order to accompany the patient in the lead position. The therapist asked whether he interpreted this as meaning that Slim was out to take the lead as a sort of rebellion. He said he didn't think so, but that he didn't give way because he wanted to maintain the proper formation in the flight. Then he said, "Maybe that's why I feel so guilty, because I didn't give way." The result was that Slim was hit by flak and slid over the patient's plane to the right, on fire.

The analyst ended the interview by saying, "I think that there are some definite unconscious negative feelings toward Slim which might be responsible for your sense of guilt, and hence for your depression. We will take that up in the morning." (It is often of great value and economy to treatment to leave the patient at the threshold of new insight, not to point out to him what is obvious to the therapist as the next step, but to let him see it and take it alone in the interval between sessions. Then the therapist can be sure of the dynamic process of the therapy.)

The next morning the patient entered the room at ease and in good spirits. "Colonel," he said, "I have been thinking a good deal about the situation of Slim. A clue you gave me yesterday brought me to some sort of conclusion. Probably it is silly; you might not think it is important, but I have been thinking about it." (When a patient says he is going to tell you something "silly," you prick up your ears because it is probably going to be the most important thing you will hear.)

"I always decided that I wanted to do things and get ahead," continued the patient. "I was very ambitious. I wanted to be better than just average, and when I decided on any ambition I worked very hard to accomplish it. Sometimes I would win and sometimes I would lose; but I would always work for whatever I wanted. When I was in school there were four of us on a cattle-judging team. I wanted to be top man, but there was another fellow on the team who lived with me and he was awfully good. I had to fight it out with him. We fought it back and forth all year round. In my junior year, I was able to beat him. The next year he beat me. There were no hard feelings about it. It was competition, but we were still friends." (The patient now begins to *test his own inner attitudes in the light of reality.*)

The patient then repeated several other incidents of competitive relationship with other men and it became clear that he took no pleasure in winning over people who gave him no struggle. He always wanted to win over someone he felt was superior to him.

"When I joined my outfit it was the same way. We had a C.O. who believed that the leadership in the squadron should come from the boys themselves. There were eight places for flight leaders and the men had to win the jobs. Even after a man became flight leader, he had to work hard to keep it. We were always practicing—practically all the time. Two or three would go up and try to outfly each other. When we finally went overseas, I wasn't able to take a lead position but I became an assistant flight leader. I was disappointed, but I worked hard just the same. Finally there were eight of us who were flight leaders, including Slim and myself. But we weren't always given the job of leading the flight. Our C.O. wanted to see how we were able to fly under somebody else's orders. We didn't always fly leader; we frequently flew wing. Once I went up with our C.O. to try to outfly him. I fought him hard and

I beat him. When we came down I didn't say a word to anybody that I had beaten my C.O."

(The patient had now achieved some *insight into his personality trends* without a direct interpretation. He had worked this thing out himself. There had been some direction in the interview, but he had been able to think along the directed lines merely because he had had an initial emotional release and ego support. The release alone, however, was not sufficient; he still did not know the reason for the load of guilt he had been carrying.)

The therapist then explained to the patient the nature of unconscious attitudes which are not tempered and modified by civilized realities. Sportsman-like competition is a civilized modification of aggression, but the real hostile competitive spirit is still based, so far as the unconscious is concerned, on the concept of "kill or be killed." As a result, victory in competition means (unconsciously) that the defeated person has been destroyed as the direct result of an unconscious wish to be rid of that person. Hence, when competition is followed by the actual death of an individual, the person feels as if he himself has killed that individual. The patient accepted this interpretation.

In the same interview, the patient was given a second pentothal injection. He said immediately, "I used to think I was responsible for Slim's death. I used to feel as if it were my fault. I know now that it is just one of those things that happen and I couldn't help it. He was a fine fellow. I was scared to go on that mission. He and I went into the mess hall that night for some supper, but we just nibbled; we couldn't eat. I had no cigarettes but Slim had two packs and gave me one of them. I smoked half a package of cigarettes. Slim was generous like that. I was terribly nervous. It was a dangerous target but off we went in a tight formation. There was a terrible amount of flak over the target. The trucks blew up and I felt good when I saw it. I don't know why Slim came over and tried to take the lead from me. I flew under his lead the day before and *I* stayed in formation. I can't understand why he broke formation and came up toward me and then got into a heavy flak position. But I didn't give ground. I know now we were jealous of each other and we were really fighting against each other for the job."

When he awakened, he felt a little dizzy and thought he had been sleeping. The whole material of the interview was summarized again by the patient and therapist before the session was terminated.

The next day the patient came in and said he felt perfectly well. He had slept soundly all night, had had no dreams, and felt that a great load had been lifted from him. He said again that he wanted to go back to duty. He recalled that when he had gone home for overseas leave, his family had recognized that something was the matter with him and had refrained from asking him questions. As a result he had kept all the experiences to himself and deliberately tried to forget, but there had always been that load on his mind. He now understood that the only way one can forget is to suffer the pain of remembering first. He remembered episodes he thought were funny and amusing, incidents that happened in his squadron overseas. He was beginning to remember and talk about little experiences. Prior to this he had not been able to think about these because they always led his mind into situations which became painful. Now he said, "It is silly for intelligent people to let things bother them the way I did." (His ego has now regained a more *mature attitude* and may be considered ready to *attempt adult activities*.)

The question now arose whether one should go on with further interviews and therapy, to bring to consciousness the unconscious hostility he had to his own father, or whether one should stop at this point and return him to duty. The therapist had been successful in removing the burden this man had been carrying for a year. This burden was the direct result of his combat experiences acting on his individual character and personality. As a result of the incorporation within his personality of the idealized figure of his father, this man had been a successful student, a successful pilot, and a successful leader. From this personality structure, one could predict that he would probably continue to be successful in life. With this compulsiveness toward success, the therapist had to recognize that the severity of his ego ideal might make trouble for him if he came into a situation in which he could not be successful, but this ideal had already been disturbed and dislodged. The therapy had been directed largely to weakening the severity of the attitudes taken over from his father, in order to permit him to accept his repressed aggressions. That was the load the therapist had helped him get off his chest. The therapist could be assured that the loosening and easing of this pressure on the patient would continue, that while his ego ideal would remain strong it would probably not be too severe.

The patient was not treated further, therefore, but returned to duty. Reexamination six months later showed him to be entirely well and performing his flying duties competently.

Comments on Case U

Any barbiturate administered intravenously will produce the same effect as pentothal. This drug has the advantage of a quicker and shorter action than the others, enabling the therapist to continue his session with the patient in a conscious state after the narcosis. There is no general rule regarding frequency or number of treatments; each case is individual. On the average, two pentothal treatments suffice, but often none is necessary. The drug is used early in the therapy when the patient persists in rationalizations for his condition or resists going into details of his traumatic experiences. It is repeated when there is suspicion that not all the disturbing things have been told, when it seems necessary to bring out more and older memories, and when it is desirable to learn the unconscious reactions to the therapy.

With the patient just described, the second pentothal treatment shows a direct response to the therapist as if he were answering a question regarding his insight. This exposes the effect of the psychiatrist's attitude on the patient, indicating the value of transference in the curative process. The patient had suffered a psychological trauma in a military setting where, by virtue of a common group-ideal, all men are brothers and are identified with each other. By giving the patient permission to feel rationally about his lost brother-in-arms Slim, and to slough off his identification with him, the therapist had softened his too severe super-ego. In the second pentothal treatment it became obvious that the patient had taken over the therapist's attitudes and only "used to feel" as if it were his fault. The individual super-ego of civilian life returned by a process of identification with the psychiatrist.

In psychotherapy for combat veterans who have not been treated immediately after the precipitating trauma, we are always concerned with several editions of a repetitive conflict. In the order of their emergence, we encounter first the current problem, which brings us immediately to the recent past of combat, and finally to material of the childhood past. Transference reactions, exposed throughout the treatment in the patient's attitudes, words, and behavior, are interpreted as little as possible. If negative attitudes appear and are not adequately abreacted under pentothal and related to their correct origin, they must be interpreted at once or else the therapy will be unsuccessful. Positive feelings toward the therapist, however, are usually not interpreted but encouraged as an incentive to cooperate in the treatment. The one exception is that strongly dependent transference feelings must be interpreted as insight develops and the ego is reeducated to attempt anew an independent trial at life; if this is not done, the patient will relapse immediately on return to a strict military existence.

Treatment in the zone of combat is colored by the ever-present fear of death and destruction. Both the patient and the doctor are concerned primarily with the immediate stress, the direct and demonstrable effect of combat; they cannot become greatly interested in the distant past. Therapy is largely directed, therefore, to immediate issues of reaction to the danger. Only rarely is the past, the predisposing personality, clearly expressed in interviews or abreactions. This is partly because the relationships of the current experience to the past are not easily perceived and also because psychiatrists in general are concerned only with the battle stimuli and often intolerant of characteristics arising from old and seemingly unimportant conflicts.

Before experiencing combat themselves, psychiatrists are inclined to believe that war neuroses are largely dependent on a psychoneurotic background; in combat, they see only war as the main etiology. But when these psychiatrists work with returned veterans, the relationship of the old to the new becomes crystal clear. In the interval before returning to the United States, war neuroses seem to undergo a change of pattern; the newer reactions are engulfed by old patterns and the total picture stands out sharply, showing the reaction to war to be a repetition of old reactions to previous conflicts.

Thus, as is seen in this case, our therapeutic achievements are frequently more than a removal of recently developed anxiety. Often, as here, they include an unexpected and beneficial reorientation of the total personality, lessening the chances of another such breakdown.

In working with returned veterans, psychiatrists have ample evidence that the particular *quality of* the stress, as well as the quantity, is an important determinant in the breakdown. Those patients specifically predisposed to a particular stimulus will be affected by the corresponding trauma, ignoring all others. For instance, this patient could endure any amount of danger in battle, but he could not stand the loss of his buddy. Each individual has his Achilles' heel. It may never be found and pierced in his individual combat experience or it may be only lightly pierced without catastrophic results, but each person has a weak spot which, if squarely hit, can cause a breakdown.

Roy R. Grinker, M. D.

Chapter 17

CONCLUSIONS AND OUTLOOK

The work set forth in this volume is a logical continuation of a trend in psychotherapy which began with Freud's discovery of the phenomenon of transference as the dynamic agent of the curative process. Expressed more concretely, the main *therapeutic* result of our work is the conclusion that, in order to be relieved of his neurotic ways of feeling and acting, the patient must undergo new emotional experiences suited to undo the morbid effects of the emotional experiences of his earlier life. Other therapeutic factors—such as intellectual insight, abreaction, recollection of the past, etc.—are all subordinated to this central therapeutic principle.

Reexperiencing the old, unsettled conflict *but with a new ending* is the secret of every penetrating therapeutic result. Only the actual experience of a new solution in the transference situation or in his everyday life gives the patient the conviction that a new solution *is possible* and induces him to give up the old neurotic patterns. By repetition, these corrected reactions gradually become automatic; the ego accepts the new attitudes and integrates them into the total personality. It is thus that therapeutic results become consolidated.

In the patient-physician relationship, the therapist has an unique opportunity to provide the patient with precisely that type of corrective experience which he needs for recovery. It is a secondary question what technique is employed to bring it about. The *standard* psychoanalytic technique is only one— and not in every case the most suitable one—of the many possible applications of fundamental psychodynamic principles that can be utilized for this kind of emotional training. Moreover, every therapy which increases the integrative functions of the ego (through reexposing the patient under more favorable conditions to those conflicts which have before been met with neurotic defense mechanisms) should be called psychoanalytic, no matter whether its duration is for one or two interviews, for several weeks or months, or for several years.

One of the most significant *practical* results of our study is the clear recognition of certain definite disadvantages in any routine procedure. Just as a strain of bacteria may adapt itself to the drug being used for its extermination and become sulfa- or penicillin-resistant, so neurotic mechanisms often adapt themselves to a standardized technique and thus rob it of its therapeutic effectiveness. The result may be an "interminable" transference neurosis in which the patient replaces his old disturbance with a neurotic relationship to his doctor which gradually loses most of its suffering and retains chiefly a morbid gratification—thus becoming a new method of evading those problems in life from which he retreated by means of his neurotic symptoms. Only by constantly counteracting the patient's regressive tendencies and changing the routine procedure can this most vulnerable feature of the standard psychoanalytic technique be annulled.

In this connection it is important to remember that the patient's new emotional experiences are not confined to the therapeutic situation; outside the treatment he has emotional experiences which profoundly influence him. The corrective emotional experiences within the transference situation enable the patient to endure or to meet successfully life experiences which he had been unable to face before, and the influence of the treatment is itself reinforced by each such success. A proper coordination of life and therapeutic experiences is the basis for determining when a change in the frequency of the interviews or an interruption of treatment is necessary. At a certain phase in every treatment it will be desirable to have the patient translate into his actual life experience his newly acquired reaction patterns without the support of the therapist. In such a phase an interruption, long or short, is indicated.

All this can be summarized as *the principle of flexibility in treatment: the application of the technique best suited to the nature of the case.* This principle of flexibility opens for psychoanalytic therapy new possibilities of great social significance.

Originally, psychiatry dealt almost exclusively with the custodial care of advanced cases of psychosis. With greater psychological understanding of the nature of mental disturbances came the development of the practice of psychiatry in offices and out-patient clinics. These cases, well-diagnosed forms of severe chronic psychoneurosis, were ambulatory patients who continued to live in their usual environment during a prolonged treatment of almost daily interviews. We can now extend the scope of rational psychotherapy to include an even greater number of maladjusted persons, to include not only many severe psychoneurotics who have been unable to benefit from the standard technique (because of insufficient time or money) but also that even greater group—the acute, the mild chronic, and the incipient psychoneurotics.

As a result of the gradual extension of the scope of psychiatry in general, the understanding of the nature and methods of psychiatry and of the functioning of the human personality is becoming a part of contemporary public knowledge. Mental illnesses, which until recently were little understood and were therefore an open field for conjecture and superstition, are gradually losing their stigma and yielding to a more reasonable point of view. Already it is becoming a natural part of everyday life to consult a psychiatrist when the occasion arises, just as one would consult any other specialist, and it no longer need be shrouded in shameful secrecy.

The development of bacteriology, the knowledge of disease-curing germs, became the foundation of public hygiene and, by preventing the periodic extermination of the population through epidemics, made congested living in large cities possible. Contemporary man now faces a problem of, if possible, even greater magnitude: the problem of living together harmoniously in a highly differentiated civilization. The majority of mental disturbances are failures of adjustment by the individual to social living—an adjustment which is becoming more and more difficult in this era of transition wherein social values and standards are so rapidly changing. Harmonious emotional adjustment has thus become a problem for the large majority of the population.

Here lies the most vital function of psychotherapy: to give rational aid to all those who show early signs of maladjustment. A flexible approach, based on sound general principles of psychodynamics and adjustable to the great variety of those in need, is therefore a pressing necessity of our day.

The progress of psychiatry in the past has been characterized by the gradual improvement of mental hospitals. The new development will come to expression in the creation of well-staffed out-patient clinics where the large number of incipient cases— all those whose emotional balance has been impaired through the complex human relationships in our fluid, ever-changing and highly differentiated society—will receive rational, dynamic psychotherapy.

We believe and hope that our book is only a beginning, that it will encourage a free, experimental spirit which will make use of all that detailed knowledge which has been accumulated in the last fifty years in this vital branch of science, the study of the human personality, to develop modes of psychotherapy ever more saving of time and effort and ever more closely adapted to the great variety of human needs.

Franz Alexander, M.D.

SELECTED READING LIST

PSYCHOTHERAPY

ACKERMAN, N. W. "Psychotherapy and 'Giving Love'." *Psychiatry*, 7:129, 1944.

AICHHORN, A. *Wayward Youth*. Viking Press, New York, 1935.

ALEXANDER, F. "On Ferenczi's Relaxation Principle." *International Journal of Psycho-Analysis*, XIV:183, 1933.

"The Indications for Psychoanalytic Therapy." *Bulletin of the New York Academy of Medicine*, 20:320, 1944.

The Medical Value of Psychoanalysis (rev. ed.). W. W. Norton, New York, 1936.

"A Metapsychological Description of the Process of Cure." *International Journal of Psycho-Analysis*, VI:13, 1925.

"The Problem of Psychoanalytic Technique." *Psychoanalytic Quarterly*, 4:588, 1935.

"Psychoanalysis Revised." *Psychoanalytic Quarterly*, 9:1, 1940.

Psychoanalysis of the Total Personality. Nervous & Mental Disease Publishing Co., New York, 1930.

"Psychosomatic Disturbances of the Gastrointestinal Tract." *Diseases of the Digestive System*, by Sidney A. Portis, pp. 826–842. Lea & Febiger, Philadelphia, 1944.

ALEXANDER, F., BACON, C., *et al.* "The Influence of Psychologic Factors upon Gastro-Intestinal Disturbances: A Symposium." *Psychoanalytic Quarterly*, 3:501, 1934.

ALEXANDER, F., and HEALY, W. *Roots of Crime*. A. Knopf, New York, 1935.

BARTEMEIER, L. H. "Introduction to Psychotherapy." *Psychoanalytic Review*, 30:386, 1943.

BERLINER, B. "Short Psychoanalytic Psychotherapy: Its Possibilities and Limitations." *Bulletin of the Menninger Clinic*, 5:204, 1941.

BINGER, C. *The Doctor's Job*. W. W. Norton, New York, 1945.

CRICHTON-MILLER, H., and NICOLLE, G. H. "Recent Progress in Psychotherapy." *Journal of Mental Science*, 90:307, 1944.

DE FOREST, I. "The Therapeutic Technique of Sandor Ferenczi." *International Journal of Psycho-Analysis*, XXIII:120, 1942.

DEUTSCH, F. "The Associative Anamnesis." *Psychoanalytic Quarterly*, 8:354, 1939.

DEUTSCH, H. *Psychoanalysis of the Neuroses*. Hogarth Press, London, 1932.

FENICHEL, O. *Outline of Clinical Psychoanalysis*. W. W. Norton, New York, 1934.

Problems of Psychoanalytic Technique. Psychoanalytic Quarterly, Inc., Albany, N. Y., 1941.

FERENCZI, S. *Contributions to Psycho-Analysis*. Badger, Boston, 1916.

Further Contributions to the Theory and Technique of Psycho-Analysis. Hogarth Press, London, 1926.

FERENCZI, S., and RANK, OTTO. *The Development of Psychoanalysis.* Nervous & Mental Disease Publishing Co., New York, 1925.

FRENCH, T. M. "Clinical Approach to the Dynamics of Behavior." *Personality and the Behavior Disorders,* edited by J. McV. Hunt, pp. 255–268. The Ronald Press Co., New York, 1944.

"A Clinical Study of Learning in the Course of a Psychoanalytic Treatment." *Psychoanalytic Quarterly,* 5:148, 1936.

"Insight and Distortion in Dreams." *International Journal of Psycho-Analysis,* XX:287, 1939.

"The Integration of Social Behavior." *Psychoanalytic Quarterly,* 14:149, 1945.

"Reality Testing in Dreams." *Psychoanalytic Quarterly,* 6:62, 1937.

FRENCH, T. M., ALEXANDER, F., et al. *Psychogenic Factors in Bronchial Asthma.* Psychosomatic Medicine Monographs, National Research Council, Washington, D.C., 1941.

FREUD, S. "Analysis Terminable and Interminable." *International Journal of Psycho-Analysis,* XVIII:373, 1937.

"The Analytic Therapy." *Introductory Lectures on Psycho-Analysis* (rev. ed.), pp. 375–388. Allen & Unwin, London, 1929.

"Fragment of an Analysis of a Case of Hysteria." *Collected Papers,* III:13. Hogarth Press, London, 1924.

"Further Recommendations on the Technique of Psycho-Analysis." *Collected Papers,* II:342. Hogarth Press, London, 1924.

The Interpretation of Dreams. Modern Library, New York, 1938.

"On Psychotherapy." *Collected Papers,* I:249. Hogarth Press, London, 1924.

"Recommendations for Physicians on the Psycho-Analytic Method of Treatment." *Collected Papers,* II:326. Hogarth Press, London, 1924.

"Turnings in the Ways of Psychoanalytic Therapy." *Collected Papers,* II:392. Hogarth Press, London, 1924.

FUERST, R. A. "Problems of Short Time Psychotherapy." *American Journal of Orthopsychiatry,* VIII:260, 1938.

GLOVER, E. "The Therapeutic Effect of Inexact Interpretation." *International Journal of Psycho-Analysis,* XII:397, 1931.

GRINKER, R. R., and SPIEGEL, J. P. *Men Under Stress.* Blakiston, Philadelphia, 1945.

War Neuroses in North Africa. Josiah Macy Jr. Foundation, New York, 1943.

GROTJAHN, M. "Brief Psychotherapy on Psychoanalytic Principles." *Illinois Psychiatric Journal,* 2:1, 1942.

"Some Features Common to Psychotherapy of Psychotic Patients and Children." *Psychiatry,* 1:317, 1938.

GUTHEIL, E. A. "Psychoanalysis and Brief Psychotherapy." *Journal of Clinical Psychopathology,* 6:207, 1945.

HERZBERG, A. "Short Treatment of Neuroses by Graduated Tasks." *British Journal of Medical Psychology,* XIX:19, 1941.

JOHNSON, A., and FISHBACK, D. "Analysis of a Disturbed Adolescent Girl and Collaborative Psychiatric Treatment of the Mother." *American Journal of Orthopsychiatry,* XIV:195, 1944.

KNIGHT, R. P. "Application of Psychoanalytical Concepts in Psychotherapy: Report of Clinical Trials in a Mental Hygiene Service." *Bulletin of the Menninger Clinic,* 1:99, 1937.

"Evaluation of the Results of Psychoanalytic Therapy." *American Journal of Psychiatry,* 98:434, 1941.

KUBIE, L. S. "The Nature of Psychotherapy." *Bulletin of the New York Academy of Medicine,* 19:183, 1943.

SELECTED READING LIST 345

LEVINE, M. *Psychotherapy in Medical Practice.* Macmillan, New York, 1942.

MASSERMAN, J. H. "Experimental Neurosis and Therapy." *Behavior and Neurosis,* pp. 58–91. University of Chicago Press, 1943.

MOHR, G. J. "Some Treatment Indications." *American Journal of Orthopsychiatry,* XI:438, 1941.

OBERNDORF, C. P. "Consideration of Results with Psychoanalytic Therapy." *American Journal of Psychiatry,* 99:374, 1942.

"Factors in Psychoanalytic Therapy." *American Journal of Psychiatry,* 98:750, 1942.

"The Nature of Psychogenic Cure." *American Journal of Psychiatry,* 101:91, 1944.

Proceedings of the Brief Psychotherapy Council. Institute for Psychoanalysis, Chicago, 1942.

Proceedings of the Second Brief Psychotherapy Council. Institute for Psychoanalysis, Chicago, 1944. (Vol. I: War Psychiatry; Vol. II: Psychosomatic Medicine; Vol. III: Psychotherapy for Children, Group Psychotherapy.)

SAUL, L. J. "Utilization of Early Current Dreams in Formulating Psychoanalytic Cases." *Psychoanalytic Quarterly,* 9:453, 1940.

SCHILDER, P. *Psychotherapy.* W. W. Norton, New York, 1938.

SCHMIDEBERG, M. "The Mode of Operation of Psycho-Analytic Therapy." *International Journal of Psycho-Analysis,* XIX:310, 1938.

"Reassurance as a Means of Analytic Technique." *International Journal of Psycho-Analysis,* XVI:307, 1935.

STRACHEY, J. "The Nature of the Therapeutic Action of Psycho-Analysis." *International Journal of Psycho-Analysis,* XV:127, 1934.

SULLIVAN, H. S. "Conceptions of Modern Psychiatry." *Psychiatry,* 3:1, 1940.

"Symposium on the Theory of the Therapeutic Results of Psycho-Analysis." *International Journal of Psycho-Analysis,* XVIII:125, 1937.

SZUREK, S., JOHNSON, A., and FALSTEIN, E. "Collaborative Psychiatric Therapy of Parent-Child Problems." *American Journal of Orthopsychiatry,* XII:511, 1942.

THOMPSON, C. "Notes on the Psychoanalytic Significance of Choice of Analyst." *Psychiatry,* 1:205, 1938.

WEISS EDOARDO. "Emotional Memories and Acting Out." *Psychoanalytic Quarterly,* 11:477, 1942.

TRANSFERENCE

BALINT, ALICE and MICHAEL. "On Transference and Counter-Transference." *International Journal of Psycho-Analysis,* XX:223, 1939.

BIBRING-LEHNER, G. "A Contribution to the Subject of Transference-Resistance." *International Journal of Psycho-Analysis,* XVII:181, 1936.

FEDERN, P. "Psychoanalysis of the Psychoses." *Psychiatric Quarterly,* 17:246, 1943.

FREUD, S. "The Dynamics of the Transference." *Collected Papers,* II:312. Hogarth Press, London, 1924.

"Further Recommendations in the Technique of Psychoanalysis. Observations on Transference-Love." *Collected Papers,* II:377. Hogarth Press, London, 1924.

"Transference." *Introductory Lectures on Psycho-Analysis* (rev. ed.), pp. 360–374. Allen & Unwin, London, 1929.

FROMM-REICHMANN, F. "Transference Problems in Schizophrenics." *Psychoanalytic Quarterly,* 8:412, 1939.

THOMPSON, C. "Development of Awareness of Transference in a Markedly Detached Personality." *International Journal of Psycho-Analysis,* XIX: 299, 1938.

MISCELLANEOUS

ALEXANDER, F. *Our Age of Unreason.* Lippincott, New York, 1942.
"The Relation of Structural and Instinctual Conflicts." *Psychoanalytic Quarterly,* 2:181, 1933.
"The Voice of the Intellect Is Soft . . ." *Psychoanalytic Review,* 28:12, 1941.
BENEDEK, THERESE. "Adaptation to Reality in Early Infancy." *Psychoanalytic Quarterly,* 7:200, 1938.
"Defense Mechanism and the Structure of the Total Personality." *Psychoanalytic Quarterly,* 6:96, 1937.
BENEDEK, THERESE, and RUBENSTEIN, B. *The Sexual Cycle in Women.* Psychosomatic Medicine Monographs, National Research Council, Washington, D.C., 1942.
DEUTSCH, H. *The Psychology of Women,* Vol. I. Grune & Stratton, New York, 1944.
The Psychology of Women, Vol. II: Motherhood. Grune & Stratton, New York, 1945.
FRENCH, T. M. "An Analysis of the Goal Concept Based Upon Study of Reactions to Frustration." *Psychoanalytic Review,* 28:61, 1941.
"Defense and Synthesis in the Function of the Ego." *Psychoanalytic Quarterly,* 7:537, 1938.
"Goal Mechanism and Integrative Field." *Psychosomatic Medicine,* 3:226, 1941.
"Reality and the Unconscious." *Psychoanalytic Quarterly,* 6:23, 1937.
FREUD, ANNA. *The Ego and the Mechanisms of Defense.* Hogarth Press, London, 1937.
FREUD, S. *The Ego and the Id.* Hogarth Press, London, 1927.
SAUL, L. J. "Physiological Effects of Emotional Tension." *Personality and the Behavior Disorders,* edited by J. McV. Hunt, I:269. The Ronald Press Co., New York, 1944.
Ten Year Report, 1932-1942. Institute for Psychoanalysis, Chicago, 1942.

INDEX

Abreaction, 204
  cathartic, 293–299
  in narcosynthesis, 328
Ackerman, N. W., 343
"Acting out" character, 45, 185, 313
  frequency of interview and, 33, 263
Adaptability of patient, 97–98
Adler, A., 23
Adolescent girl, analysis of, (Case R) 305–313
  in pathological family constellation, (Case S) 314–319
Advice, giving of, 39, (Case C) 155–157, (Case D) 158–162, 266
Age of patient as factor in therapy, 97
Aichhorn, A., 54, 70, 80, 133, 138, 343
Alcoholism, (Case N) 269–277
  dependence on therapist in, 276
  dependent wishes in, 92–93
Alexander, F., 343, 344, 345
  (footnotes), 20, 135, 247, 300
Ambition as factor in peptic ulcer, 247, 253
Analyst (see Therapist)
Anxiety, diminishing of, 103, (Case Y) 119–125
  examination, (Case L) 244–254
  general, (Case R) 305–313
  severe generalized, (Case K) 234–244
  (see also Phobia)
Anxiety hysteria, frequency of interview and, 141–142
Anxiety state, chronic, (Case O) 277–287
Asthma, psychogenic, (Case Q) 299–304
  confession in, 135–136, 303
  dependence in, 300
  dynamics of, 135–136, 300
  interpretation in, 136
Attitude, of patient toward therapist, 79, 84–86
  of therapist toward patient, 53–54, 82–83, 84–86
Authors:
  Alexander, Franz, v–x, 3–41, 54–70, 96–106, 145–155, 162–164, 338–341

Authors—(Continued)
  Bacon, Catherine L., 207–220
  Benedek, Therese, 173–206
  French, Thomas M., 71–95, 107–144
  Fuerst, Rudolf A., 157–162, 220–232
  Gerard, Margaret W., 233–267
  Grinker, Roy R., 325–337
  Grotjahn, Martin, 155–157, 165–172
  Johnson, Adelaide M., 291–324
  McLean, Helen V., 268–290
  Weiss, Edoardo, 41–54

Bacon, C. L., 343
Balint, A., 345
Balint, M., 345
Bartemeier, L. H., 343
"Basic rule" of psychoanalysis, 16
Behavior patterns, modification of, 134–140
Benedek, Therese, 346
Berliner, B., 343
Bibring-Lehner, G., 345
Binger, C., 343
Breuer, J., 14, 162
"Brief" psychotherapy, 145
  (see also Flexible therapy)

Cases:
  Case A (Conversion Hysteria and Severe Personality Disturbance), 55–65
  Case B (Depression), 146–155
  Case C (Reactive Depression), 155–157
  Case D (Frigidity), 158–162
  Case E (Schizoid Personality), 166–172
  Case F (Peptic Ulcer), 173–181
  Case G (Acute Reactive Depression), 182–191
  Case H (Premenstrual Depression), 192–203
  Case I (Depressive Type), 208–220
  Case J (Inhibited Type), 220–230
  Case K (Phobia), 234–244

347

Castrative wishes, (Case K) 234–244
Character disturbance, analysis of, 207–232
  depressive type, (Case I) 208–220
  inhibited type, (Case J) 220–230
Climacteric, 189, 190
"Common sense" approach, 55, 64
Competition, aggression and, 333
  guilt feelings and, (Case B) 146–155, (Case I) 208–220
Confession in bronchial asthma, 135–136, 303
Conflict, neurotic, 3, 4, 268
  nuclear, 298–299
Constitutional factors in neuroses and psychoses, 9, 10
Conversion hysteria, (Case A) 55–62, (Case O) 277–287
Cooperation, antagonistic, 3–4
Corrective emotional experience, 22, 55–62, 253, 260, 265, 338, 339
  through rapport, 268–290
  therapeutic principle of, 66–70
Crichton-Miller, H., 343

DeForest, I., 343
Delinquent, 70
Dependence, in alcoholism, 92–93, 276, 288
  in bronchial asthma, 300
  frequency of interview and, 28, 32–33, 80
  hostile, 197, 301
  in peptic ulcer, 118, 125–126, 130, 177, 178, 181, 247–249, 253

Dependence—(Continued)
  repressed, (Case K) 234–244, (Case L) 244–254, (Case M) 254–261
Depression, acute, (Case P) 293–299
  acute reactive, (Case G) 182–191
  premenstrual, (Case H) 190–203
  reactive, (Case C) 155–157
  severe, (Case B) 146–155
  in war neurosis, (Case U) 326–337
Deprived patients and transference relationship, 45
Desensitization in narcosynthesis, 328
Deutsch, F., 343
Deutsch, H., 343, 346
  (footnote) 275
Dora, case of, 15, 16
Dreams, 15, 232, 264, 313
Dysmenorrhea, 193, 203

Ego, change in, (Case Q) 299–304, (Case R) 305–313
  definition, viii
  free association and, 16
  functions of, vii–x
  in hypnosis, 14
  integrative capacity of, 98
  integrative functions of, 338
  psychoneurosis and, viii, 8
  psychosis and, viii
  repression and, 21
  supportive therapy and, 103
Ego strength, frequency of interview and, 30, 31
  gauging of, 98
  intensity of treatment and, 26
  length of treatment and, 163
Ego, strong, 31, 153, 191, 219, (Case B) 146–155, (Case I) 208–220, (Case K) 234–244, (Case L) 244–254, (Case M) 254–261
Ego, weak, (Case E) 166–172, (Case T) 320–324
  frequency of interview and, 30, 31
  supportive therapy and, 103
Emotional level, frequency of interview and, 30, 140–144
  interpretation and, 52
Emotional readjustment as goal of therapy, 126–128
Emotional reeducation, 18–23, 92–95, 137–138
  in supportive therapy, 165–172
Environment, manipulation of, 96–97, 132–134, (Case K) 234–244, (Case L) 244–254, (Case M) 254–261, (Case S) 314–319